NO FRILLS

NO FRILLS
The Truth Behind The Low-Cost Revolution In The Skies

Simon Calder
Foreword by Sir Freddie Laker

First published in Great Britain in 2002 by
Virgin Books Ltd
Thames Wharf Studios
Rainville Road
London
W6 9HA

A catalogue record for this book is available from the British
Library.

ISBN 1 85227 932 X

Typeset by TW Typesetting, Plymouth, Devon
Printed and bound in Great Britain by CPD, Wales

Dedicated with love to Charlotte, for flying without frills but with enthusiasm, and locking me – in the style of the late Douglas Adams – in the Hotel Las Vegas in Malaga until this book was finished. And to Daisy, for discovering the secret of flying free, at least until she is two years old*. In any case, thanks are due to Daisy for providing an excuse to pre-board.

(*Terms and conditions apply)

Simon Calder, London, April 2002

CONTENTS

PICTURE CREDITS

The author and publishers are grateful to the following sources for pictures reproduced in the illustrated section of this book.

Boeing	Boeing 737s, p. 5
Buzz	Nine of Buzz's new routes, summer 2002, p. 8
easyJet	Stelios Haji-Ioannou, chairman of easyJet, p. 1
	easyJet's protest against Go, p. 2
Go	Barbara Cassani, chief executive of Go, p. 3
Ryanair	Ryanair's response to 11 September, p. 8
	Michael O'Leary, chief executive of Ryanair, p. 7
Sir Freddie Laker	Sir Freddie Laker, founder of Skytrain, p. 3
Southwest	Herb Kelleher of Southwest, p. 6
Virgin Atlantic	Sir Richard Branson christens the first Australian Virgin Blue 737, p. 4
Vladimir Raitz	Vladimir Raitz, inventor of the package holiday, p. 2

ACKNOWLEDGEMENTS

Thanks are due to the airline bosses who gave generously of their time during a spell when the aviation business worldwide was in a state of upheaval: Barbara Cassani and her management team at Go, Michael O'Leary and Tim Jeans of Ryanair, Stelios Haji-Ioannou and Ray Webster of easyJet, Tony Comacho of Buzz, Tony Davis of BMIbaby, Rob Brown and Greg Wells of Southwest Airlines, Sir Richard Branson and Neil Burrows of Virgin Express, and Sir Freddie Laker of Laker Airways. Thanks are also due to Vladimir Raitz, the inventor of the air package holiday; Bob Ayling, former chief executive of British Airways; Jamie Bowden of Mediawise Consulting; Neil Taylor, director of Regent Holidays; chief inspector Mike Alderson of Sussex Police; Luke Deals; Howard Putnam, former chief executive and president of Southwest Airlines, Franco Mancassola, formerly of Continental Airlines and founder of Debonair; and Tony Anderson, former marketing director for easyJet. Dozens of other people in the aviation industry agreed to be interviewed on their part in the story. Caroline Virr transcribed three months' worth of recordings superbly.

For Virgin Books Stuart Slater developed the original idea with my agent, Megan Dorcas, while Humphrey Price edited it expertly. Thanks are also due to the muggers who kindly took only my mobile phone, rather than the notes for this book, when they set upon me in the centre of Lisbon in November 2001. If you should be offered a cut-price mobile by some dodgy Portuguese characters, politely decline.

FOREWORD

I love 'frills'. At the point in 1982 when the traditional airlines were conspiring to force my Laker Skytrain out of business, I was introducing 'Regency Class' on my transatlantic flights. It offered a superb business-class service for far less than my rivals – and gave my good friend Richard Branson some ideas for his unbeatable Upper Class service. But I also recognise that the ordinary man or woman is much more interested in getting where they want to go than in the free food and drink on board.

The whole point of Skytrain was to open up the skies to people who were prevented from flying by the airlines' fare-fixing. They had to keep fares deliberately high, to featherbed the expensive nests that they had comfortably constructed for themselves.

As I showed with Skytrain, and as Stelios and Michael O'Leary have demonstrated with easyJet and Ryanair, the traditional airline model keeps people out – but low-cost flying brings them in. Since the tragic events of 11 September 2001, the no-frills airlines have shown how public confidence in flying can be restored – enabling holidaymakers and business-people to travel at reasonable fares, providing the flights that can bring families together.

As Simon Calder's book shows, the twentieth century largely belonged to the traditional, high-cost airlines (with a few snipers, like me, upsetting their cosy cartel). The twenty-first century will be the preserve of the no-frills airlines, at least within Europe.

This book may even inspire you to start your own low-cost carrier. If you do, and you suspect that the existing airlines are trying to obstruct you, may I offer you the same advice that I gave to Richard Branson and Stelios? If the allegations are true, sue the bastards!

Sir Freddie Laker, Grand Bahama Island, 2002

1. THE FREEDOM OF THE SKIES

In 1973 I hitch-hiked from the grand Irish port of Kinsale to Cork airport. At the time, the one-way air fare to London was £30, which represented three weeks' work on the farm at the end of the runway at Gatwick airport where I happened to be working at the time. So I carried on thumbing, and arrived back at the ranch three days later. In 2001, I again hitched to Cork airport. But this time I stopped, checked in, and got on a plane. The fare was still £30 – representing three hours' work at the average British wage. Unbelievably, no-frills flying has rendered hitch-hiking an uneconomic form of transport. Had I opted to thumb, and paid for the ferry to Britain, and miserable motorway food and drink along the way, it would probably have cost me more than the plane.

Rule 1 of air travel: the person in the next seat has always paid less than you for the same flight. One day in November 1995, any of the passengers on a British Airways jet on the apron at Glasgow who cared to look across at the funny orange and white Boeing next door would have seen an entire plane full of people who had paid less than them.

The sight was as ludicrous as, say, the Millennium Dome. Someone had painted human-sized, bright orange digits along the fuselage of a 737. Until then, airline liveries had been safely conservative. A wider perspective revealed a telephone number, 0582 445566, in Luton – from where the plane had recently arrived. The people who had dialled this number had found that they could fly between Luton and Glasgow for £29 each way. Edinburgh flights – same price, same absence of free newspapers and snacks – began five days later.

Since antiquity, man has yearned to take to the skies. In the fifteenth century, Leonardo da Vinci made sketches of how this could be achieved, getting impressively close to a blueprint for the modern helicopter. By the early eighteenth century, a Jesuit priest named Bartholomeu de Gusmao had proposed – and modelled – a hot-air balloon. In 1783, the first man had been lifted by the Montgolfier balloon. One hundred years ago, powered flight became a reality when the Wright brothers achieved sustained flight. Nowadays, most of us are well past the amazement stage, and are simply concerned to get where we're going safely, cheaply and on time.

'It's not rocket science,' Stelios Haji-Ioannou, the man behind easyJet, is fond of saying. No-frills airlines fly the same expensive pieces of metal at the same speed as the traditional carriers. But they cut costs wherever they can, for example by plastering the reservations phone number (or, these days, the Internet address) on the side of planes to save on the marketing budget. When it comes to pricing, 'We look at the fare the customer can pay, not what the market can bear,' says Rob Brown, who speaks for the world's most successful airline, Southwest. This pioneering carrier began opening up the skies so long ago that Rod Stewart was a bright new hope whose first album was topping the charts on both sides of the Atlantic. The business plan (of Southwest, not Rod) has been emulated from Australia via Brazil to Canada. But the no-frills revolution is at its most fervent in the skies over the British Isles. For instance, a decade ago there were a dozen flights a day between London and Edinburgh on two carriers. Now there are almost fifty each day, each way, with six airlines competing.

The rebels with two causes – lower fares and higher earnings – are slugging it out with the traditional airlines and, increasingly, with each other. They comprise four home-grown airlines, an Irish carrier that outranks them all, and an offshoot of the Virgin empire that suddenly and unexpectedly found itself the biggest airline in Belgium. Like fundamentalist Christian sects, each no-frills carrier holds its particular version of the gospel of cheap air travel to be superior to the rest.

A century after Orville and Wilbur Wright built the first successful aircraft, the world has shrunk. You can be virtually anywhere on the planet within 24 hours. We are approaching the point where one billion people annually will take a flight somewhere in the world. Yet for the first half-century of its existence, aviation was the exclusive privilege of the rich. The first economy class was launched only in 1952 – on TWA, one of the many famous names eased into oblivion with some help from low-cost carriers.

The figures who have put air travel within reach of the people are not traditional airline bosses. Herb Kelleher, who has the greatest low-cost track record of all, once settled a dispute on behalf of his airline, Southwest, with an arm-wrestling contest. On this side of the Atlantic, from Sir Freddie Laker ('sue the bastards!') to Michael O'Leary ('stuff it to Lufty!' or perhaps something even less polite), they are larger-than-life individuals with the guts to take on the establishment – and each other – plus the brains to win.

This book focuses on the men and women who stripped away the expensive frills and invited ordinary people on board. There is plenty of mutual admiration among the top tier in low-cost travel. Freddie loves Richard. Barbara admires Stelios. Michael kneels at the altar of Herb. But there is a vast amount of venom too. Put two or more of the airline bosses in the same room, and you have a combustible mix.

They all agree, though, that the no-frills business hinges upon nailing costs down – by flying planes for more hours each day, eradicating tickets and dispensing with travel agents' commission. Cut costs, and you can even make money flying people between England and Scotland for £29 each way.

That's on a good day. During the course of writing this book, fares on a number of flights fell effectively to zero. Some passengers found they could travel from Scotland and Northern Ireland for only the cost of the government's Air Passenger Duty. I have been tracking European air fares for twenty years, during which time prices have gently declined in real terms. Now those complex calculations have ceased to have any meaning. When fares vanished, the calibration was rendered as obsolete as a ticket on AB Airlines (one of several no-frills failures). Yet the same airlines that are giving away seats can also report increased passenger numbers and earnings, even after the attacks on America that dented confidence in air travel.

How do they do that, then? By squeezing every possible penny out of every possible seat, and then giving away the rest. The airlines continue to thrive because the average fares paid are significantly above the prices quoted in ads. Indeed, a common complaint is that the fares advertised so temptingly often seem mysteriously unavailable. But we travellers are learning that there is nothing so fluid as the price of a seat on a no-frills airline. The black art of yield management can mean that you are not only sitting next to someone who paid less than you, but that he or she may not have paid anything for the trip besides tax.

You may regard this as worrying evidence that the world of travel, always in something of a world of its own, has finally taken leave of its senses. I urge you to stop worrying and start travelling.

First, though, I hope to clear a flight path through the fog of misapprehension and misinformation that hangs over no-frills flying. Partly, confusion arises because the airline world used to be simple to grasp. There was British Airways and its foreign counterparts: Air France, Alitalia, Lufthansa, and so on. Fares and frequencies were fixed by the airlines, at levels to suit them – not travellers. They used to collude on rules to make sure no one was giving the passenger too good a deal. 'We used to have meetings to discuss the permissible dimensions of a salt cellar in first class,' reminisces one airline executive, wistfully recalling the days when no airline was able to demonstrate a competitive edge, and none was necessary. On routes shared by airlines, revenues were often pooled, which meant there was no point in trying to outshine the competition.

The message to the consumer was 'take it or leave it'. Mostly, they left it, because fares were way too high. In 1980, the cheapest available return fare on what was then the world's busiest international air route, between London and Paris, was around £70. This represented a week's work for the average British worker. Today, the same fare applies – but the average wage has risen to the point where it is just a day's salary. But to allow such sweeping change to take place, concepts that passengers had previously taken for granted, from paper tickets to in-flight meals, have been jettisoned as part of the crusade to reduce costs to a level where a whole new market of travellers could be attracted. And that £70 fare may be halved or doubled at any moment, as the airline juggles the price and the people it predicts can be tempted on board.

Besides poor visibility, the course steered towards free skies is likely to run into political turbulence. Europe's skies have officially been open, courtesy of Neil Kinnock – the European Commissioner for Transport – since 1997. But leading airports remain effectively closed to newcomers because of the shortage of available slots – Heathrow being the world's most desirable, and hence most difficult, place in which to land a plane. The present state of freedom of the skies can be roughly stated as 'you can fly anywhere you like within Europe, as long as it doesn't include Heathrow; Gatwick, Frankfurt, Paris and Amsterdam could be tricky, too.' Even after 11 September 2001, there is not enough room in the skies or on the runways for all the flights that wish to be airborne at peak times. And in parts of Europe, obstructive governments act in collusion with 'flag-carriers' to constrict the freedom of the skies. Many countries regard an airline as an essential component of a nation's identity, in the same way that dud teams from dwarf countries get to play in European soccer tournaments, where they are customarily knocked out in the preliminary round.

With some ostrich-like exceptions, the no-frills revolution has forced the flag-carrier airlines to cut fares and, equally importantly, restrictions. The freedom of the skies has impacted on the railways, too. A fleet of Eurostar trains that was supposed to shuttle travellers from Scotland and northern England through the Channel Tunnel to Paris and Brussels was rendered obsolete even before it could enter service. The reason: the spectacular growth of no-frills aviation. The rolling stock arrived just as cheap flights from Glasgow (or thereabouts) to the French and Belgian capitals (or thereabouts) began. And Sir Richard Branson, a champion of no-frills flying in Europe and Australia, finds his trains from Scotland to London and Bristol in uncomfortable head-to-head competition with easyJet, Go and Ryanair.

Even the charter airlines, who maintain that they have perfected the art of low-cost flying, have woken up to the disconcerting reality that there are strange-looking Boeing 737s parked on sun- and ski-holiday runways from Athens to Zurich. When the independent traveller or villa owner can book a cheap scheduled flight from Bristol to Faro, Liverpool to Palma or East Midlands to Malaga, the economics change for the worse for charter airlines.

'All we cut is the price,' promised one now-obsolete airline, British Midland, with a fare of £149 return to Frankfurt. Another, Debonair (which, unlike British Midland, went bust rather than rebranded), was offering Nice from £118. And British Airways took out an ad to boast that its best fare to Pisa was £159 return. The year was 1997. By 2002, the base fares to these destinations had been halved. These examples show why British Airways and other full-service airlines are finding it so difficult to make money in Europe these days. There is barely a big city within two hours flying time from London that cannot be reached on a no-frills flight, routinely for fares of £100 or less.

To make the most of the new freedoms, though, you have to be prepared to make compromises. To fly no-frills from Heathrow, for example, the only possible destination is Brussels, on Virgin Express. But if you fly from Stansted to 'Brussels' on Ryanair, you will find yourself in the town of Charleroi, halfway to the border with France. Should anything delay the flight, by three hours or three days, you can expect no compensation nor rations. If you want to go to Boston on Southwest Airlines, the airline suggests you use Providence in Rhode Island or Manchester in New Hampshire – neither of which is even in the same state as Boston. But in the new business climate, plenty of travellers have found that the benefits of cheap travel outweigh the cost in terms of inconvenience. And thousands of people who would not otherwise have been able to fly have seen the world open up before them.

If you are an inveterate traveller, no-frills aviation allows you to see more of the world. If you are in business, you can afford to get out and about more. And if you are in love, cheap flights can bring you closer together – whether geographically (if you are hundreds of miles apart), or emotionally with that romantic getaway to Paris or Venice, or at least airports within hitching distance of those cities. (Alternatively, anyone looking for Love need only fly on Southwest to its home base at the Dallas airport of that name.)

Weekends away have become mystery tours for thousands of people thanks to Ryanair's and Buzz's policies of flying to places you didn't know you wanted to go to. If you thought Bergerac was simply a dodgy 1970s TV serial, and had always assumed Västerås to be an unpleasant urinary infection, you can find out how wrong you were by flying to either destination from Stansted on the cheap. (Cabotage, incidentally, is not that quaint village in the Dordogne with the lovely church and friendly cafe, but the legal right for a UK-based subsidiary of a Dutch airline to fly domestically in France from Bordeaux to Grenoble.) The geography of twenty-first-century Europe has been transformed. I don't know which is the stranger phenomenon – that an ex-US Air Force base on a plateau above the Moselle Valley is now a leading European aviation hub, or that you can fly there any day you like from Dorset.

Until 1995, no one in Europe had heard of no-frills flying. Now, everyone knows easyJet, BMIbaby, Buzz, Go, Virgin Express and Ryanair, and has probably flown on one or other of them, too. Just like supermarkets, they have adopted distinct characteristics and appeal to different people: easyJet is Tesco, BMIbaby is Safeway, Buzz equals Somerfield, Go is Waitrose, Virgin Express is that interesting new deli you're not quite sure about, and Ryanair is ASDA.

Staying with the supermarket analogy for a moment: imagine driving to your favourite store, only to be told to drive round and round the roundabout outside for ten minutes, because the car park and its access roads are full. When you are finally allowed in, you are instructed to park in a distant corner and told to wait for a bus to bring you to the main door. If you suffered this treatment week after week, without a word of apology, you might start looking for another supermarket. It might be a little further from home and take longer to reach, but if the overall journey time plus stress were reduced, and the new supermarket charged lower prices, you would soon get used to it. That is what some of the no-frills airlines count on. They believe that travellers can be persuaded to see the advantage of less popular airports. At a time when 'stacking' over south-east England is a necessity for planes heading for Heathrow and Gatwick, many passengers are beginning to agree.

Does cheap equal nasty? The number of people who think so is diminishing with every celebrity who chooses the no-frills option. Tony Blair and his family taking their holiday flights on Ryanair did the Irish airline as many favours as did its steward, Brian, winning Big Brother, while squads of Premier League footballers and television presenters on implausibly big salaries demonstrate a fondness for easyJet. Barbara Cassani of Go, the only woman chief executive at the helm of a no-frills carrier – and, say some, the acceptable face of cheap flying – is in constant demand as an inspirational speaker. Simply shadowing her for a day is an exhausting experience.

For some people, frills comprise half the fun of travelling. If you are prepared to pay a club class fare of £400 for the half-hour flight between London and Paris, arrange for a limousine to meet you, and pick up the tab at Le Crillon, then enjoy your Air Miles and bathrobes while they last. As thousands of employees of traditional airlines have found to their cost, the world is changing rapidly. Business travellers have always been part of the no-frills plan. The routes that have proved most successful are those with a mix of business and leisure travel, such as London to Edinburgh, Copenhagen and Barcelona.

Every fortnight or thereabouts, another 737 destined for one of Europe's cut-price airlines comes off the production line at the Boeing factory in Seattle. To rent one of these shiny new specimens costs about $100,000 per month. They have to be kept aloft, and three quarters full of people. And to do that, the carriers must flood the market with cut-price deals. This book aims to take you behind the scenes, where the decisions that change the way we travel are taken, and scores are settled. You may conclude that the no-frills runway is more like a school playground; but to traditional airlines, and even some train operators, the no-frills carriers represent a potentially deadly threat. 'By 2008, no one will be flying on traditional airlines in Europe,' says Stelios. Plenty of people disagree. But there is no doubt that the map of Europe has changed, probably for ever, thanks to the swashbuckling figures whose planes and people work the hardest in the business. The roots of the routes from Luton and Liverpool, Stansted and Prestwick, are tangled. This book aims to unravel them, to help you make sense of an industry where Hot Air is more than just an in-flight magazine, and to try to make sure that Rule 1 – that you always pay more than the person in the next seat – does not apply to you.

Some people in the traditional airline business have yet to grasp that what people are buying is not the dubious pleasure of sitting in an aluminium tube for a couple of hours, eating questionable food and sinking as much 'free' alcohol as possible in the time available. We are buying the sensation of warm sand and cool Mediterranean between our toes; the surge of adrenalin when a deal is done; the scent of a strange and beautiful Italian town; the sheer euphoria of a goal at the Nou Camp stadium in Barcelona; or the smile on the face of your loved one who realises that the distance between the two of you has diminished.

With thrills like that, who needs frills?

2. A TOUCH OF CLASSLESSNESS

'It began by a fluke, like everything else does'
VLADIMIR RAITZ, FOUNDER OF THE PACKAGE HOLIDAY

'Iberia – where only the plane gets more attention than you'; 'Alitalia takes your fun very seriously'
ADVERTISEMENTS IN *NATIONAL GEOGRAPHIC*

'Nation states believed that to be a nation you needed a flag, a national anthem and an airline. The first two come cheap but the third is extremely expensive'
BOB AYLING, FORMER CHIEF EXECUTIVE, BRITISH AIRWAYS

The great journeys of exploration by Marco Polo, Columbus and Livingstone have the same root as a short hop on Ryanair for a weekend of bingeing in Dublin or an easyJet flight to Athens for a month of island-hopping through the classical myths. Ever since human beings formed themselves into communities that created a surplus of production, man has been a traveller. Thousands of years ago, the people of Mesopotamia journeyed through what is now Iraq to trade goods and ideas; later, similar trips were made up and down the Nile, across the Indian subcontinent and Asia. Mostly, the journeys were driven by desire for economic improvement or for military conquest, which were inextricably entwined. The vast majority of human journeys to alien lands taken up to the end of the Second World War were undertaken for the purposes of conquest or colonisation, with a sprinkling of holy wars conducted in the name of religion. But, by the second half of the twentieth century, the notion of foreign travel was sufficiently advanced for the ordinary man or woman to aspire to a week in the sun. And by the start of the twenty-first century, the average British person can be in Europe within a few hours for a few hours' work, or on the other side of the world for a week's not unduly hard labour.

Since Herodotus, there have been guidebook writers to prepare the ground for travellers, and since Thomas Cook there have been individuals determined to find solutions using the latest technology that allow people to travel decently for a fair price. Cook would not have seen himself as a no-frills kind of fellow, but his concept of empowering new strata of society to travel parallels the development of low-cost flying.

Thomas Cook was not merely the pioneer of package holidays – he was also the first to encounter the massed ranks of vested interest blocking his path, and to find inventive ways to get around the obstruction. A statue outside Leicester railway station pays tribute to him. He had begun organised tourism in a small way in the city in 1841, running a temperance outing to the nearby town of Loughborough for one shilling and sixpence (7 ½p). It wasn't no frills, mind, because the price included tea. Anyone caring to visit the Leicestershire town nowadays would not automatically be struck by its attractiveness as a holiday destination, and might even suggest that it would look better after several strong drinks. But exactly 160 years after Cook's first trip, Go announced no-frills flights from several Mediterranean destinations to East Midlands airport – nearest town, Loughborough.

As is natural for travel entrepreneurs, Thomas Cook wanted to expand. The perfect opportunity was provided by the 1855 international exposition in Paris, the first to be held in the French capital, set in the dramatic surroundings of Baron Haussmann's newly redrawn city. The steadily rising incomes and increased aspirations of the middle classes brought about by the industrial revolution convinced Cook that there would be a market for trips from London to Paris. He duly approached the leading shipping lines on the cross-Channel routes and asked for discounts on tickets in return for guaranteed group bookings. They turned him down, on the grounds that it would not be in their interests to sell below official rates, despite his assurance that they would be conveying a whole new market of people who would not otherwise travel. (This same argument between innovator and entrenched interests was to take place repeatedly as the no-frills airlines sought to take to the skies.)

Eventually, Cook was offered a deal on the route between Harwich and Antwerp. A glance at the map will reveal that it is not ideal to start a journey from London to Paris by heading north-east to Harwich, and that the Belgian port, which lies almost on the Dutch border, is not exactly convenient for the French capital. Even Ryanair would be hard pressed to describe Antwerp as Paris. So Cook sought to turn this to his advantage, and constructed an itinerary that continued to Brussels and Cologne, meandered up the Rhine, branched off to Heidelberg and Baden-Baden, turned west to Strasbourg and onwards to Paris. The French side of the ferry operation was prepared to negotiate with Cook, so his parties completed their grand circular tour by returning to London across the Channel from Le Havre or Dieppe.

Foreign travel for pleasure, as opposed to trade or war, was still the preserve of the wealthy. Indeed, until the 1871 Bank Holidays Act, the working man or woman had no right even to take 25 December off. The new law assigned days off at Christmas, Easter, Whitsun and on the first Monday of August. The railway companies did well out of the change, taking millions in the Victorian equivalent of no-frills travel – third class – to resorts in Britain for bank holiday weekends. There was no prospect of the average worker ever venturing abroad for a holiday. A significant number of people headed west to seek economic improvement in America, but the sailings were almost invariably one-way. When people waved loved ones off from quaysides at Liverpool, Southampton or Queenstown (as the port of Cobh was known when Ireland was part of nineteenth-century Britain), they knew it was extremely unlikely they would ever see them again.

The First World War took more British people abroad than ever before. A million of them died there, mostly slaughtered on the Western Front. The social effects of the 'Great War', and the political shifts that it caused, have been well documented. But the First World War also changed travelling patterns, as bereaved relatives demanded the opportunity to visit the fields of Flanders where a generation of young men had fallen.

During the First World War, many thousands of men had been trained to fly; enough of them survived to form the basis of the new industry of passenger air transport. It had developed first of all in the United States, partly because the Americans were late entrants to the First World War and therefore developed commercial flying sooner. The first civil purpose of aviation was to carry mail, not people. The aviators took risks but earned good money: it was a lucrative business working for national governments, and the cargo, unlike human freight, did not complain about the bumpy ride, the intense cold and the ever-present danger. 'Self-loading cargo' is one of the more pejorative terms for the people who ultimately pay the wages of workers in the travel industry, i.e. the passengers. If, at the end of a long, uncomfortable flight, that is what you feel like, then bear in mind the origins of passenger traffic. People travelled on trains and ships, often in considerable comfort and at great speed. Only slowly did the mail planes start taking paying passengers, to supplement the earnings from postal contracts.

The first purpose-built international air terminal in the world was built beside the Purley Way, at the time well south of London. From the day the Air Minister's wife opened the new terminal in May 1928, until the final Lufthansa flight took off on the last day of August 1939, Croydon – or at least its airport – was the most glamorous place in Britain. The Aerodrome Hotel next door (another world first) could sell space on its roof at a penny per person as crowds gathered to welcome aviators like Charles Lindbergh and Amy Johnson, and film stars such as Douglas Fairbanks and Mary Pickford.

NO-FRILLS NAVIGATION

The first workable air traffic control system in Europe had been introduced at Croydon aerodrome. Initially, it was a rudimentary affair: in poor weather, a man with especially good hearing would venture out on to the walkway around the tower, and listen for aircraft. Once he heard one, he would report its direction to the controllers. A rotating transmitter would be wound around to point towards the inbound aircraft and with luck a Morse code conversation would ensue.

In the 30s, the principle upon which the modern Global Positioning System is based was used to enable pilots to fix their precise positions. At an agreed instant, three radio stations in southern England took a bearing on the aircraft, and a navigator at Croydon would collate the results to pinpoint the location. The aerodrome is now a museum, and in the faithfully recreated Radio Room, you can visualise ghostly figures crouching over dials, valves, maps, pencils and rulers.

Just as the X-ray revolutionised medicine by allowing doctors to 'see' through human flesh, so the invention of radar (RAdio Detection And Ranging) transformed aviation. No longer were pilots and air traffic controllers constrained by what they could see; by bouncing high-frequency radio waves off objects in the sky, cloud and darkness ceased to be causes for concern (at least in theory). Radar is now used by everything from the ground controllers keeping the taxiways tidy at Luton to the 'air-prox' warning systems on board aircraft that warn of other nearby planes.

The 'Air Ministry Administration Building', now known simply as Airport House, became the model for the initial generation of airports. The main terminal hall has an interior that is still so robustly art deco that it seems to resound with the voices of the passengers who used to weigh in there. Yes, that's *weigh* in: then, as now, the standard baggage allowance was 20 kg (44 lb). But in the early days of civil aviation, each passenger was discreetly asked to step on to the scales, so that seats could be allocated in such a way as to maintain the trim of the aircraft.

In 1936, two significant events took place in England. Fifteen miles south of Croydon aerodrome, a circular building adjacent to the railway station opened. The first airport that allowed passengers to step straight from the train to the plane, without even getting wet, was located at the small airfield adjacent to Gatwick racecourse. (The terminal, known as the Beehive, is now occupied by GB Airways, the with-frills competitor to many of the low-cost airlines.) The other development took place 120 miles north of London. On Easter Monday, Billy Butlin opened his first holiday camp at Skegness with the slogan 'Holiday with pay . . . holiday with play . . . A week's holiday for a week's wage'. He correctly anticipated the passing of the Holidays with Pay Act two years later; he had lobbied vigorously for it, and when it was passed he chartered a special train to take every MP who had voted for it to his second camp, at Clacton.

The 1938 Holidays with Pay Act was a dramatic change in entitlement. For the first time, millions of families could look forward to a week away. In 1939, 11 million workers earned a holiday, their last for six years because of the outbreak of war. The few of them who chose – or, rather, could afford – to travel to Paris with Air France did so in seventy minutes, rather faster than present-day travellers can enjoy from Gatwick, even though the Sussex airport is twelve miles nearer the French capital.

The Second World War, like its predecessor, changed the way that ordinary people looked at travel. Millions of young men saw much more of the world than they could have imagined, albeit under circumstances that were not of their choosing. Peace, when it finally came in 1945, bestowed Britain with a different society than had existed before the war – one in which the concept of foreign travel for the masses was no longer alien. Servicemen who returned alive from overseas had acquired a taste for abroad that the prevailing travel industry could not satisfy.

The first flight took off from the new Heath Row airport, west of London, on 1 January 1946. It was a proving flight, destined for Buenos Aires, for British South American Airways – the airline for which the mother of one of the no-frills pioneers, Richard Branson, later worked.

The roots of the present day no-frills routes from Luton and Liverpool, Stansted and Prestwick, are old and tangled, but one man did more than anyone to get ordinary people travelling. A young man named Vladimir Raitz had been born in Moscow in 1922, but his family left the Soviet Union when he was six. He enjoyed a pedigree education, at the Goethe School in Berlin and the Lycée Français in Warsaw, before reading Economic History at the London School of Economics, which he calls 'a very dubious organisation'; Stelios of easyJet went to the same college, as did all manner of people from Mick Jagger to Cherie Blair. Raitz was working as a journalist for Reuters when he took his first holiday in Calvi, Corsica, in August 1949 – the year after Britain's post-war ban on leisure travel abroad was lifted. A Russian colleague invited him to the French island.

Even aged eighty, Raitz is slim and sharp, with a face that still matches the chiselled profile on snapshots of his Mediterranean sojourn at a holiday camp in Corsica. 'It was run by friends of mine – Russians like myself, White Russians.' There is some irony that the Soviet Union, which gave the world one of its most joyless airlines, Aeroflot, also provided it with the package holiday. The White Russians, themselves exiles from the 1917 October Revolution, had established a camp in Calvi before the war. In 1949, they revived it, using ex-US Army tents that provided the accommodation for the first sun, sea and sex package holidays. 'It was called Club Olympique,' recalls Raitz. 'I had a most excellent two weeks' holiday in the most spartan of surroundings.'

The holiday may have been excellent, but the journey there was arduous. It involved a train from London to Dover, a ferry to Calais, another train to Nice and then an overnight crossing on the good ship *Ile de Beauté* to the port of Calvi. At the end of the trip, he says, 'They asked me, "Why can't you send us some British clients?" And I came back and thought I would do this in addition to my day job at Reuters.' Raitz was not the only one to be inspired by the Club Olympique. A Frenchman named Gérard Blitz subsequently developed the concept into the Club Méditerranée.

'It began by a fluke, like everything else does,' Vladimir Raitz now says. He had £3,000 in capital, bequeathed by his grandmother. That equates to about £60,000 today. He found premises in Fleet Street, London, above what was then D & S Radford's Snuffe Shoppe and is now Ryman the stationer. He recruited a secretary with the adventurous name of Connie Everest. And he chose a name: Horizon Holidays. All he needed now was to solve a problem that Blitz and his French clientele did not face: how to get people to Corsica without it taking two days each way, a journey that would wreck the average week's holiday. The solution lay in the large number of ex-military transport aircraft that were in circulation, many of them owned and operated by Freddie Laker in Southend. But Raitz called on an air broker, Instone Air Transport, to provide the capacity. The company gently explained, as Raitz puts it, that 'British European Airways had the monopoly, and they didn't really want to tolerate any competition of any sort'. The chances of persuading the Ministry of Transport to open up the market were remote. 'I had great difficulty in getting permission to start these series of flights,' says Raitz with some understatement. 'The thing I faced was the implacable opposition of the established airline. British European Airways had the monopoly and they trod on everyone's feet to maintain this monopoly.'

British European Airways (BEA) would later become part of British Airways, the organisation that was to hamper Laker Airways and Virgin Atlantic in their attempts to open up the skies across the Atlantic. Vladimir Raitz proved useful warm-up material in 1950. 'British European Airways said, "Yes we want you to fly, but we want you to fly on our scheduled services." Perhaps they saw what was coming, I don't know. "We don't want people to fly and undercut us." '

At the time, BEA did not fly to Corsica. The return fare to Nice, the closest point to the island that the airline served, was £70 – the equivalent of about £1,400 today, but curiously about the same as you might pay now for a cheapie on easyJet or Go. After a series of 'fights with the Ministry of Transport to get the licence', Raitz was finally given permission to operate to Calvi just before Easter 1950. The licence was too late and too limited, he says: 'I was restricted to flying teachers and students only.' It had taken the government five months to decide that Horizon would be allowed to fly – but only if it was restricted to the education world. The charters were allowed on the grounds of their educational value, and ever since students, and people who pretend to be students, and teachers and lecturers, have enjoyed special fares. But to sign up for a week in Corsica, they had to be quite well heeled. 'My all-inclusive holiday in the first year cost £32 and 10 shillings [£32.50, equivalent to £650 today], which included the flight and two weeks' full board at this holiday camp including as much food and wine as you could consume.' Showing that there are few original ideas in travel, the fastest-growing sector in package holidays during the 1990s was the all-inclusive holiday, with unlimited food and alcohol.

'It really was absolutely no frills,' says Raitz about his first flight. The 32-seater DC-3, belonging to Air Transport Charter, took off from Gatwick on the third Saturday in March 1950 (unwittingly establishing the Sussex airport as the charter airport *par excellence*). It flew at a top speed of 170 mph, and – being unpressurised – at turbulent altitudes below 3,000 feet. The aircraft could make it only as far as Lyon before stopping for supplies. 'We were a couple of hours on the ground refuelling and having a meal,' says Raitz. The rest of the journey took another two hours. When jet flights begin between London and Corsica – almost certainly on a no-frills flight – they will take around eighty minutes.

The first season was a great success with the public, but less so with the balance sheet. This is a common complaint among airlines. Thanks to a friendly bank manager, Horizon was able to stagger into a second season, which saw a 9 per cent increase in price and a 40 per cent increase in bookings – the sort of trick that plenty of airlines wish they could pull today. Even better, from Raitz's point of view, the incoming Conservative government made aviation less restricted. The teacher-and-student condition disappeared, but Raitz was still obliged to battle for every licence.

'One had to appear firstly before the Air Transport Advisory Council, then the Air Transport Licensing Board and the CAA. BEA, and then later on BA, tried to shut everyone down. Although I must say we were all attackers and defenders, we were all on the greatest of terms, and we all liked each other very much.' Just before Horizon's summer season began in May 1952, two more events took place that were profoundly to affect the traveller. On the first of the month, the US airline, TWA, introduced a 'tourist' class. Before 1952, all scheduled air travel in the West was one class – first class, with prices to match, which helps explain BEA's fare of £1,400 return (in 2002 prices) from London to Nice. TWA wisely concluded that earnings would be higher if they cut fares and squeezed in more seats.

Then, on 2 May, the world's first passenger jet service took off. A de Havilland Comet, in the colours of the British Overseas Airline Corporation (BOAC) took off from London Heathrow, destination Rome. It flew at twice the height and twice the speed of previous airliners, and was a thirsty brute. The Italian capital was just the first of a series of five refuelling stops that were needed between London and Johannesburg, the destination for that first flight. Today, five wide-bodied jets fly this route every day, non-stop. But the Comet, which built on the work of the jet-engine pioneer, Frank Whittle, halved the journey time. Exactly a year later there was the first of three fatal crashes within twelve months involving Comets. Nevertheless, the pioneering jet proved that moving large numbers of people at close to the speed of sound could be done, and spurred American engineers at Boeing, Convair, Douglas and Lockheed into finding safe designs for passenger jetliners. The Comet returned to the skies after substantial re-engineering, and did much to open up Europe for independent travellers with 'seat only' and student charters to Greece and Spain, in the colours of Dan-Air and British Airtours.

Meanwhile, Vladimir Raitz was changing the face of Europe. 'You know Estartit on the Costa Brava?' he enquires casually. 'When I arrived there, there was a completely deserted beach and a boarding house. To turn something like that, without doing too much damage, into a holiday resort for British clients was immensely satisfying. And the same in Majorca – when I went there, there was one hotel on the island. And some beaches – now unfortunately surrounded by hotels – you couldn't even get to. There were no roads, you had to clamber down a mountain-side to see a lovely little beach. That was what was so satisfying.'

What was less satisfying were the constant arguments over licences. British European Airways objected to flights to Palma in Mallorca because they would cause 'material diversion of traffic', even though the airline did not at the time fly to the island; the closest it got was Barcelona on the Spanish mainland. Raitz won. But on routes that BEA or another scheduled airline flew, the lowest price he was allowed to charge for a package was limited by the lowest prevailing fare set by the International Air Transport Association. And BEA had one more trump card they could produce – the concept of 'wasteful duplication' of resources; in a country still recovering from the ravages and privations of war, this could prove a forceful argument. Raitz countered equally forcefully, but politely. 'While we berated each other in front of the [Air Transport Licensing] Board, afterwards we all went for a drink. It was all done in a very British way.'

Perhaps because of the tussles over licensing, competition was slow to arrive. 'For about four or five years we had the field to ourselves. Then other people started coming in and the industry grew.' At first, 'there was a certain spirit of camaraderie. There was no hatred or dislike or anything like that. And I didn't worry because the cake was getting very much larger anyway.' One of the competitors was the Travel Club of Upminster, whose proprietor, Harry Chandler, had a rival claim to have started the foreign package holiday, having organised rail groups to Schwangau in Bavaria as early as 1935, and following it up with trips by air to the Algarve in Portugal, beginning in 1965. His son, Paul, who now runs the business with Harry's widow, Rene, says, 'I've always taken the family line that we invented the package holiday. But my father would never have called it a package holiday. He called it an inclusive tour. We were there, and so was Vladimir.'

Croydon aerodrome got in the package holiday (or inclusive tour) business as one final bid for survival, serving as a departure point for DC-3s to Spain. But a new, hi-tech Gatwick was opened by the Queen in 1959, and Croydon received its final call in 1959, after which the airfield was buried beneath ranks of factories. The surviving airport buildings descended into dereliction, before Airport House was rescued by a private property company.

By now Vladimir Raitz had progressed from the war-surplus DC-3s to the Viscount. It was, he says, 'a marvellous plane, flying at 300 mph against 170 mph', and managing to stay above some of the weather. These kept going in commercial service until the late 90s, by which time charter fleets had advanced by several generations. Raitz says that 'the old saying of the clapped-out charter planes never really applied'. Even the DC-3s, with which he began, were safe: 'Many of them are still flying around in India, and not long ago I saw one in Florida. They were good planes. And then when we went into the jets – the BAC1-11s and Boeing 737s and Boeing 727s – tour operators used some of the best aircraft.' Until recently, a venerable Dan-Air 727 was flying scheduled routes in Colombia on behalf of the regional airline, SAM, with its original colours inexpertly painted out.

The fact that charter carriers were using modern aircraft alarmed the scheduled airlines, which helps explain some exceptionally cheesy advertising. The Spanish carrier, Iberia, promised that 'only the plane gets more attention than you', while Alitalia announced that it 'takes your fun very seriously'. Both of these appeared not in the 70s equivalent of *Hello!* magazine, but within the otherwise highbrow pages of *National Geographic* in October 1970. What particularly worried the scheduled airlines was the way that some seats were being sold to independent travellers, the precursor of cheap no-frills flights today. Arcane rules were drawn up that required accommodation to be an integral part of the holiday, and even more tortuous solutions were found to evade them. The standard agreement issued by the travel agent who sold the ticket required the traveller to affirm that they owned property abroad, that they hereby granted rights in it to the agent, who promptly rented it back to the traveller for a pound. The Greek authorities were particularly stern. Olympic Airways was well aware that using a cheap charter to go island-hopping was standard practice among independent travellers. Even today, passengers on charter flights may be denied the flight home from Greece if their passport contains evidence of their having left the country (e.g. on a side-trip from Kos to Turkey) for one night or more.

From the 300 clients of Horizon who took package holidays in 1950, the number of British travellers on packages increased to around 18 million by 2000. Along the way, there were numerous crashes, both financial and fatal. In 1964, Fiesta Tours collapsed, stranding 2,000 holidaymakers; in June 1967, two British aircraft, both on Spanish charter flights, crashed within twelve hours of each other, killing over 160 people; the following year, the charter airline British Eagle went bust. But the package holiday market was expanding inexorably in a climate of rapidly increasing disposable income. In 1970, Raitz invented Club 18-30, a brand that became a legend in its own Happy Hour, and is presently owned by the Thomas Cook organisation – something that the original temperance campaigner would not have favoured.

The year that still haunts Vladimir Raitz, and many other veterans of the travel industry, is the tumultuous twelve months of 1974. It began in darkness, as the three-day week brought about by the miners' strike took hold. In the 'Who Rules Britain?' election of February, Harold Wilson's Labour party won fewer votes than the incumbent prime minister, Edward Heath, but gained the most seats and took power. The enduring economic gloom, amplified by the Middle East oil crisis, brought Raitz's Horizon Holidays to its knees, along with many other travel companies that had hitherto prospered in a climate of expansion. Even though Raitz poured his personal assets into trying to shore up Horizon, it went into receivership and was taken over by the ever-expanding Court Line conglomerate. 'I loved what I was doing, I did it successfully for 25 years until the disastrous year of 1974.'

Two months before the October election in which Wilson achieved a slim majority, Court Line collapsed; 40,000 holidaymakers were stranded abroad, and 60,000 others lost money, albeit temporarily. Part of Horizon survived: the Birmingham operation had been split from the original company, and was trading under the name of Horizon Midlands. It was eventually floated as a public company, and reverted to Horizon Holidays after a decent interval. It established a charter airline called Orion. Eventually, it was absorbed into the giant Thomson combine, now part of the Prussian Mining, Iron and Steel Company, better known as Preussag. Before the German takeover, Raitz offered to buy the unused Horizon brand back, without success. 'I went to Paul [Brett, then in charge of Thomson] and I said, "Will you sell me the name and I'll start again?" And he said, "Vladimir, I'm not going to sell you the name, even for a million pounds, because I don't need any further competition."'

The backpack revolution had begun at exactly the time Horizon had folded, with the publication of Lonely Planet's first book, *Across Asia on the Cheap* in 1974. The new generation of low-budget travellers started off on the Magic Bus, but when that involved too many hours plodding through Germany or risking the two-lane road through Yugoslavia, they demanded no-frills flying without paying the outrageous fares charged by scheduled airlines. One short-lived expedient involved a bus from Aldgate in London to Southend airport, which at the time was a fairly busy place – way ahead of its rival, Stansted. A Viscount belonging to the late lamented British Island Airways hopped over to Ostend, where another bus was waiting (you hoped) for the drive into Brussels. On a good day you could cover the ground in six hours, for a fare of around £40 return, or less if you went only as far as Ostend, the starting point for many a hitch-hiking trip to Antwerp, Athens or Afghanistan. By

1982, the quirky guidebook *Alternative London* offered some financial advice to impecunious British travellers: 'English 2p pieces work in most French Space Invaders machines; 5p pieces work as 1DM in German vending machines.'

To test out this theory of improving exchange rates, thousands flew to Germany on the charter airline Dan-Air, which operated 'quasi-scheduled' flights from Gatwick to Berlin. These were nominally charters but every potential customer – mostly British servicemen stationed in the divided city, going home to see their relatives, and budget-minded business travellers – knew they flew at the same time every day, offering a scheduled service in all but name. The fare by the end of the 1980s was £109, a bargain compared with the prevailing price on British Airways – the only airline allowed to fly the route, because Lufthansa was banned by the post-war agreement that split Berlin. It was then that the tour operator, Inspirations, started up the most ambitious no-frills (or at least low-frills) flight ever. It used a DC-9 aircraft – a short, thin and slow five-seats-across twinjet, the natural successor to Raitz's DC-3. The flight began in Bristol, where the company was originally based, hopped to Gatwick to pick up the other half of its passengers, then laboured to Cyprus, Dubai and on to Goa. The journey time for this 4,500-mile trip was close on 24 hours. It ended not long before easyJet took to the skies.

Few would dispute the assertion from Seamus Conlon, the managing director of Airtours, that 'the charter airlines were the original low-cost carriers'. But within five years of easyJet's establishment, there were signs that the uneasy truce between the old and new guard was breaking down. In July of the year that its name celebrates, Air 2000 designated hundreds of its charter flights as scheduled services, bookable through travel agents. 'We perceive there's an expanding market of people who demand flexibility,' said Peter Cox, the man behind the plan. 'They have more holiday entitlement but less time to take it, and may be looking for five- or ten-day stays, rather than the usual week or fortnight.' Traditionally, 'seat only' sales on charter flights were for seven or fourteen days' duration, and were unavailable through the global distribution systems that host most scheduled flights worldwide. Suddenly, travel agents anywhere in the world could access Air 2000's flights from Bristol to Lanzarote or Glasgow to Faro. Tim Jeans, sales and marketing director of Ryanair, is 'not bothered' by the prospect of competition from charter carriers. 'They do generate significant seat-mile economies on their larger aircraft. But what the charter airlines haven't yet addressed is the whole cost of distribution. Ryanair and easyJet are light years ahead of where the charter airlines are on distribution,

THE BIGGEST NO-FRILLS AIRLINE OF THEM ALL?

Aviation in the Soviet Union was always a different activity to that in the West. Indeed, for the USSR flying without frills was the norm. The idea that the in-flight service should consist of a starter of contempt, a main course of ignorance and a dessert of blank incomprehension has been around since 26 March 1932, when Aeroflot – which was to become the largest airline of the twentieth century – got off the ground. While the Soviet Union was still a going concern, getting off the ground was just the first hurdle faced by Aeroflot passengers. Once in flight, the catering comprised a plastic cup of something that purported to be fruit juice but had probably been manufactured by a petrochemical plant in Omsk, and a 'cutlet' which involved a pulverised piece of meat smothered in stale breadcrumbs some months previously in Tomsk. The meals were about as tasty and nutritious as the fraying upholstery. The aircraft were ear-splittingly loud: the jets that spluttered into existence during the 50s were especially liable to bend the needle of the noise meter. But, like the best no-frills flights, they were reliably cheap. Much more than the Trans-Siberian Railway, aviation bound the fifteen diverse republics of the USSR together, and fares were kept low enough to enable the ordinary comrade in the ulitsa (street) to travel widely. Even as late as 1991, when the Soviet Union had already crumbled, it was possible to travel from Minsk in Belarus to Kiev in Ukraine for less than £1.

marketing and all of that stuff. At the moment all the charter guys are doing is flogging off distressed inventory at normal scheduled rates. When they really get into the £49 or £59 fares, and market and distribute those, then that's a different matter altogether.'

The losers, as Jeans would have it, include Air JMC – the charter airline that bears the initials of John Mason Cook, Thomas's son. It is part of the giant Thomas Cook combine, now in German hands. So, too, is Thomson, owner of Britannia Airways, and now part of Preussag, the Prussian Mining, Iron and Steel Company. Vladimir Raitz says that is a shame: 'It is sad that two very large organisations should be forsaking their roots – especially Thomas Cook, a company that was started in 1841.' But he takes pride in his part in expanding horizons. 'I have to confess that I am proud and I am very pleased, and I've had a certain amount of recognition. Not in this country, but at least the Italians have given me awards. No one has recognised me here – other than the newspapers, for which I am grateful, and television.'

Vladimir Raitz considers the no-frills airlines 'very welcome', though he is not an entirely satisfied customer. 'I think some of their advertising is very, very misleading. Let me give you an example. Buzz saying, "We've got these very cheap flights, and we're running on empty" so I said, "Look I have to go to Berlin today and come back the following day, what do you quote me?" and they quoted me some absurd figure of about £175 return. I said, "What about all these cheap flights?" and they said, "Ah, well, you should have booked those two or three weeks in advance." '

Neil Taylor, another great travel industry innovator, says Raitz, is missing the point of no-frills travel: '£175 is a bargain compared with what the scheduled carriers would charge. The low-cost airlines have all discovered a market of business travellers who require flexibility, but nothing else.'

Over half a century since he revolutionised travel, Vladimir Raitz is still active in tour operating – organising travel to another relatively virgin island, Cuba. He has not made the money that some of his contemporaries achieved, but counts 'fathering three daughters and having a happy family life' as his greatest achievement. 'I certainly didn't think I was creating an industry. What I was doing was having a lot of fun, going to little villages, and what I had in mind was adding one resort after another. The idea of making a lot of money never entered into it at all.'

3. A LOUSY THIRTEEN BUCKS

'If it's conventional, it's generally not wisdom. If it's wisdom, it's generally not conventional.'

HERB KELLEHER, CHAIRMAN, SOUTHWEST

'How important's Herb Kelleher? Herb Kelleher's like God'

MICHAEL O'LEARY, CHIEF EXECUTIVE, RYANAIR

'This will be a no smoking, no complaining and no whining flight today'

DUANE REDMOND, SOUTHWEST FLIGHT ATTENDANT

I'm in Love: Love Field, Dallas, the World War I airfield named after a pioneering aviator, Lieutenant Moss Lee Love, who died in a crash in California in 1913. The joke waddling towards me on a T-shirted Texan is in questionable taste: 'Why is it called Tourist Season,' the slogan on the convex garment asks, 'if we can't shoot them?' The anniversary of the assassination of President Kennedy in Dallas passed a few days ago. That date, 22 November 1963, is particularly poignant here at Love Field, the last airport where JFK touched down, alive, aboard Air Force One.

'Dwight is your dwiver,' announces the sign at the front of the Southwest Airlines shuttle bus. 'Will you drop me off at the uniform department?' a flight attendant asks Dwight. 'No, ma'am, but I'll slow down to thirty.' For the first mile of the ride to the headquarters of the world's most successful airline, Dwight's bus runs along the same road as John F. Kennedy travelled on his final, fatal journey. At about that time, a lawyer named Herbert D. Kelleher was working in San Antonio, 250 miles south-west of Dallas. He had not the slightest intention to change the way that people travelled and, like most Americans, had little interest in airlines at all. Nearly 40 years, and many legal tussles later, Kelleher is the man that the bosses of Europe's no-frills airlines idolise.

'He's the original genius,' says Michael O'Leary, chief executive of Europe's biggest no-frills airline, Ryanair. 'Herb Kelleher would have been the Thomas Edison of low-fare air travel. This is the guy who created it, this is the guy who first dreamt of charging people $10 for two- and three-hour flights in the US, and he's the one who revolutionised the industry. He's the Sam Walton of the airline industry.' Stelios of easyJet asserts, 'Southwest is really my role model.' 'As far as low-cost travel is concerned, he was definitely the pioneer,' says Sir Richard Branson. And it's not just talk: when Ryanair was floated, says O'Leary, the airline offered Kelleher 5 per cent of the equity and a seat on the board – for free. 'He didn't take it because he didn't want to be distracted,' says O'Leary. 'You've got to stay true to what you do.' Herb Kelleher didn't stay true to his original training, as a lawyer, but has remained faithful to Southwest since his part in dreaming it up in 1966. Kelleher was born in a suburb of Philadelphia – Haddon Hills, New Jersey – in 1931. His first job was delivering the *Philadelphia Bulletin* for $2.50 a week. He studied law at New York University, worked for a while for the New Jersey court system, then decided to set up on his own account.

The sight of 'a Yankee in a one-way U-Haul' became a pet hate on the part of some Texans during the 60s, as thousands of northerners flooded south to the booming 'Sunbelt' economy. Fuelled by the huge federal investment first in NASA's space exploration and later by the military demands for fighting the Vietnam War, Texas needed people, and people needed lawyers. Kelleher joined a legal practice in the rapidly growing Texan city of San Antonio. He recruited a young woman named Colleen Barrett as his legal secretary. She is now president of Southwest, while another former employee of Oppenheimer, Rosenberg, Kelleher & Wheatley, Jim Parker, is the airline's chief executive officer.

Dwight's dwive to Southwest's HQ epitomises the choices that were open to Texan travellers when Kelleher moved in. The runway of Love Field is barely a wingtip from a four-lane highway and a single-track railway line. By 1963, the heyday of the train had ended. The automobile was supreme. But Texas is so large that driving devoured time. The state's strange shape, resembling a coyote splayed flat on Interstate 10, measures 800 miles from north to south and from east to west; Texas occupies more space than France, Belgium, Holland and Switzerland combined. The golden triangle between the state's three largest cities – Dallas, Houston and San Antonio – is served by Interstate freeways, but the drive between any two of those cities takes four or five hours. In 1963 flying – which cut the journey to less than an hour – was the preserve of the rich and powerful.

The large, blanched building at 2702 Love Field Drive was built 35 years after Kennedy touched down. It is a people's palace, a bright, comfortable and friendly headquarters building for America's most successful airline. Not the biggest: that title rests with American Airlines, based a few miles west of here. United and Delta also take precedence in terms of passenger numbers. But Southwest still manages to fly 75 million passengers a year. Even before 11 September 2001, its market capitalisation – the amount at which the stock market values it – was bigger than that of the three largest airlines, plus fifth-placed Continental, combined.

Its success can be measured in several ways: Southwest began flying in 1971, moved into profit within three years, and has been profitable ever since. During that time, none of the 10 million flights has crashed seriously enough to kill anyone. Possibly most remarkably, the billboard outside shouts 'Now hiring'. In a nation traumatised by the events of '9-11', and in an industry that laid off 100,000 workers within days of the terrorist attacks on New York and Washington, Southwest Airlines has not only kept all its workers, it is paying to advertise for more.

Almost everyone you speak to puts Southwest's success down to one man. Herb Kelleher is credited with reinventing air travel, by concentrating on providing what was necessary for safe, reliable and cheap air travel, and ditching anything that was not needed on board – such as assigned seating. 'We've always done it differently,' he says. 'We don't assign seats. Used to be we only had about four people on the whole plane, so the idea of assigned seats just made people laugh. Now the reason is you can turn the airplanes quicker at the gate.'

Southwest does not care to do what other airlines do unless there is a good reason. That is why you will look in vain for any seat assignment when you check in. The company line is that your seat on the plane is reserved, you just don't know which one. Instead, passengers checking in are given a boarding card, colour coded (and, for the colour-blind, labelled Dark Blue Boarding Pass). It carries a large number. 'Hi,' says a message on boarding pass number 83. 'You're in the third boarding group and, once on board, you can choose whatever seat is available.' The assigned number depends on how early you check in: 'Hurry, better get a good number,' one Southwest employee at Phoenix urged me. A good number is in the range 1 to 30, meaning you have first choice of the 137 seats on one of the airline's brand new 737-700s. If you are in the 121-137 group, you can be pretty sure of getting a middle seat down the back. In any event, passengers get aboard quicker than when seating is assigned.

As a lawyer, Herb Kelleher arrived at Southwest with none of the excess baggage that many people in aviation accrue. 'If it's conventional, it's generally not wisdom,' he likes to say. 'If it's wisdom, it's generally not conventional.' Colleen Barrett, who succeeded him as president in 2000, follows the same philosophy. On the seat-assignment question, she says the alternative would be to spend one billion dollars on new planes. 'We have examined assigned seating periodically, and all of our studies show that it takes more time than our current system. That is an extremely important consideration because, if we had to extend our ground times by as little as ten minutes for assignments, we would have to buy 31 more 737s at a cost of $36 million each.'

The large white building at 2702 Love Field Drive is a suitable headquarters for a Fortune 500 company. Inside the front door stands a marble statue of Abraham Lincoln, a scale model of the president's memorial in Washington DC. The reception area is the size of a couple of tennis courts, and twice the height of a Boeing 737 tail. Talking of which, a fleet of ten miniature jets dangles from the glass and steel ceiling. Every few minutes, a real 737 streaks past the door on the Love Field runway on its way to another Texan city or a neighbouring state. All around are cases containing awards and tributes to Herb Kelleher, notably a ventriloquist's dummy of the man holding a trademark cigarette.

'This will be a no smoking, no complaining and no whining flight today. If you would like to smoke this afternoon, just step outside onto the wing. If you can light it, you can smoke it.' That's what Duane Redmond, a Southwest flight attendant, tells his passengers. For the chairman of a non-smoking airline, Kelleher is mighty fond of tobacco. 'I've had lunch with Kelleher on two occasions,' recalls Sir Richard Branson '– both occasions where I took up smoking again.'

As two bored receptionists gaze out of the window at the departing Southwest jets, an impressively wide range of clothes wanders past: both women and men in polo shirts and shorts, or sweatshirts and chinos. And that's just the cabin crew. Most of the office staff wear jeans. The only people in ties are me and a pilot who has arrived on Dwight's bus to seek a job.

Southwest has a simple proposition, which can be summarised as, 'Keep planes flying, because that is where they make money, and keep fares low enough to keep people travelling.' Each of Southwest's aircraft flies an average of eight missions a day, staying in the air for a total of twelve hours. The airline is consistently rated as one of the most punctual in America, despite the impression created by jokey cabin announcements like 'Our flight time today is: when we get there, we get there.' The average fare paid is $85 (£60) for an average journey of 695 miles, which in my experience is around one-third less than the competition. It sounds a simple recipe, but it is one that has been fiendishly difficult to concoct in the face of the vested interests of the traditional airline industry. You could write a book about the travails that Southwest faced before its first flight took off on 18 June 1971. Indeed, several people have done just that.

One of them, *Nuts* by Kevin and Jackie Freiberg, has become a business best-seller. 'Herb Kelleher reinvented air travel when he founded Southwest Airlines,' begins the back-page blurb. There is a strong case to make that Kelleher has done more than anyone else to transform aviation – but Southwest was more his adopted infant than his conception. He was by no means a single parent, and the initial venture owed a lot to an existing operation in California. In aviation, as in most areas of life, there are few completely original ideas.

Life in the 60s was tough for anyone with the temerity to want to start an airline. The commercial aviation network had been established primarily for the transport of the US Mail. It was neatly carved up among a few big airlines. Competition was minimal. As in the UK, the federal government frowned upon what was perceived as 'wasteful duplication' of services, preferring each airline to have its own turf. Washington could enforce this on a nationwide basis, but there was nothing to stop new airlines starting up within each state – except for a truckload of vested interests, and the reality that intrastate flights were only feasible within really big states. Alaska, with an average of just one person per square mile compared with seventy in the rest of the US, was a special (and unprofitable) case. California and Texas were the obvious candidates.

Pacific Southwest Airlines began life in 1949 during California's post-war boom, and pioneered many of the ideas that Southwest still employs. The founder, Kenny Friedkin, believed he could take passengers from road and rail if he offered fares much lower than the existing airlines such as United and Western (now part of Delta). The first route was classic Southwest territory: from San Diego on the Mexican border via Burbank, a low-cost airport serving Los Angeles, to Oakland – a cheap alternative to San Francisco. Many of the passengers were from the huge naval base at San Diego, which led to PSA acquiring the nickname 'Poor Sailors' Airline'. To keep costs down, the pilots who flew the DC-3s also helped out on the ground, and the cabin crew cleaned the interior.

Friedkin picked up some larger DC-4s on the cheap, at the time when the DC-6 was the state of aviation art. The latter had distinctive rectangular windows. Friedkin ordered that boxes be painted around the DC-4s' windows to make passengers think they were about to board one of the more modern planes.

What is nowadays termed 'corporate culture' was valued by Friedkin. The company newsletter, entitled *Skylines* (Southwest's is called *Luvlines*), used first names for everyone, and the company organised annual picnics. Operationally, PSA was rigorous, keeping the aircraft flying as much as possible, with short turns at airports between arrival and departure.

Kenny Friedkin died suddenly in 1962, and J. Floyd Andrews, known universally as Andy, took over. He coined the slogan 'The world's friendliest airline', and painted smiles on the noses of the new Boeing 727 jets.

When a San Antonio businessman, Rollin King, saw what Pacific Southwest Airlines was doing in the Golden State, he decided it should work in the Lone Star State. It was the winter before the 1967 summer of love. The Byrds may have been Eight Miles High, but rock stars were part of a small minority who could afford to experience life at 40,000 feet: only 15 per cent of the US population had ever flown. PSA had begun to change that, offering relatively cheap air fares between the main centres of population in California. A Texas-based operation could do the same, concluded Rollin King. First, he needed a good attorney to cut through the bureaucracy. Late in 1966 he asked a local lawyer named Herbert D. Kelleher to meet him at the city's St Anthony Hotel. The original route map, linking Dallas with Houston and San Antonio, was sketched on the back of a napkin; a copy of it hangs in the boardroom at 2702 Love Field.

On 15 March 1967 Kelleher, whose name had by now been abbreviated by all to 'Herb' (a word normally pronounced 'erb' by Americans, but in this case pronounced 'Herb'), filed the incorporation papers for a company called Air Southwest. By 27 November, the paper airline had become Southwest Airlines. That day, Kelleher applied on the prospective carrier's behalf for permission to fly between Dallas, Houston and San Antonio with the Texas Aeronautics Commission. Given the unchallenging workload that the body normally had to endure, it was perhaps surprising that it took twelve weeks for the TAC to approve the application.

Among the amusements available to passengers, meeters or greeters awaiting a delayed flight at Love Field is the Frontiers of Flight Aviation Museum. It is an impressive collection that takes the traveller from classical legend to the first Apollo moon landing in July 1969. At the time that NASA down in Houston was sending men to the moon, Southwest Airlines was having a tough time even getting off the ground. One obstruction was Braniff Airlines, the airline that was bright orange three decades before easyJet discovered the colour. The Dallas-based airline was doing very nicely out of the 60s boom, charging fares that were agreed with the other two carriers flying within Texas: Continental and Trans-Texas. All three airlines objected to Southwest's arrival on their patch, and managed to get a restraining order banning the Texas Aeronautics Commission from issuing a certificate to fly.

In the summer of 1968, a court in the Texas capital, Austin, declared that there was no need for a new airline, a decision upheld by the appeals court. So far, Southwest had spent more than half a million dollars on legal fees and had not carried a single passenger. In 1969, Herb Kelleher, who had seen his own investment in Southwest consumed in the legal fight, said he would continue the battle at his own expense. Eventually the Texas Supreme Court found for Southwest, and a challenge by the three existing rivals to the Supreme Court in Washington DC was disallowed. The airline could start living up to its name.

By now, Kelleher had carved a large financial – and intellectual – stake in Southwest. He had decided his future lay with the airline he had coaxed into existence. But while he had built up a great deal of experience in commercial law, neither he nor Rollin King knew much about commercial aviation. So they hired an industry veteran, Lamar Muse, as chief executive officer. Howard Putnam, another vastly experienced airline executive who later joined Southwest, says Muse deserves more credit: 'He was really the man that put together the operation, the team and a lot of the route strategy. Rollin King had the idea, but would never have been able to organise the operation. Herb focused more on legal, political and fund raising in the beginning.' Lamar milked his contacts for cash to replenish the empty coffers at Southwest, and recruited solid aviation professionals to run the operation. Boeing sold the airline three brand new 737s for $4m each, a 20 per cent discount on the prevailing list price, which turned out to be an excellent investment, since Southwest now has over 350 of the model, and the jet is established as standard equipment for no-frills airlines. The first cabin crew uniforms have not remained standard equipment. They comprised tight tops, hot pants and white leather boots. (The original chief hostess had previously worked for Hugh Hefner aboard the Playboy jet.) The advertisements that attracted the first recruits showed that Southwest was going to be different. Sex discrimination was still allowed, which permitted the airline to announce: 'Attention Raquel Welch: you can have a job if you measure up.' In contrast, the flying was approached with some seriousness. In-flight safety briefings were memorised; they did not include the twenty-first-century variety that I heard from Duane Redmond aboard Southwest flight 244: 'Place the mask over that big old mouth and nose of yours and breathe like this: aaaaaah, ooooooh, uuuuuuh. By the way, that wasn't me calling your house last night.' Such levity would have to wait until Southwest had proved itself to be the safest airline the world has ever known.

Everything was set for the first flights between the three biggest Texas cities – Dallas, Houston, and San Antonio – to begin on 18 June 1971. Except that Braniff and Texas International (which Trans-Texas had become) managed to obtain a restraining order preventing Southwest starting operations. The day before the start-up, Kelleher summoned all his legal experience to persuade the Texas Supreme to throw out the injunction. Famously, when Lamar Muse wondered what might happen if the sheriff was still inclined to enforce the order, Kelleher replied 'You roll right over the son-of-a-bitch and leave our tire tracks on his uniform.'

The sheriff stayed away. So too did many of the hoped-for passengers, when flights began the next day from Love Field. There were twelve departures each day to and from Houston Intercontinental (nowadays there are thirty each way between Dallas and Houston), and six round trips between Dallas and San Antonio. Passengers paid a flat $20 one way, saving 25 per cent on the rivals' fares.

Loads were dismal for the first few months, though they improved when Southwest switched to Houston's smaller, older and closer airport, Hobby. This enabled travellers to make the city-centre to city-centre journey between Dallas and Houston in as little as ninety minutes. Muse started employing a primitive form of yield management, the principle that now governs pricing for all low-cost airlines. Southwest charged higher fares – $26 each way – when the market could bear it on daytime services, but in the evenings and at weekends the fare was halved to $13. By 1973, Southwest had moved into profit – helped by a celebrated spat with Braniff.

Passenger numbers on the Dallas–San Antonio route were poor, so in January 1973 Southwest started charging a flat $13 on every flight. Braniff reacted by introducing the same fare on the Dallas–Houston run, the one route where Southwest was making money. Lamar Muse trumped Braniff with a newspaper advertisement that read, 'Nobody's going to shoot Southwest Airlines out of the sky for a lousy $13.' It was a direct appeal to Texans' sense of fair play – and self-interest. Southwest offered a two-tier pricing system: $13 for people paying their own way, or $26 for business travellers who could collect a bottle of Scotch whisky or vodka for their personal use. (A similar trick was employed in 1996 by easyJet on the Luton–Aberdeen run.) Rob Brown, regional director of field marketing for Southwest, says these days passengers do not need such bribes to demonstrate loyalty. Typically, when the airline starts on a new route, existing airlines will dramatically cut fares. But, he says, 'Customers understand the benefits we bring to a market. They know that by supporting us it'll be beneficial to them, and it'll be beneficial to the market.'

Braniff threw in the towel on the fares war, and the route returned to profitable levels; 1973 saw Southwest turn a profit for the first time. It also saw Kelleher seek ways to fly more people and make more money. So he went to California, as the website that records the history of PSA (iflypsa.com) mourns.

'In 1973, a Texan came out to San Diego. His name was Herb Kelleher, and he worked for Southwest. PSA showed him the entire operation, and told all their department heads to "open everything up for Herb". (Tom Irwin [a PSA executive] was sent to Dallas with manuals in hand. Southwest was so impressed that they took PSA's name off the manual, stuck their name on, and made it their manual.) In return, PSA got a lot of heartache in the 1980s.'

Why on earth would an airline open itself for a competitor? Because, in 1973, there was no prospect of Southwest being a competitor for PSA. Each flew only within its own state. Just as Southwest was happy in 1990 for Michael O'Leary of Ryanair to check out the company, PSA saw no downside in helping Kelleher. (Southwest may be pleased to know that O'Leary has no plans, at present, to move in on its patch.)

There was no manual for the battle for survival that Southwest was still fighting. The oil crisis that began late in 1973 put pressure on all airlines, as the price of aviation fuel tripled. Lamar Muse could do nothing about the international politics that had caused the jump in kerosene prices. But he could maximise the use of aircraft. The 'ten-minute turn' was introduced, bringing pit-stop principles to aviation. A Boeing 737 could arrive, offload, refuel, board passengers and depart within ten minutes, far better than the competition could achieve. It has not survived. 'Our ten-minute turn has stretched a little over the years – it's had to, due to more baggage, more customers and, frankly, regulations have caused us to spend more time on the ground,' says Greg Wells, vice-president for security for Southwest. But the airline still beats the competition on aircraft utilisation, and keeps its jets in the air for an average of twelve hours a day. Southwest's president, Colleen Barrett, says, 'Our employees and our customers participate in a ballet of motion each time we load and unload an aircraft.'

The staff certainly enjoy some ambitious choreography as they dance around the US. In the early days, the flight crews saw possibly too much of three cities; these days, they see huge amounts of the country, often on a single shift. A Houston flight attendant might begin the day at Oklahoma City, having nightstopped from the previous day, and fly two hours west to Phoenix. There, the crew changes direction and goes three hours east to St Louis. Another flight takes them even further from home, to Columbus, Ohio. And while on board, they are doing much more than delivering droll announcements.

For an airline that has long been described as 'no frills', Southwest dishes out a lot of frills: free coffee and juice at the gate and again on the plane, free peanuts (each passenger gets through an average 1.2 packets) and decent snacks on longer flights. When you enrol in the frequent-flyer programme, you get free vouchers for in-flight cocktails, which normally cost $4 each. 'Complimentary soft drinks are available. Beers, wine and cocktails are available for purchase.' Duane Redmond's in-flight announcement on Southwest flight 244 begins ordinarily enough. But then he adopts the demeanour of a temperance preacher. 'For those of you drinking so early in the afternoon – shame, shame, shame on you.' Southwest offers no in-flight entertainment in the normal sense, but many of its flight attendants perform stand-up comedy for the ultimate captive audience: 'Those of you sitting on the left-hand side of the aircraft will get an excellent view of Mount Rainier. Those of you sitting on the right will get an excellent view of the backs of the heads of those looking at Mount Rainier.' The cabin crew are following the example of the chairman: when Herb Kelleher picked up yet another business leadership prize, at the University of Michigan in 1997, he said, 'It's great to be here to accept this award, but I'm a little bit anxious since I'm out of my normal environment. I'm sober. If you like what I have to say, I'm Herb Kelleher, president of Southwest Airlines. If you don't, I'm John Dasburg, president of Northwest Airlines.'

At various stages in its gestation, Southwest gave away alcoholic drinks during the day, 'because we had almost all business travellers and they didn't drink anyway at that time of day,' says Howard Putnam. One of the legendary Southwest stories is that Herb Kelleher holds the record for the largest number of Jack Daniel's consumed in a single flight, having downed eight during a flight from Dallas to Houston. Putnam now confesses, 'I made up the Jack Daniel's story. Herb and I were hosting lunch on Wall Street for some analysts in late 1978 and I was asked, on a fifty-minute flight from Dallas to Houston, how many free drinks could one get? I replied: "The record is seven Jack Daniel's and water and it is held by our Chairman, Herb." Herb quickly responded (all unrehearsed), "Seven, Howard, I thought I had eight?" Got a big laugh.' The chairman's liking for Wild Turkey whiskey is, however, well documented. Sir Richard Branson confirms that his lunches with

STAY SLIM

Southwest didn't get where it is today by overpaying its staff. Reservations sales agents must spend three weeks training, without pay, before earning $8.05 an hour for the first year; after that, it increases by 75 cents. Customer service agents, who handle passengers at the airports, earn $9.09 an hour in California and at Baltimore, but only $8.30 elsewhere; again, there is a modest increase after the first year. To get the job, they must be capable of lifting 70 lb (32 kg) 'repetitively'.

Flight attendants need lift only 50 lb (23 kg). They are paid entirely on a piece-rate basis; on a typical 250-mile flight, they earn $14.67. After six months, this increases by 23 cents; only after a year does it rise to $17.34. Hang on, you may be thinking, for a flight of less than one hour that's a fine rate of pay. But on a bad day the average shift of eight hours may include only four flights, meaning an hourly rate of just $8.67 for experienced staff.

Even so, there are plenty of good reasons for wanting to work for Southwest. A recruitment leaflet lists the following advantages: 'Casual dress; chili cook-offs; Hallowe'en celebrations; deck parties [these take place at the Dallas HQ each Friday from 3 p.m., with beer and wine a dollar]; golf tournaments; spontaneous celebrations [possibly more fun than golf tournaments]; and parades. Perhaps even more enticing is the prospect for free travel anywhere on the network for you and your family alike, subject to space being available.

'There are many opportunities to share your shining spirit with thousands of customers every day as a member of the Southwest Airlines Family.'

But to get a job, you should be in shape. Don't apply for a job as a flight attendant or a customer service agent if you are overweight. The rules phrase that as diplomatically as possible: 'Weight must be of such proportion to height that a neat appearance is maintained and physical ability to perform all functions is not hindered. Only standard uniform sizes are available. Men's uniforms range in waist size from 27 to 42 inches. Women's uniforms range in size from 0 to 18. No tailor-made uniforms are permitted.' And don't think you can let go of your shape after you get the job. 'If hired, you must sustain compliance with the Appearance and Physical Performance Standards Policy throughout your employment.'

Kelleher tend to become 'blurry'. Kelleher has long been a heavy smoker, too, but Southwest experimented with some no-smoking flights long before the practice became mandatory.

Under the presidency of Lamar Muse, Southwest expanded slowly. It took five years for the fleet to double to six aircraft (in 1998, Go took a few months), and despite lobbying for greater commercial freedom the airline was still restricted to Texas. Muse is described by Howard Putnam – at the time, a rival – as 'The finest airline entrepreneur of the last forty years'. Putnam adds: 'He controlled the authority and decision-making channels within the company. To put it bluntly, the man was a dictator.' By 1978, the extremely flat management structure – which meant the lines of control between Muse and any employee were very short – began to impede the company's growth. He was also getting too autocratic for the board's liking, unilaterally taking decisions on new planes and bases. The story of his downfall is reported eloquently by Putnam: 'Lamar told me the story over a game of golf in Dallas. He said: "I was always arguing with another member of the board and co-founder, Rollin King. We just couldn't agree on much in those days. Anyway, during one of the board meetings I called for a vote and said, 'Either Rollin leaves the board or I quit as president.'" At that point Lamar left the room while the board voted. Ten minutes later, they called him back to give him the results. "Sorry Lamar, you lose." Lamar admitted to me "I was shocked, but at least I kept my sense of humour. When they broke the news, I just took my keys out of my pocket and threw them down on the table. Then I stared straight at them and said: 'Damn, I'd have never called for a vote if I thought I wasn't going to win', and walked out of the room."'

Muse served out two years of 'gardening leave' required by a 'non-compete' clause in his severance agreement, then started his own airline, Muse Air, with his son Mike – who had also been working for Southwest, and was fired at the same time as his father. It was the world's first totally non-smoking airline. Kelleher took charge of Southwest as chairman, chief executive and president. Some years later, he told *Forbes* magazine 'when Lamar left, a lot of people said Southwest Airlines is over, because Lamar Muse is Southwest Airlines. Well, Lamar left in 1978 and Southwest is still here.' Kelleher was not at the top for long. He stayed on as chairman but relinquished his other two titles to none other than Howard Putnam, then group vice-president for marketing at United Airlines, who began work on his 41st birthday.

The second notable event of 1978 was that, three-quarters of a century after the Wright Brothers first flew, President Jimmy Carter deregulated aviation. All the old rules that restricted routes and schedules and fixed high fares were shelved. Any airline that could demonstrate to the Federal Aviation Administration that it was safe was free to fly anywhere at a fare of its choosing. The new president and CEO, with his background with America's biggest airline, could have expanded dramatically, and bought larger aircraft capable of flying right across the country, but he stayed focused on its original proposition. 'We also wrote the Southwest Airlines vision statement in 1978,' says Putnam, who calls it the most important achievement of his tenure. The carrier still adheres to those 52 words today: 'The mission of Southwest Airlines is to provide safe and comfortable air transportation in commuter and short-haul markets, from close-in airports, at prices competitive with automobiles and buses, and to involve customers and employees in the product and the process, making the airline a fun, profitable, and quality experience for all.'

Putnam oversaw Southwest's transformation to corporate adulthood, taking advantage of the new freedom of the skies to expand from Texas into neighbouring states: 'The first interstate route we picked was Dallas Love Field to New Orleans, with seven round trips a day.' This was achieved using just one aircraft. 'Immediate success,' recalls Putnam. Houston Hobby to New Orleans was the next 'interstate'. The first three days of April 1980 saw a trio of flights from Dallas: Oklahoma City, Tulsa and Albuquerque joined the Southwest network. Most crucially, this small airline was the first carrier to order the Boeing 737-300, which later became the biggest selling aircraft ever. 'We did it with a total team of five people, part-time, doing the research and analysis. A one-billion dollar order was very big for a little airline.' The airline's first wholly owned Boeing was named Rollin W. King, after the man who dreamed up the idea.

The airline has followed a cautious policy, which continues today, of adding only one or two new destinations and a few more aircraft every year. Even though Boeing's technology allows the 737-700 to fly between any two points in the continental US, Southwest has only slowly entered the transcontinental market – offering an all-day haul between Tampa in Florida and Seattle in Washington that stops at New Orleans and Albuquerque, for example. The longest non-stop flight is the 2,271-mile haul from Providence in Rhode Island to Phoenix. But each year Southwest is approached by more than 100 cities asking if the airline will start flying there.

'The Department of Transportation has coined a phrase, the Southwest Effect,' says marketing director Rob Brown. 'When we go into a market, fares go down and traffic goes up. One example is when we started service from Providence in 1996. One year later, between Providence and Baltimore, fares had decreased by 74 per cent, and traffic had gone up by 790 per cent. That's the Southwest Effect that we have.'

The contrast with its arch-rival Braniff's overexuberance is instructive. Plenty of people still recall the airline with affection: Tom Barry, who lives in Oklahoma City, reminisces about the days when Braniff flew to Dallas. 'They used to put a clock out front, and if your flight was ten minutes late you got your money back.' Time was running out for the Big Orange. The airline expanded frantically, placing a half-billion dollar order for new aircraft and even persuading British Airways to operate Concorde between Dallas and Washington DC on Braniff's behalf.

By 1981, the plan had begun to unravel. Braniff poached Howard Putnam and Southwest's chief financial officer, Phil Guthrie, to try to rescue the business. Putnam now says, 'We would have not gone to BN had they shown us the correct financials. They were "cooking the books" and only after we got there did we find out we only had ten days of cash, $175 million less than the numbers we had been shown. That is where I learned crisis management.' Nevertheless, they kept Braniff afloat, with the flagship route from Dallas to Gatwick (featuring a bright orange jumbo jet) for seven months, before placing it in 'Chapter 11 bankruptcy', which gives protection from creditors, getting it flying again and selling it. 'We then had had enough "character building" and left the industry for other things.' At the point Putnam left Southwest, Kelleher had enjoyed ten years' character-building training in aviation. He reacquired the titles of president and CEO of Southwest, and was now in sole charge of the airline he had helped navigate through turbulent skies.

Almost at once, life became tougher for US airlines. America's air traffic controllers went on strike. They were promptly fired by President Reagan. While their replacements – managers, and military controllers – were brought up to speed, airlines were ordered to reduce their flights. Southwest's cautious expansion, and its conservative mission statement, meant it stayed in profit while others lost small fortunes. The following year, Southwest expanded to Los Angeles, San Diego, Las Vegas, and Phoenix – the cities that are now among the most important on the network, plus San Francisco, which was abandoned in 2001 because of congestion and high fees.

Inevitably, Southwest has attracted a fair number of imitators who believe they can emulate, or even improve upon, the original plan. The travel industry is littered with case studies where a pioneering company is upstaged by a rival firm that can emulate some of the business model but learn from the first mover's mistakes. The UK aircraft industry brought out the first civil jet, the Comet, but was soon eclipsed by a bigger, safer aircraft, the Boeing 707. Laker Airways pioneered cheap fares across the Atlantic, but it was Virgin Atlantic that succeeded where Laker's Skytrain failed. So why has no one simply copied Southwest? United, US Airways and Continental all tried to set up low-cost subsidiaries, with 'Shuttle by United', 'Metrojet' and 'Continental Lite' respectively. But all failed. American Airlines, the biggest carrier in the world, has never tried the concept – for good reason, says Henry Joyner, the airline's senior vice-president for planning. 'There's not enough benefit to justify the difference that you make, treating one group of customers in a different way from others. Without significant cost-savings, you just cause brand confusion.' American Airlines and Southwest have one common interest: the former publishes the latter's in-flight magazine, *Spirit*, a relationship that makes money for both companies. Plenty of start-ups have tried to mine the same rich seam as Southwest. Those that have come and gone include Kiwi, Air South, Lone Star and Western Pacific. Southwest has actually bought a couple, both interesting cases. In 1985 it acquired Transtar, which was what Lamar Muse's venture had become, and soon closed it down. The other, in 1993, was Morris Air, a Salt Lake City-based operation. It had been started by a travel agent named Morris, who was fed up with the high fares that Delta and Western was charging out of the Utah city, and decided to start running charters. When the operation became more serious, David Neeleman was brought in to mastermind a scheduled operation. The sale to Southwest included a clause where Neeleman agreed not to compete in the low-cost sector for five years. During that time, he went north to Canada to help start WestJet; once it had ended, he established JetBlue at New York.

One reason why attempts to emulate Southwest's achievements have rarely succeeded is the company's culture. When the airline's staff hear the word 'culture', they reach out for one another. There is no compelling need for gate C6 at Phoenix airport to have a collage of photographs showing the celebrations at the Southwest Airlines Christmas party – except that the airline considers its corporate culture to be as important as its planes, as witnessed by this post-11 September outpouring by Colleen Barrett: 'Our people transformed an idea into a legend. That legend will continue to grow only so long as it is nourished – by our people's indomitable spirit, boundless energy, immense goodwill, and burning desire to succeed. Our thanks – and our love – to the people of Southwest Airlines for creating a marvelous family and a wondrous airline.'

Besides all of the above, the wondrous airline's growth has also partly been achieved by acquisition. Sometimes it was entire airlines; in other cases, such as the gates at Chicago's Midway airport, the all-important terminal infrastructure was grabbed literally overnight. Midway used to be the busiest airport in the world, until the day when O'Hare opened up the road. It stayed open, and a company called Midway Airlines based itself there. In November 1990, rumours were circulating about the carrier's financial health. A Southwest team flew to Chicago (from Dallas-Fort Worth, not Love Field, because time was imperative and the extraordinary Wright Amendment then, as now, forbids direct flight from Love to Chicago). They negotiated a takeover of the Midway gates, giving Southwest the dominant position at the most convenient airport for America's third city.

Southwest was also innovative on the Internet. It was the first US airline to establish a home page – though in 2000, only one in three of its passengers (in terms of revenue) was booking through the web, compared with 80 or 90 per cent for no-frills airlines in the UK. The bribe it offers to customers is a special set of fares that can be booked only online. But in order to save the average $4 or $5 cost of each conventional reservation, Southwest could look to Europe for expertise. It deserves some payback from the favours it has conferred on the likes of Ryanair and easyJet, by showing that low-cost aviation is not an oxymoron.

'All you had to do was compare what people paid in the US relative to what people paid in the UK and Europe,' says Stelios. When the easyJet founder saw what Southwest had achieved and what European passengers were paying, he said to himself, 'There must be an opportunity here, someone must be able to do better than this – offer low fares and maybe make some money in the process.'

'What took real brains and real balls,' says O'Leary of Ryanair, 'was to say "We can charge $10 a seat and still make money." ' Barbara Cassani of Go believes Kelleher's greatest achievement is in creating strong bonds with staff and customers. 'I think a good relationship with your people and making a lot of money go together. I think good relationships with your people and good relationships with your customers goes together. It is a very virtuous relationship with all of those areas.' And Sir Richard Branson confirms Kelleher's legendary ability to be less than virtuous about lunch. 'At about six o'clock in the evening, after a six-hour lunch,

I remember thinking, "If anyone walks through this door and sees two airline owners puffing and drinking away, they'll suddenly be flying on someone else's airline." '

Not everyone joins the chorus of approval. While Sir Freddie Laker respects what Southwest has achieved, he believes the airline is playing into the hands of its bigger rivals. 'These big boys love Southwest,' he says. 'Whenever someone says, "Your fares are too high" or "You're dominating the market", they just turn round and say "How can we be uncompetitive when Southwest are there?" '

As Southwest moves into middle age, its biggest rival, in every sense, is American Airlines. Henry Joyner, that airline's senior vice president responsible for planning, says, 'We've got a longer history than anyone in competing with the biggest, most successful low-cost operator in the world.' Continental, based in Houston, and a competitor since Southwest's earliest days might disagree with that, but probably not Joyner's assertion that, 'While there is a price difference, there is also a product difference. People make trade-offs in terms of service and convenience to get that low fare.' He insists, interestingly, that Southwest offers fewer non-stop flights and more 'connects', even though it sells itself as a point-to-point carrier rather than a hub-and-spoke operation like American Airlines.

'Along with peanut wrappers, snot rags and used diapers, you will find this safety information card in the pocket in front of you.' For almost the first thirty years of Southwest's history, the familiar plastic card was a superfluous document. But on 3 May 2001, Southwest passengers travelling from Las Vegas to Burbank went rather further than they were expecting. Flight 1455 overshot the runway, ploughed through the perimeter fence and ended up at a gas station on the adjacent highway. For the first time in its history Southwest 'totalled' an aircraft. Remarkably, not one of the 142 people on board, nor anyone on the ground, was hurt (though the two pilots were sacked six weeks later). As with Virgin Atlantic's most serious incident, when the undercarriage on an Airbus approaching Heathrow failed to open fully, Southwest demonstrated the art of crashing painlessly. But the fated flight number was 'retired', a practice normally associated with fatal crashes, and the incident tainted the big party that took place six weeks later. On 18 June 2001, the airline – and Kelleher – celebrated thirty years of operation. The following day, Kelleher stepped down as president and CEO, passing on these titles to his ever-faithful right-hand woman, Colleen Barrett, and the former lawyer, Jim Parker, respectively. Kelleher remains as chairman and, according to Ryanair's Michael

MALICE IN DALLAS
In March 1992, the Yankee lawyer rejected the courts in favour of arm-wrestling to settle a trade-mark dispute. Kelleher turned a potentially bitter and expensive wrangle into a publicity stunt, a contest billed as 'Malice in Dallas'.

At issue was the right to use the phrase 'plane smart'. A small South Carolina-based facilities company, Stevens Aviation, had been using the slogan since the early 1970s. It objected when Southwest started describing people who flew on the airline as 'just plane smart'. Scenting an opportunity, Kelleher and his counterpart, the younger and fitter Kurt Herwald of Stevens Aviation, decided to settle the issue by arm-wrestling. They hired the Sportatorium Arena in Dallas, packed it with staff from both companies and invited in the national TV networks. In the manner of great heavyweight tussles, they monopolised the news in the days leading up to the event, with stories such as Kelleher's tough training regime of cigarettes and Wild Turkey whiskey. The bout was over in less than a minute, with the younger man winning easily. But the pictures of 'Smokin' Herb' being carried out on a stretcher, saying 'I don't care what you say about me, just remember my name,' were the ones that grabbed editors' attention. Afterwards, it transpired that both parties agreed they should share the 'plane smart' slogan anyway.

O'Leary, 'he'll still have a profound influence'. One reason for Kelleher taking what amounts to a back seat is concern about his health. 'He's survived these incredible indulgences,' says Branson. But Kelleher is now over seventy, with a lifetime of (legal) substance abuse behind him.Within three months of the partial abdication, the aviation system in the US was in chaos, as a result of the terrorist attack of 11 September. As well as threats, the new realities brought opportunities for Southwest. It could take advantage of its relative strength to expand beyond the continental US; the new Boeings make Juneau and Anchorage, the two most attractive cities in Alaska, accessible from Southwest's Pacific coast cities. The airline's growing strength in the north-eastern US puts it temptingly close to Montreal, Toronto and Ottawa. And south of the border, the booming Mexican economy makes a city like Monterrey an obvious target for any Texas airline. After all, Stelios and O'Leary have already demonstrated that the Southwest

WRIGHT WAS WRONG

One obvious benefit that Southwest offers over its rivals, says marketing director Rob Brown, is access to small airports with 'close proximity to downtown, to provide our customers with a quick and easy airport experience'. As everyone from the Kennedys to the Dixie Chicks have discovered, Love Field is handy for downtown Dallas; the airport is hemmed into a few square miles of suburbia.

By 1964, it was clear that demand for air travel was outstripping what Love Field could provide. The city fathers were ordered by the Civil Aeronautics Board to team up with Fort Worth, thirty miles west, with which Dallas had always had an uneasy relationship. They were told to develop an entirely new airport midway between them. By the time it opened in 1974, Dallas-Fort Worth airport – abbreviated by everyone to DFW – was the biggest in the world in terms of area, occupying a patch of north Texas the size of Manhattan. For a time after the new airport opened, travellers, meeters and greeters were confused by the two, as the gynaecologist-turned-country-star, Hank Wangford, noted in his song, 'I waited for you at DFW but you must have been in Love'.

The plan had been for all the airlines to vacate Love Field in favour of DFW, even though Love was much easier to reach for anyone in downtown Dallas. In yet another legal battle, Kelleher managed to argue Southwest's case for being allowed to stay at its home base, but at what was to be an extraordinary cost. A year after President Jimmy Carter deregulated aviation, a law was passed that was intended to prevent Southwest flying people from its home base to anywhere beyond Texas and the states that immediately adjoin it.

Every day, thousands of travellers are inconvenienced by the Dallas Love Field section of the International Air Transportation Competition Act of 1979. It is better known as the Wright Amendment, after the Fort Worth congressman who devised the rule.

Like many Fort Worth citizens, Jim Wright disliked and distrusted the bigger city to the east. He took the opportunity of his position as Speaker of the House of Representatives to push a law through Congress that comprises a shameless piece of protectionism for DFW, an airport that really needs no help, and an attempt to stifle Love Field. The Wright Amendment prohibits airlines with aircraft of 57 seats or more flying people between Dallas Love Field and any point beyond Texas, Louisiana, Arkansas, Oklahoma, and New Mexico. Southwest cannot even hint at the possibility that a traveller could transfer at, say, Albuquerque or New Orleans to reach other destinations. The law was weakened a little by the 1997 Shelby Amendment, which added three states to the list: Alabama, Kansas and Mississippi. But the rule is still like banning flights longer than ninety minutes from Luton. The only airline with a significant operation at Love Field is Southwest.

Today, it is my turn to be a victim of Congressman Wright's rule. For a simple journey from Kansas City to Dallas, I have to buy two separate tickets. (Despite the name, Kansas City is in Missouri.) At the intervening stop, Oklahoma City, I have to collect my bag and line up again to check in. That is not because Southwest takes the easyJet and Ryanair view of connecting flights (bluntly stated, 'We don't offer them'). It is because, in the twenty-first century, an absurd piece of federal legislation still interferes with free consumer choice, making air travel tougher and more expensive than it needs to be. One consequence is to reduce the number of tourists to Texas – which may not have been what Jim Wright had in mind.

concept can work internationally. But there is no sign that Southwest will bite at this tempting bait; expansion domestically will continue, although at a slower rate after the attack on America. To hear a flight attendant *singing* the arrival announcement within three months of 11 September may be considered bad taste by some. But Duane Redmond is having fun – and hopes most passengers are, too:

> We love you and you love us,
> We're so much faster than the bus,
> So come back soon for our hospitality,
> If you'd married one of us you could have flown for free.

Back at Love Field, the evening rush is beginning, with flights shuttling to Houston and San Antonio every half hour. The souvenir shop does a nice line in T-shirts, including one reading, 'I'm drunk and I can't find my horse'.

I've touched not a drop of Jack Daniel's or Wild Turkey, and I can find my wallet. As an experiment, I feed a dollar into an automatic change machine. It regurgitates a nickel, two dimes and three quarters – $1-worth of change. But for a time in 1974, I would have received $1.05 in change. Kelleher discovered that the machines at the newly opened Dallas-Fort Worth airport delivered only 95 cents. He ordered the Love Field machines to be programmed to pay out $1.05, and made sure the media knew all about it. Some passengers took advantages (you could tell which ones they were when they tried to walk through the metal detector), but the exercise was a heck of a lot cheaper than advertising. Turning $1 into $1.05, for the benefit of the public – and himself – is pure Kelleher. He would never short-change the traveller.

4. SKYTRAIN: POWER TO THE PEOPLE

'It never occurred to them that there was a fourth class out there called the human race who just want to fly at the lowest fare'

SIR FREDDIE LAKER

'Even twenty years after the fall of his airline he still remains bitter. Really, I can't blame him'

STEPHEN BATH, PRESIDENT OF ABTA

LAKER AIRWAYS FLIGHT 1: FORT LAUDERDALE, FLORIDA–FREEPORT, GRAND BAHAMA

Tens of millions of people have flown on aircraft bearing the name Laker. Few of them realise that Freddie Laker's first flights were shuttles between the British-controlled fragments of post-war Germany. The man who was to bring no-frills flying to the North Atlantic cut his teeth carrying coals and clothes across East Germany as part of the Berlin Airlift.

At the end of the Second World War, after Hitler killed himself amid the ruins of Berlin, the remains of the Third Reich were carved up by the Allied powers. Britain, France, the US and the Soviet Union each received a tranche of German territory. The first three were later amalgamated to form the Federal Republic, better known as West Germany, while the USSR's chunk became the German Democratic Republic, at least in name. Berlin was a special case because of its political and propaganda significance. Although the city lay far to the east, within the Soviet sector, the Allies insisted that Berlin was divided using the same pattern. So the British, the French, the Americans and the Soviet Union each had a sector of the former and present capital. Checkpoint Charlie was established as the crossing point between the American and Soviet zones.

One problem: how to keep the military and civilian populations of the isolated Allied sectors supplied? The Potsdam conference, where the boundaries were drawn, laid out rail, road and air corridors that cut through Soviet East Germany. In 1948, as Cold War tension mounted, Moscow unilaterally blockaded the surface corridors, turning West Berlin into a city under siege. Short of shooting down Western aircraft, and triggering another world war, the USSR could do nothing to seal the air corridors. So for the next year, a constant shuttle of flights kept the supply lines open. Many wartime aircraft were pressed into service to fly thousands of mercy missions. A good number of the planes were owned and operated by a young Freddie Laker – whom Vladimir Raitz called a 'freebooter'.

'Everything that could fly was used,' recalls Raitz. At the time, Raitz was a journalist for Reuters. Later he became a customer, and sometimes competitor, of Laker.

The Berlin Airlift provided Laker with a great deal of experience and money. He would need plenty of both when trying to establish the right to offer low-cost flying between the UK and US. He succeeded, for a while. Which is why, 53 years after the missions began, I am waiting in room 107 of the Clay Hotel.

A cloud the same fierce grey as the underside of the British Airways jet that brought me here is hovering low over Miami Beach, occasionally dousing the few tourists foolish enough to step out on to Washington Avenue. The rain makes the pastel pinks and yellows, greens and blues of the art deco district of South Beach look forlorn. South Beach, like the world of aviation, was very different when I first flew to Florida's largest city in 1981. Like millions of transatlantic travellers, I arrived on the Laker Skytrain, a no-frills service that transformed travel across the North Atlantic.

'All the people that I said would turn up, when I formulated the plan in 1971, are here,' Laker told the BBC on the day Skytrain first took off from Gatwick. 'Students, old age pensioners, people from all over Europe, Americans wanting to go home, all the low-income earners who need to travel instantly and for an undetermined amount of time.' His words presage those of today's no-frills entrepreneurs: 'There will be a seat for everyone, all through the winter,' he insisted. 'This is geared, and built, for the instant traveller. We've got 345 empty seats every day.' The seats were just like those of the other airlines: aboard a big, safe plane. The flights took the same time as the more familiar with-frills rivals (and, rainstorms permitting, a little less than my flight here yesterday). The larger, stronger rivals on the Atlantic offered similar fares for some of their seats. The difference with Skytrain was that Laker's lowest fares were also his highest fares. 'Look: I've got to give you a better deal,' Laker had said in one advertisement. 'I've got my name on every plane.'

A generation of travellers who never knew Skytrain is still reaping the benefits in lower fares between the UK and US. A few British backpackers are staying at the Clay. Outside, the hotel projects a fine example of Mediterranean Revival in the self-styled Spanish Village; inside, it is a no-frills sort of place. Room 107 has a 'semi-private bath', which means not very private at all. A connecting door with a bolt on either side leads to a bathroom that is shared with the occupants of Room 109 (who, to judge by their enthusiastic performance last night, are a lively couple). The bolts have to be opened and closed in the right combination to avoid scenes worthy of a French farce. But I feel less a character in *'Whoops! There go my trousers'*, and more like something miserable by Beckett or Kafka about the meaningless of life, and the fatuity of communication. I have pressed every possible combination of numbers on the telephone keypad, but I still cannot get beyond the automated exchange for LB Limited and speak to a human being.

LB Limited ('Formerly Laker Airways Bahamas Limited') is an airline serving the needs of gamblers heading for the island of Grand Bahama. The airline's headquarters are in Fort Lauderdale, thirty miles north along Highway 1 from the noisily romantic couple in Room 109 of the Clay Hotel. For around $300, the company flies weekenders from Fort Lauderdale to the island on a Saturday morning. They get a night in a ritzy resort, and are flown back to Florida on Sunday afternoon, older, wiser and quite possibly poorer than they were when they arrived. To fly on Laker these days, you have to be heading to or from the Bahamas.

Frederick Alfred Laker was born in Canterbury on 6 August 1922. He enjoyed a chequered career in aviation before launching the innovation he will be remembered for: the no-frills Skytrain service across the Atlantic that began in 1977. 'My name's Freddie Laker,' he told the American public. 'I own Laker Airways. And I think it's outrageous what you have to pay to fly. If you fly round-trip to London on one of the high-priced airlines, it can cost you a bundle. But if you take a Laker to London round trip you can save from 10 to 50 per cent off regular economy fares.' He reinvented air travel – cutting frills, slashing costs and passing on the savings – and redefined the word 'colourful' when applied to airline bosses. He is a man I must meet.

It is still raining, and the phone in room 107 is still not ringing. At an Internet cafe on the corner of Washington and 15th St, I prepare and send a reasonably smart-looking document headed:

ONE PAGE FAX FOR SIR FREDDIE LAKER
September 28, 2001

Dear Sir Freddie,

I understand that these are busy and turbulent times for everyone in aviation. But I am very keen to talk to you about the Skytrain story, at a time and place to suit you. I wonder if there is a time over the next four days, either in Fort Lauderdale or Grand Bahama, when we could meet?

I am at the Clay Hotel in Miami Beach (305 534 2988, room 107). Sincerely,

Simon Calder

That, you might think, is a presumptuous sort of fax to send. Anyone who flies all the way to Florida hoping to speak to one of the great aviation pioneers without an appointment deserves to be on a hiding to nothing. Except I have an appointment, or at least I thought I had. When I spoke to him by phone one week ago, Sir Freddie said that we could meet this weekend, either at his office in Fort Lauderdale or his home in Grand Bahama. On the strength of this discussion, I bought a non-changeable, non-refundable transatlantic ticket. Twelve hours before the flight left, his representative in Britain called to say Sir Freddie was 'too busy' to see me. 'I'm sure with a call to the right person you'll be able to get a refund,' was her suggestion. I declined, and boarded the half-empty British Airways flight from Heathrow to Miami.

The nagging feeling that things possibly aren't going to work out had begun almost at once, when the 747's departure was delayed by an hour after some unexplained technical problem. We were buffeted by headwinds all across the Atlantic. Then, almost at the end of the final approach, about 200 feet above ground, the engines roared, the nose lifted and we shot upwards with great haste. The people in the window seats had the look of unwilling victims on a roller-coaster ride that they thought was about to end before they were hurled around on one last, defiant fling. No one spoke, except the expressions on the faces of the cabin crew, which said, approximately, 'What the heck is going on?' We took a short-notice spin above the Everglades. At a point that I judged to be more or less exactly above the crash site of the ValuJet flight in 1996, the pilot explained that a sudden rainstorm had caused him to abort the landing. After an arc above the highrises of Miami Beach, we went out over the ocean and tried again. Eventually the jumbo splashed down on the runway.

From the terminal, I called Sir Freddie Laker's assistant, Irma, at his Fort Lauderdale office. 'I'm away from my desk right now . . .' I let her voicemail know where I would be staying.

That was twenty hours, five inches of rain and many phone calls ago – all of them outgoing. Outside, it has stopped raining; inside, it has never started ringing. The digital clock strikes 11.00. Perhaps a message has been left on my voicemail back in London.

There is one. From southern Florida. But not from Sir Freddie, nor any of his people. 'My name is Michelle Talamino. I represent Negril in Jamaica, and I'm calling to invite you on a press trip from 10 to 15 October.' I decide to call Michelle to decline what is likely to be the best offer I get all day, and to ask if she knows anything about Sir Freddie Laker. But the number fails to work. I call Irma again, but she is still away from her desk right now. I leave a message of the kind that implores any kind of news, good or bad. Maybe Irma has responded to the fax I sent with a fax of her own? I plod down to the Internet cafe to be met with shrugs.

Friday afternoon is nearly over, and things are going unhelpfully badly. Tomorrow, I will have to fly to Freeport, Grand Bahama, on Sir Freddie's own airline, to see if I can track him down.

By now I know that one of the automated options offered when you call the LB Limited office is for flight reservations. It refers callers to a toll-free number. I dial 1 800 432 2294, carefully. 'Thank you for calling Grand Bahama Vacations.' I wait for an operator, the first real person to whom I have spoken by telephone all day. I explain I want to fly next morning to Grand Bahama. Given the uncertainty of my mission, I am a little reluctant to pump another few hundred dollars into this venture for the half-hour hop to the island and a night in a hotel. So early on I ask about costs.

'Are you a regular player, Mr Simon?' she asks after taking my name. When someone asks a question like that, you do not want to be thought an amateur. 'Er, yes, but I've never played in Grand Bahama before,' then add as an afterthought, 'Vegas, mostly.' The only time I have ever played the tables was while being filmed for BBC2's *Travel Show*.

'Mr Simon, I'm going to transfer you to Sal, the Director of Players.'

Do you ever get the feeling that you are getting in too deep? As Sal comes on the line, I realise that an impromptu interview is about to begin.

'Are you a serious player?'

'Pretty serious,' I fibbed.

'That's good, because we're going through renovations and we need a lot of cash,' he laughs. 'What do you play?'

'Blackjack.' I know enough about the uncharitable probabilities of gambling to be aware that Blackjack is a favourite of proper gamblers. Amateurs believe the aim is to get cards totalling 21; professionals know that the sole purpose is to beat the dealer. He or she is constrained by some rules that mean the odds are only slightly stacked against an expert player with a steady nerve who adheres to the mathematical rules that tell you whether to 'hit' (take another card) or 'stand' (stick with what you have). In the long term, that means you lose money more slowly than at roulette or on the slot machines. In the short term, there is a fair chance of getting ahead quite quickly. Casinos are happy for a player to make modest gains, in the expectation that he or she will blow it all in the end. So Blackjack marks out a serious player and a reasonable prospect as a new customer.

'How much do you bet?'

'Twenty-five.' Another fib. But I recall that in Las Vegas the lowest stake for each hand is usually $5, and inflate that to come up with something that sounds respectable but not boastful. 'So what's it going to cost me?'

'The flights are free and the room is $85 double. Too bad there's only one of you. How much are you going to bring?' About $2,000, I lie. 'That's good,' he says, implying I had supplied the right sort of answers. 'Make sure everyone rates you properly,' he urges. 'On the tables, in the restaurant, anything you charge to your room.' The technique of 'rating' enables the casino to keep tabs on your spending, to find out who the high rollers are. They can then make sure that guests who are betting seriously are rewarded with 'comps' (free drinks, dinners, flights etc.) and are betting generously.

The last time I called a Laker airline to book a flight, I explained I wanted to fly from Gatwick to Miami. I was given the price, quoted my credit card number and was told to pick up the ticket from the desk at the airport. The only similarity with this transaction was the last bit, about picking it up at the airport. 'The flights are free.' Sal's words echo around the empty walls of room 107. Is this no-frills heaven? No. Sal has 'comped' me and expects a substantial pay-off to help with those builders' bills. While he transfers me to an assistant to make the booking, I wonder how big he and his friends are.

'I've got you booked at 9 a.m. tomorrow. Turn up at Fort Lauderdale airport, Terminal 4, two hours ahead, don't bring knives or scissors, you'll pay taxes of $43 going, $18 return.'

How, I wonder, do I get to the casino from the airport at Grand Bahama?

'They'll pick you up at the airport.'

The thought that Sal and his pals might be waiting in a stretched limousine to see the size of my wad haunts me for the rest of the day. I stare out of the window at the rain that is now bucketing down. A banner over the art deco Cameo cinema announces AMERICA WE STAND TOGETHER & UNITED. The *Miami Herald* tells the travelling public that, 'Troops in airports, stun guns for pilots are likely measures.'

Ten minutes before close of business for the weekend, I make one last call to LB Limited. When Irma herself answers I am so startled that I can barely speak. 'Didn't you get my messages?' she asks. 'I called a few times but there seems to be something wrong with the hotel switchboard. Anyway, Sir Freddie will see you tomorrow morning in Grand Bahama.'

* * *

'Ft Lauderdale-Hollywood Int'l Airport wishes to express its deepest sympathy to families and friends of the victims of the attack on America.' The message flickers on and off opposite the sign announcing that Spirit Airlines' flight to New York has been cancelled. A Mike Peters cartoon in the *South Florida Sun-Sentinel* shows a smiling check-in woman asking 'Thank you for flying today. Do you have reservations?' and a fearful passenger answering, 'Yes, but I'm still going.'

Shortly before 7 a.m., with a tropical storm brewing outside, I approach the counter with the familiar red and black logo spelling out the name of Laker Airways.

'We don't have anyone of that name, sir, When did you make the reservation?' Eventually we find me under Mr Calder Simon, with my date of birth shown as 11/11/11. Not even Sir Freddie is that old.

Skytrain got off the ground when Laker was a relatively young 55. Five years later the no-frills airline went bust, leaving hundreds of staff out of work and thousands of passengers stranded on both sides of the Atlantic. Undeterred, in the 90s Laker – then aged 75 – started up another link between Fort Lauderdale airport and Gatwick, offering a luxury economy class across the Atlantic. 'He tried again,' says Sir Richard Branson, 'but he didn't get it right second time round. But the spirited Sir Freddie still flies.'

He does, frequently, aged 79, on his own airline between Fort Lauderdale and Grand Bahama. Before I can follow, a complicated transaction is required where I hand over $43 for the taxes and sign a form headed 'Rated Player Transfer and Receipt Coupon'. A proper gambler would be delighted to be thus recognised; I find it menacing. A 'goody pack' provided with the ticket informs me I have missed Harold Melvin's Blue Notes by several weeks, but that I am in for a 2-for-1 Sports Day drinks special this evening. And lunch is on the Casino. I feel slightly nauseous at the prospect, because it reminds me of my pact with Sal.

'Flight 1, Gate 1. Have a nice trip.'

The lounge is thinly populated. At 7.47, a Boeing 727 draws up at the gate. Twenty years after I first stepped aboard one of Freddie Laker's aircraft as a passenger on Skytrain, I look eagerly for the brash Laker Airways livery, the symbol of a great aviation survivor. Oh dear. This plane has Transmeridian Airlines written all over it. Does that mean the Laker magic has deserted Sir Freddie once again?

'Good morning, we're about to begin boarding Laker flight zero-one to Grand Bahama. Boarding all rows.' About forty people, around one third of the capacity of the jet, wander towards the gate. Five minutes early, the plane is pushed back, and flies through thick cloud to a wet, stormy and uninviting Grand Bahama island. Had this been a normal charter flight carrying sunseekers in search of an idyllic beach, we would have been disappointed. But gamblers, and interviewers, have different ambitions. As did the tall, tanned and smiling man waiting for me in the corner of the customs hall.

Freddie Laker is to aviation what Paul McCartney is to music. Sir Freddie, I say with sincerity, it is a pleasure to meet you.

'I left school when I was 16, because I wasn't very bright.' East Kent in the 30s was not the most promising place or time to be growing up, but two events made Laker determined to fly. 'I had a flight in an aeroplane with Alan Cobham and his Flying Circus – a five-bob flight around the airport. It was one of the reasons I wanted to get into aviation.' The other was seeing a Hindenburg balloon and a Handley Page biplane flying over his home city. A painting of the scene is given pride of place in his home on Grand Bahama's millionaires' row.

'I got a job at Short Brothers at Rochester.' This aircraft manufacturer, which still makes parts of planes in Belfast, was Britain's fraternal answer to Orville and Wilbur Wright. 'I had two jobs in the first hour,' says Laker. 'One was sweeping the floor, the other was getting the tea.' We are drinking coffee and watching the rain from the terrace at the Casino Towers at Bahamia, the resort that has a room booked in my name – and a Director of Players named Sal. I keep this side of the story quiet and listen to a man who changed the world.

Laker was barely seventeen when the Second World War broke out, but his early attempts to serve were thwarted because he was working for an aircraft maker. 'I wanted to get into the war, hopefully to fly, but every time I went along they said, "No, we can't take you, you're in a reserved occupation." The recruiting officer explained to me that it wasn't pilots they wanted, it was aeroplanes. What point were the pilots without the aeroplanes? Then I saw an advertisement in a newspaper that the Air Transport Auxiliary, which ferried planes, were looking for engineers. I thought this would be a way of getting in. So I went along and they were reasonably interested in me, and asked me what I did now. "I'm working on the Stirling bomber for Short Brothers." I wasn't the world's greatest aviator with my one Flying Circus flight, but to cut a long story short, I got in.'

When the Second World War ended in 1945, Freddie Laker was 23, a qualified pilot – and a survivor. His wartime experience earned him a job at British European Airways, an airline newly created by the Attlee government and based at Northolt airport in Middlesex; anyone who has driven to or from London on the A40 will have noticed this now-military airfield, whose runway almost strays on to the road. Twenty-seven years later, BEA merged with BOAC to form British Airways. But Laker had left very much earlier.

'I stayed with them for three months, and said, "Well, I can't do this. It's impossible." Everything had been nationalised, and of course with a Conservative mother that didn't work very well.'

What about your father, I ask.

'My father was a disaster, a total disaster. He ran off and left my mother. And he locked me in the coal cupboard, under the stairs, when I was five years old. I only saw him once after that, during the war. I was in uniform at the time, and I was in a pub, and a person came up behind me, tapped me on the shoulder and said, "Aren't you going to buy me a beer, then?" I looked him straight in the face and said, "No." I didn't see him again. He died a long time ago, he's not part of my life. He was so incompetent he couldn't even drive a truck; he had to be the lorry driver's mate.

'My mother was a different thing altogether. She was absolutely out of this world. A wonderful lady. She fell in love with a fellow. His name was William James Allin, and he was such a wonderful fellow that he changed his name to Laker. Now that's a man and a half. That was a real father.'

Laker is something of a father figure to many of the Bahamians we encounter. Our conversation is repeatedly interrupted. Every one of the passing staff greets 'Mr Laker' ('Sir Freddie' is the correct form, but carries a hint of too much familiarity). A holidaying Londoner wanders over and introduces himself. The Laker legend is alive and well, as is the man – despite a prostate cancer scare ten years ago – and his mind.

After treating each person he encounters with grace and meticulous good manners, he returns to talk animatedly about the subject he knows best: his life in aviation.

'When Mr Attlee got into power and nationalised all air transport and said "Thou shalt not fly", a few of us said we are going to fly, so I went off and got involved with all kinds of business.' In the post-war years, Britain's aviation industry was hurriedly changing gauge from a military to a civil footing, and making something of a hash of it. There was plenty of scope for an entrepreneur with fast footwork and good contacts to oil the wheels – and line his pockets in the process. 'I hold the record of actually buying three aeroplanes from BEA and selling them to BOAC.' The two airlines created by the government within the Air Ministry could not manage a simple deal to transfer the aircraft from one to the other. It took a middleman: Freddie Laker. He bought almost any aviation surplus that the Ministry of Supply was offloading, selling scrap aluminium to saucepan makers and buying obsolete aircraft engines solely for the valuable platinum points on the spark plugs. But the making of Laker was on a Cold War frontline: the Berlin Airlift.

When the Kremlin decided to seal the land corridors to the city in June 1948, closing Checkpoints Alpha and Bravo in the process, the West had three options. Of these, the unthinkable one was to do what the USSR hoped for, and abandon the city. Equally unpalatable, it could launch a military strike, precipitating a conflict that could quickly escalate to atomic weapons and cause even more carnage than the Second World War. The third possibility was that Western aircraft could attempt to ferry in fuel, food and every other essential by air. However expensive and impractical, this was the only feasible course. Initially, military transports were used, but quickly private operators had to be drafted in. At busy times, aircraft arrived in the city at the rate of one every two minutes.

Freddie Laker realised the Western Allies were prepared to spend heavily to protect their easternmost enclave, and he leaned upon his trading skills to earn his share of the cold war cake. 'I was buying brand new bombers, with two hours flying time on them, for £100 apiece. We painted them silver and put them on the Berlin airlift.' Aviation Traders Ltd, his first proper company, was based in Southend, but most of its aircraft shuttled between British bases in western Germany and Tegel airport in the British sector of Berlin. As the propaganda battle intensified, with the West outfoxing the USSR, Laker got rich. 'By any normal standards I was making an awful lot of money. But I didn't go off having a party. I started buying aircraft parts.'

Laker correctly observed that the bonanza could not last for ever; in the end, it continued for nearly a year before the Soviet Union relented and reopened the land corridors. Laker had planned for a soft landing once the earnings dried up. He continued to wheel and deal in an environment when civil and cargo flying was increasing rapidly yet the UK government was still flogging off valuable equipment at bargain prices.

And then he went into the car ferry business.

At the time, the procedure for anyone wishing to take a vehicle on the ferry between Dover and Calais was long and precarious. Each car was hoisted by crane into the hold of the ship. 'All these cars were getting damaged because they were swinging them over on chains.'

Besides denting vehicles that were, at the time, luxury goods, the journey took all day because of the painful slowness of winching each car on and off.

'I thought to myself that with a Bristol Freighter, updated, I could do a car ferry.' Laker approached Douglas Bader, then managing director of Shell Aviation, whom he knew to have what was popularly known as a 'Bristol Frightener' for sale. He adapted the aircraft to carry two cars and their occupants. The first passengers that a Laker airline flew were motorists, along with their vehicles.

Initially he flew the air ferry from Southend to Calais and Ostend, and later added Rotterdam to the network. It was such a success that he decided to expand, and converted a much larger DC-4 into the 'Carvair'.

'We cut the nose off the DC-4 and put it up above the fuselage like a 747, and we could carry five cars and 22 passengers.' On the ground, the aircraft looked faintly ridiculous, with a huge gaping hole where the nose cone and flight deck should be. Yet the idea of front-loaded freight was not only ahead of its time – the same concept led to the development of the Boeing 747 – it was also effective in getting the travel-hungry middle classes to the Continent. Before Eurotunnel, before the giant roll-on, roll-off superferries every half-hour from Dover, the smart route for anyone who wanted to take a motor car abroad was on an air ferry.

In 1958, the Queen opened the new terminal at Gatwick, which soon became the low-cost alternative to Heathrow. By then, many of the fragmented private enterprises of UK aviation – including a couple of Laker's companies – had consolidated, and British United Airways was formed. Laker became managing director of the company, the biggest independent rival to BEA and BOAC ('There was a terrible row when we said we were going to put "British" in the name,' he recalls). BUA was to build up a strong scheduled operation, including lucrative flights to the Libyan cities of Benghazi and Tripoli, as well as carrying charter passengers on behalf of tour operators like Horizon. Initially it operated only propeller aircraft, but Laker took the bold decision to become the launch customer for the 1-11, the new twin-jet being built by the British Aircraft Corporation that aimed to rival the French Caravelle and the American DC-9. Being a launch customer means you can drive a better deal, but it also carries large risks from untried technology – just ask BOAC about Comet. For a British jet aircraft, the 1-11 turned out to be quite a success, and underpinned Ryanair's development as a no-frills operation.

Laker's career at BUA ended – and his own airline began – in tragic circumstances. The shine disappears from his eyes as he tells the story.

By 1965, Laker was on an annual salary of £3,500 as managing director of BUA. This translates to £40,000 today – not a fortune for an airline boss, but enough for him to run a yacht, which he kept moored in Italy. By his first marriage, Laker had a son named Kevin. It would have been natural for him to work for what had become the family firm. But, says Laker, 'He didn't want to work for me in BUA, "because I will always be in your shadow". So I said we'd go into the package-holiday market.' Laker senior started looking into buying some hotels, and planned to charter BUA to fly the passengers. 'All this was set up,' he recalls – until one day he was on the yacht. 'I'm down in Italy on my boat, and I get a phone call from England saying Kevin's had a terrible accident. The little boy who was with him is already dead, and you must come back immediately.'

Kevin was still alive, but gravely ill in hospital, by the time Freddie flew home. 'I got back, and went to see him, and I said, "Who is this?" and he said, "Oh, you're my Daddy". That's the last I heard from him. Then he died.'

The personal tragedy had professional repercussions. 'Of course now there's no reason for me to leave BUA,' says Laker. But by now rumours were rife that his relations with the airline's chairman, Miles Wyatt, were strained, and that Laker was planning to set up his own operation. On the day of Kevin's funeral, he took a telephone call from Wyatt.

'He knew it was the funeral of my son, and he said, "Are you going, or are you staying?" And I said, "Miles, my kid's outside in a box. Please don't ask me that today. Let's talk about it tomorrow or the next day or something." He said, "I want to know now." I said, "Miles, if you want to know now, the answer is I'm going." And that was that. I'm out of BUA, and I thought, "I'm going to keep going." So I formed Laker.'

This was not the package-holiday operation he had originally intended. Instead, he established an airline that would prove to be a thorn in the side of BUA. Laker Airways began with a couple of leased Britannia propeller planes, but soon had the distinction of possessing Britain's first all-jet fleet, starting with three BAC 1-11s. The airline grew rapidly on the rising tide of holidaymakers keen to follow Vladimir Raitz's footsteps to the Med. In an early move towards vertical integration – where the airline and tour operation are under common ownership – Laker picked up a couple of tour operators, Arrowsmith and Lord Brothers, which would later become Laker Holidays. But the most crucial move was to acquire a Boeing 707 and move into so-called 'affinity charters', the extraordinarily convoluted means that, before 1977, allowed ordinary people to fly the Atlantic without first robbing a bank.

The arcane rules of the International Air Transport Association (IATA) forbade any kind of discounting by scheduled or charter airlines. They did, though, permit cheap fares for bona-fide groups of passengers. And what comprised a bona-fide group? 'Members of a club, which has been formed for a purpose other than air travel, who attended regular meetings.' Such a passenger qualified for a cheap ticket on affinity charter flights. There was one further condition: the booking must be made three months in advance. But like the other rules it was widely flouted. In practice, word-of-mouth recommendations and handwritten cards in newsagents' windows led prospective passengers to Gatwick.

'I was doing these affinity groups like crazy,' says Laker. 'Of course all the tickets were being sold in the corner of the airport.'

It was an hilariously clandestine operation. At the appointed location, passengers handed over cash. In return they received a ticket whose date stamp purported to show that it had been issued months earlier, plus a membership card for some spurious society. This latter document was to be presented to inspectors, should they show up from IATA and demand evidence of membership – by no means an unknown event. To add to the illusion that everyone was a paid-up member, sometimes a lawyer with a bible was on hand as part of the check-in procedure; the passenger had to swear their loyalty to the affinity group, and hope that God would overlook the mild exaggeration. Perhaps the fact that you needed to be in a club to see the world is what gave British Airways the idea of calling its premium business service 'Club World' a decade later.

One day in 1970, Freddie Laker received an urgent call from the duty office asking him to get to Gatwick immediately. Instead of the normal bustle that preceded the departure of an 'affinity' charter, he was greeted by mass chaos amplified by individual grief.

It was the event that led directly to the creation of Skytrain. With his eyes ablaze once again, he describes the scene as though it were yesterday, not half a lifetime ago. 'The Civil Aviation Authority are interrogating every passenger and chucking old women off the aeroplanes.' When asked, 'Why are you going to New York?' one elderly woman answered, 'To see my son'. That confirmed to the officials that the affinity group rules were being flouted. Anyone who failed to convince the inspectors that they were regular attendees at club meetings was not allowed to travel. Besides the distress of each of the stranded passengers, the inspectors' haul spelled a large fine for Laker.

'We left about 25 people behind,' says Sir Freddie. He then describes how he climbed on to a box and started shouting, 'They will never do this to me again, no one's ever going to be chucked off my planes again, I'm going to fight.'

The press had by now been tipped off that a story was developing at Gatwick. 'I got the best write-up ever known to man,' says Laker. After the Boeing had departed, with a couple of dozen empty seats, he went back to the office and hatched a new plan.

'Right. We are going to start a new system altogether. We are going to have a thing where people can get on and off aeroplanes when they like, how they like. They can eat the food or not eat the food, they can buy the ticket at the door and get on the aeroplane, just like when you want to go to Glasgow. The only thing you can't do is hand-strap. Just like a train – skytrain.' And that was that, apart from the small matter of seven years of legal battles on both sides of the Atlantic that might have exhausted a less determined man. But Freddie Laker is endowed with profound self-belief.

'If he didn't have such an enormous ego he wouldn't have built the business that he did. So good luck to him,' says Stephen Bath, president of the Association of British Travel Agents. Those seven years were spent finding a way through a bureaucratic jungle that had been judged impenetrable by everyone else. Airlines were emblems of national prestige, which governments felt they needed to protect by every means possible – starting with the stifling of competition. In both the UK and the US, Laker fought a series of legal battles to win the right to fly people cheaply across the Atlantic.

The media loved it. To demonstrate what a grip the Skytrain struggle had upon Britain in the 70s, Laker drives me through the downpour to his oceanfront house, where a collection of cartoons from national newspapers decorates the garage walls. The single-storey structure has touches of Mediterranean Revival. It is a beautiful new construction, set in ample grounds that give way to the Atlantic. The motif that begins at the gates and continues through the ensemble is the heron, an elegant bird whose name was bestowed on a De Havilland aircraft. I am too polite to ask what the house cost, but according to the real-estate listings, the smallest lot on this exclusive peninsula starts at half a million pounds – mansion not included.

One cartoon latches on to the no-frills idea, with a trio of passengers giving precise instructions to the cabin crew about how they would like the fish they have brought with them cooked. Another shows airline passengers shovelling coal, with the caption, 'What do you expect for £32?' This was the price originally quoted by Laker, but in the high-inflation 70s it increased quickly – as did Laker's legal bills. 'I fought, kicked, shouted at them day after day,' he recalls.

Until 1974, he battled with a Tory government that saw BOAC and BEA as national treasures that could not be put at risk. The two treasures merged in 1972, a move that some long-serving staff still regard as a mistake. A year later, Skytrain was designated as a transatlantic carrier under the terms of the Bermuda agreement that governs flights between the US and UK. After the downfall of the Heath administration in the Miners' Strike and Harold Wilson's return to power, he found his entrepreneurial drive left him on the wrong side of the ideological fence from a Labour party that was still a quarter-century away from embracing freedom of the skies. His adversary in the Department of Trade, Peter Shore, was implacably opposed to Skytrain. He declared in 1975 that Laker would not be allowed to start transatlantic flights. 'I wriggled myself into his office. I go up and he's got a couple of his minions there. And one of them was Bob Ayling.'

The man who was later to lead British Airways was, at the time, a government lawyer. Laker told Shore 'What you're doing is morally wrong. But that's a question for your conscience – I can't do anything about that. What I can tell you is that what you're doing is illegal. That is a different thing.' Laker says that Shore asked his advisers to comment. 'They both looked at him, and refused to look at me, and said "It's pure rubbish, Minister". So off we go, Peter Shore does his stuff, and there's a new appeal.'

Bob Ayling disputes this version of events. 'Freddie Laker is a great pioneer and it would be a nice story, but he's got the wrong man. I was advising on European Community law then. Aviation law came later for me. Though I would in all probability have given the same advice. The issue was whether or not Peter Shore could de-designate Skytrain, using the prerogative power. He decided to do so. Freddie challenged the minister's decision. The minister was upheld in the High Court. The Court of Appeal over-ruled the High Court and held that the Secretary of State had acted in excess of his power.' Eventually, Peter Shore was moved to the Department of the Environment, and was replaced at Transport by Edmund Dell.

'The new minister called me, and said, "We're behind you 100 per cent."' There remained the problem of getting permission from the US, where the two leading transatlantic airlines – Pan Am and TWA – fiercely opposed the opening of the market. Laker Airways was still flying tens of thousands of people across the Atlantic on affinity charters, but running the risk of the wrath of inspectors in both the US and UK. Like a serial poacher, Laker got to know the aviation gamekeepers well. 'They had this number one enforcement officer who called me and said, "Freddie, I'm going to fine you more than any airline has ever been fined – $102,000." I asked why $102,000, and he said that there had already been a fine of $100,000 and he was going to top it. So I said that I'd pay the fine on condition that I got a hearing for Skytrain.'

Laker maintains that he did not pay a fine of $102,000 – he bought a Skytrain hearing for $102,000. 'We got the hearing, and won.' In June 1978, President Carter gave permission for him to start flying – a year before deregulation in the US.

As Herb Kelleher had found at Southwest, even when Laker's adversaries had no further legal recourse they made life as uncomfortable as possible for the new competitor. One restriction they successfully demanded prevented passengers checking in at the airport. 'They said you can't check in the passengers at Kennedy. You've got to have a check-in facility that's at least five miles away. It actually turned out to be an asset.' Anyone who has ever visited New York's most prominent airport will appreciate the benefit of checking in away from the kerfuffle of Kennedy. Laker rented a large hall in Queens, and bused passengers direct from the hall to the aircraft steps. On the British side, passengers were on the brink of having to check in on Hackney Marshes and fly from Stansted airport in Essex. But the government made an eleventh-hour climbdown and allowed Skytrain to fly from the Laker base at Gatwick – again, with the insistence that passengers were checked in away from the airport.

During his time at BUA, Laker had made lasting friends with executives in British Rail when they came up with a prototype version of the Gatwick Express about twenty years before fast rail links to airports became fashionable. He knew of a disused building at Victoria station in central London, and turned it into the Skytrain check-in. It worked miraculously. In the days before the first flight, queues began to form with anxious Americans wanting to get home on the cheap, and adventurous Brits seeking the chance to start seeing the world. The line around the block became a regular fixture on news broadcasts. The 'turn up and go' concept was, initially, more like 'turn up and don't go anywhere'. But the impression the images created – of unstoppable demand for a new, democratic form of travel – was better publicity than a million-pound advertising campaign.

'Everything they did, thinking they were frustrating me, actually turned out to be the right way to do it,' says Sir Freddie, who is in full flow on his favourite subject. 'They were absolutely dedicated to kill me, and they forgot a lot of things.' The DC-10 jets that Laker planned to use for Skytrain had been with the airline for two years, filling in with holiday charters until the transatlantic service got the go-ahead. With 345 seats, the DC-10s carried a hundred fewer passengers than the iconic Boeing 747, but among flight crew the tri-jets were well regarded. One innovation was a crew lift that connected the main passenger cabin with the galley in the bowels of the aircraft. But a first-class section was missing. The ranks of seats – each in a strangely easyJet shade of orange – marched ten abreast all the way to the front of the aircraft.

When I ask about the first Skytrain flight, on 26 September 1977, I think I can see a tear forming in Laker's eye. I am right. 'I still get emotional about it. I think all of us, all the crew, the passengers, were in tears.' Sir Freddie was on hand before the flight to milk the publicity, then joined the pilots in the cockpit for departure. He gave the passengers a commentary during the take-off roll; the cheer when the wheels lifted off the ground was audible even over the roar of the engines at full throttle. With six years' worth of publicity to support the operation, it quickly became a success – at the expense, initially, of the affinity charters that had been the previous low-cost option. In his advertisements, Laker made the point that, 'You don't have to join a club to take off in one of my beautiful DC-10 aeroplanes.'

Within nine months, Freddie Laker's status as national hero was confirmed with a knighthood in the Queen's Birthday Honours in June 1978. Was he, I wonder, surprised when he got the call from Buckingham Palace? 'Christ, with what I'd done to the government? Execution by hanging, yes. Knighthood, never.' He keeps the awards that he was given by the trade paper, *Travel News*, as Travel Personality of the Year for five straight years from 1977. Laker was on top of the world, and to prove it he expanded Skytrain, adding Los Angeles and Miami to the network. Executives of US airlines, such as Franco Mancassola, then at Continental, were impressed. 'When Freddie Laker came into the market, I did nothing but applaud him. I admire people that have the guts to stand up for what they believe. I don't have much time for chief executives of big state airlines. They risk nothing of their own money. They blame fuel, they blame wars, they blame anything there is to blame, they ride for a few years and then they move along with big bonuses. But Freddie Laker was a man who had courage and vision. He was brave.'

Laker needed courage. Within a year of the knighthood, things began to go badly wrong. As the second winter season approached, rival airlines cut their fares to match Laker's – with the added bonus of providing meals on board free of charge. Soon, British Airways and Pan Am had queues of their own stretching from their ticket offices in Victoria. On 29 May 1979, all DC-10s were grounded worldwide after a series of fatal crashes involving other airlines. Two Laker Skytrain flights in mid-Atlantic were ordered to return to Gatwick. It was a catastrophic start to the peak summer season, when any transatlantic airline expects to make the bulk of its money. By the time the ban on DC-10s was lifted, one month later, Laker had lost millions of pounds in revenue. Worse was to come, because after a fatal Turkish Airlines crash at Paris, many passengers now regarded the DC-10 as a dangerous aircraft and opted to travel on the Boeing 747s of British Airways, Pan Am or TWA instead, rather than what was seen (unfairly) as a dangerous aircraft. Nevertheless, expansion plans continued.

Shortly before Laker Airways went bust in February 1982, stranding 6,000 passengers, Sir Freddie had filed for permission to start a Skytrain Europe service. It would have comprised a network to match the most successful of today's no-frills airlines, but the plans did not come to fruition. Neither did the promised new route from Prestwick in south-west Scotland to Tampa in Florida, which, had it worked, would have had airline experts redefining the concept of a 'long, thin route'. Instead, the rejoicing of 1977 was counterbalanced by sadness. And the frills came back. Laker introduced a cabin aimed at the business class to his previously egalitarian Skytrain service. Regency class was, by all accounts, very comfortable. The rationale made sense to a man who felt under siege from his transatlantic rivals: 'If you attack from the back of the aeroplane, operating below cost, then I'm going to attack from the front.' Regency class was also very empty, as was the rest of the plane. Flights were being cancelled or consolidated (two departures combined into one) on the say-so of the commercial department. These measures helped to fuel rumours that the airline was ailing. But whatever mistakes were made towards the end of the airline's life, Sir Freddie remains convinced that collusion between rival airlines was responsible for his corporate demise. 'What I was doing was revolutionary. They had to kill Freddie Laker.'

Death, when it finally came, was precipitated by the banks' refusal to extend the airline's overdraft to help it through to what Laker was expecting to be a profitable summer season. The scenes at Gatwick were just as powerful as the images that surrounded the launch of Skytrain. Staff who had believed their boss could ride out another storm were in tears, passengers were distraught – though other airlines agreed to carry them for nominal payments – and public sympathy was immense. Pensioners were sending in cash in a vain hope that they could save Laker – but not in the millions that Sir Freddie needed.

The deserts of the south-western US are littered with the evidence of airlines that expanded at an unsustainable rate. But Laker believes it was not his blind ambition, but his rivals' blind panic, that killed his airline. He says his earnings were crippled by the other airlines cutting their fares to below cost in a concerted effort to force Laker Airways out of business, and to prevent him establishing the sort of network in Europe that twenty-first-century no-frills carriers have.

'I think the real reason they went for me at the jugular was because of our application for Europe. With the economic union and everything else, we were going to get freedom of the skies in Europe. Even Norman Tebbit was on my side. You imagine, think about it. Imagine having Laker in Europe twenty-two years ago. How much is that worth? Billions. Billions.' Another legal fight began, which took half as long as the first, before ending to Sir Freddie's partial satisfaction. 'It's all documented out there what the bastards tried to do.'

Margaret Thatcher – the prime minister who had presided over Laker's downfall – was keen to privatise British Airways. Before a single share could be sold, though, the Laker dispute had to reach closure, to avoid saddling the new company with uncertain liabilities. 'They come along to me and say, "The whole thing's over." But I said, "It isn't over." This is the bit they never give me the credit for. We sat down until three o'clock in the morning with Colin Marshall [chief executive of BA]. John King [chairman of BA] was in a room above, because John King didn't have the guts to talk to me personally. So I said, "Look, it isn't over. You can solve the problem easily. I want all the creditors paid." He said, "Done." 'I said, "I want every member of the staff paid, and every member of staff's pension to be paid in full.' There remained the question of what Sir Freddie himself would recover from the experience, which he now reveals to be 'Eight million dollars. And change.'

After a lengthy and complicated legal battle about alleged connivance to force Laker out of business and then raise fares, six competing airlines agreed to compensate transatlantic travellers. Any passenger who could prove they had taken a transatlantic flight since Laker Airways' demise was entitled to a voucher worth £30, which was taken as an admission that other airlines' fares had been held artificially low and then inflated after the rival disappeared.

'I won. I had them. Remember we're three and a half years down the road, and you know something about three and a half years down the road? You can't put Humpty Dumpty together again. I'm a winner, but I can't get my licences back, so I lost from that point of view.' Still, Sir Freddie earned enough to set him up with a property in the Florida resort of Boca Raton, besides this one in Grand Bahama, and says, 'At the end of the day it's probably put ten years on my life.'

That life has been shared with four wives, the youngest of whom is the current Lady Jacqueline Laker. She is a former Eastern Airlines flight attendant who Sir Freddie met on an overnight transatlantic flight from Miami to Gatwick on Air Florida in the early 1980s, though they did not meet again for two more years. They married on 6 August 1985, Sir Freddie's 63rd birthday. Jacqui, and Freddie Junior – who runs a web company in Florida – accompanied the aviation veteran to Gatwick in February for a reunion to mark twenty years since the demise of Skytrain. Back in the Bahamas Sir Freddie and his wife move in the upper echelons of Bahamian society, and he has become an unofficial ambassador for his island. 'All I am interested in is, can we get tourists to Grand Bahama. Why do I want to do it? Because they've been kinder to Freddie Laker.'

The bitterness that he still feels against the British establishment surfaced a month before my visit, at a dinner where Lady Thatcher was guest of honour. 'They sat her next to me. And she said, "Freddie, the press didn't treat you very well, did they?" And I said "And neither did you, Margaret".'

'Your interview is over.' And so it is. With no pressing reason to remain in Grand Bahama, and specifically no wish to meet Sal and his pals, I ask Sir Freddie if his airline would be flying back to Fort Lauderdale that day.

When you are travelling with a ticket that is 'non-endorsable, non-transferable, non-refundable and valid only on the designated flight and date,' and you want to change your plans, it helps if you turn up with the boss of the airline. He gets me a boarding pass, and comes through to the departure lounge – to give the waiting passengers the surprise of their trip. Grabbing a microphone, he says, 'Ladies and gentlemen. This is Freddie Laker speaking. First of all I'd like to say how sorry I am about the attack on America. In the Bahamas we have our problems too. We want tourists to come and we'll do everything we can to make you safe. Please remember that Grand Bahama is the best place in the world. I know, because I live here. Thank you very much for supporting us.'

As the applause dies away, we adjourn to the bar, where this well-mannered, straightforward man allows one last sliver of bitterness to surface. 'It never occurred to them that there was a fourth class out there called the human race who just want to fly at the lowest fare.' I didn't tell him about Sal and my deception, but I think he might admire my desire to fly at the lowest fare.

The Skytrain story did not end in 1982. The following year, PEOPLExpress attempted to emulate Laker, without success. Continental Airlines took over the route and, in 1998, announced, 'The cheapest-ever scheduled flights across the Atlantic – a London–New

TREATING CATTLE LIKE PASSENGERS

When Laker set up his car ferry operation in the 1950s, there was a strong American military presence in Europe. The quartermasters for US bases on the Continent were concerned about the quality of British abattoirs, and refused to buy meat from the UK for their soldiers.

'They would if it was killed in Rotterdam,' says Laker, 'because the Rotterdam abattoirs they thought were cleaner. If we had a space on the aeroplane, we would put a cow in it. We put a tarpaulin on the floor of the Bristol Freighter, and partitioned it off from the passengers. We carried dry cows – cows that won't give milk any more, they're only fit for meat (and not very high-quality meat either, because they were old as well).

'We had a fair supply of deodorant, of course. At Southend we had a lairage – a hay rack. I had a fellow that used to go round the markets in the county buying dry cows. I paid him ten bob (50p) for each cow. We'd keep them in the lairage, and every time we had a space we'd pop one in. And within two hours of popping them in the aeroplane they were dead and hanging up in the abattoir in Rotterdam.

York fare of £178 return. That was £60 more expensive than Freddie Laker's opening offer on Skytrain. Also in 1998, miraculously, those familiar DC-10s in Laker colours appeared once more on the runway at Gatwick. Laker Airways mark two flew from the Sussex airport to Fort Lauderdale, offering leather seats, high-class catering and seatback videos for a price matching that of Virgin Atlantic. Richard Branson was taken aback to see Sir Freddie reappear as a competitor, but the challenge did not last for long. 'He didn't have the right equipment, he had a lot of technical problems, and in a sense there wasn't the opening in the marketplace,' says Branson. 'Virgin was there – and with Virgin a strong brand, it didn't work out.'

LB Limited (formerly Laker Airways Bahamas Limited) is still going, however. The Transmeridian aircraft that is waiting to take me back to Florida is a temporary aberration, chartered in while Sir Freddie 'changes gauge' with his airline operation and awaits replacement aircraft. Not many people in their 80th year would decide to order new planes. But Laker, the man who fought the battle of the North Atlantic, wants to fly his small corner of the Atlantic just right.

5. VIRGIN TERRITORY

'During the 70s, what was offered in the air was an absolutely miserable experience – which was why we decided to get into the airline business and try to change things'

SIR RICHARD BRANSON, CHAIRMAN OF VIRGIN ATLANTIC (AND OF VIRGIN BOOKS)

'I love Richard. It's as simple as that'

SIR FREDDIE LAKER

VIRGIN ATLANTIC FLIGHT 200: MAASTRICHT–GATWICK

Virgin Atlantic, voted airline of the year in dozens of awards, is anything but no frills. So it may come as a surprise to learn that the airline that pioneered no-frills flying within Europe was Virgin Atlantic. The venture was not a great success, and it was abandoned after five years. Today, flight 200 no longer hops from an obscure Dutch city to Gatwick; the number has been transferred to Virgin's prestigious Hong Kong–Heathrow service. But the record industry tycoon who started the airline was undeterred by the lack of success, and now has not one, but two low-cost airlines, with the promise of more to come.

To understand this strange state of affairs, a flashback to the 70s is in order. The decade was barely three weeks old when the first Boeing 747 in commercial service took off from New York JFK, destination London Heathrow. Pan Am flight 2 was three hours late, and the jumbo would later become the airborne target of choice amongst a generation of terrorists. Nonetheless, the 747 precipitated the greatest transformation of our travelling habits that the world has ever seen. With more than twice as many seats to fill as the Boeing 707, DC-8 or VC-10, airlines were obliged to cut prices. People who never dreamed they would be able to fly to Africa, Asia or America soon found that fares were within their reach. The then-Radio 1 megastar, Tony Blackburn, was wheeled in by BOAC – now part of British Airways – to advertise flights from Heathrow to New York for £103 return (now £900) in the pages of the leading rock music weekly, *Melody Maker*. But the ad that interested most of the people I knew was from a new and unfamiliar company called Virgin Records.

Britain's music industry had just undergone the equivalent of airline deregulation. Resale Price Maintenance, the agreement that kept the cost of discs artificially high, had been abolished. Henceforth albums by Yes, Led Zeppelin and, if you really insisted, Deep Purple, could be sold at any price the shop liked. The big retailers at the time were such celebrated music heavyweights as W. H. Smith, Woolworth and Boots. They appeared not to have noticed, and continued to charge £2 (now £18) or more for an album. Since the public seemed prepared to pay inflated prices even for *Deep Purple in Rock*, and no one had stepped in with an alternative, they had no incentive to discount.

Soon, an alternative was provided by Richard Branson. When most sixteen-year-olds were getting into rubber, whether the Beatles' 1966 album *Rubber Soul* or latex condoms, Branson was getting into business. He began his first venture while between detentions at Stowe School. *Student* magazine was an ambitious attempt to harness the ideals of the 60s. By the time Branson was a precocious 20-year-old, he had decided on the first of many business diversifications and moved into music. Branson realised a truth that has eluded many in both the music and airline businesses: with lower prices, the market can expand to generate profits that overall are higher despite slimmer margins. There was plenty of market share waiting to be seized while the slow, sclerotic giant companies figured out what to do next. I wasn't entirely sure what virginity was, but I knew Virgin Records hit every adolescent's spot with the promise of cheap music. For the record buyer, the first few retail branches comprised an early prototype of Upper Class relaxation: I sat on some giant cushions within tripping distance of Brighton's Clock Tower, inhaling joss sticks and other vapours that prevented me realising just how awful Deep Purple could be. The present-day Virgin Megastores are disappointingly mundane by comparison. Around the corner from the record store in Brighton stood a club called the Big Apple. For many of us, it was the closest we ever thought we would get to New York. Tickets for the forthcoming Rolling Stones gig there were changing hands at 18 shillings (90p).

Virgin Records, being run on a pre-decimalisation shoestring by Branson and some pals, was a no-frills sort of operation. The ads in the music press were nothing to write home about. They were, though, something to write to South Wharf Road, London W2 about – the address of the warehouse around the back of Paddington station whence the orders were despatched. I was never quite sure how Virgin Records could sell Neil Young's *After the Goldrush* for 30 shillings and 8 pence (£1.53, now worth £13.50), including postage, when every other retailer wanted 10 shillings (50p) more. But in the same way that twenty-first-century passengers express mild mystification about some of the fares offered by no-frills airlines, I honestly did not care twopence (1p).

Quite soon afterwards, Branson did that paper napkin thing. This bar or restaurant ritual appears to be an essential part of some no-frills operations; a napkin was also the vehicle for the original Southwest route map, and the medium on which easyJet's choice of name was first scrawled. The familiar Virgin scribble was born in return for a £200 fee for the designer, Trevor Key. The logo adorned the expanding chain of record shops, the Manor recording studio in Oxfordshire and the record label. It would be another decade before it was applied to the tail of a Boeing 747. Meanwhile, there was a whole lot of business to be done; Richard Branson was the first to realise just how profitable Mike Oldfield could be. In retrospect, Oldfield was the first one-album-hit wonder. But by catching the concept music wave of the early 70s, his *Tubular Bells* surfed to the front of many a music collection. The Virgin label was made. By the time the follow-up *Hergest Ridge* was released, most of us had realised that the quasi-electronic symphony of special effects had all the staying power of Little Jimmy Osmond. We sat on our hands and waited for punk to arrive. But with everyone from the Human League to Genesis on his books, Branson knew how to pick a winner. But the downside of the music business was that it involved a great deal of flying.

'We certainly ended up travelling a lot more during the 70s, but the quality of travel was absolutely dire,' says Branson today. 'What was offered in the air was an absolutely miserable experience – which was why, in the early 80s, we decided to get into the airline business and try to change things.'

By 1984, Sir Freddie Laker had discovered that the demand for transatlantic travel is as elastic as it is for music – in other words, dropping the price by 10 per cent will cause an increase in demand of more than 10 per cent. Laker had also gone bust, despite the custom of people like Richard Branson, who flew Skytrain 'on a point of principle'. The failure of Laker Airways had left a vacuum for cheap, fun travel that was initially filled by an interesting operation called PEOPLExpress.

Despite looking uncomfortable on the eye in print, this company – or, perhaps more accurately, commune – was phenomenally successful for a short time. It began in 1981 as a response to deregulation. The airline was based in Newark, New Jersey, and flew mostly in the north-eastern US. Che Guevara would have been proud of its egalitarian principles: pilots took a turn at check-in and loading baggage. The PEOPLExpress partnership philosophy – and the low fares that it generated – caught the early 80s mood. The airline was so no frills that it aimed not to employ baggage handlers. Passengers were encouraged to carry all their luggage into the cabin, with a financial penalty of several dollars if they wanted to check baggage into the hold. (Plenty of frequent travellers wish the same philosophy applied today.) Within two years, it had become America's fifth-largest airline. The company paid for the vast Terminal C at Newark airport, and established a flagship route to Gatwick airport that picked up some of the passengers who had previously flown with Laker.

As with many communes, internal squabbles soon began. Combined with the ease with which traditional airlines could trim and cross-subsidise their fares to maximise the impact on a new player, PEOPLExpress hit financial turbulence and was soon taken over by the giant Texas Air combine. Its Newark–Gatwick route became a Continental Airlines flight, establishing the Houston-based airline in Britain.

At the time, the only UK airlines flying the Atlantic were British Airways and British Caledonian. Even under the terms of the highly restrictive agreement that governs flights across the North Atlantic, there was space for another UK competitor. Early in 1984, an American lawyer named Randolph Fields had touted around a business plan for an all-business class airline called British Atlantic Airways.

The same concept had been suggested before and since. The most recent apparition was in 2000 by an entrepreneur named Michael Lord-Castle, who brought in the former Tory Cabinet minister, Lord Tebbit, as chairman of Blue Fox Airlines. Caught up in the downturn of transatlantic travel following 11 September, Blue Fox failed to make its take-off slot, scheduled for March 2002. In 1984, Branson decided the risk was too great for a business-class only operation. But the music tycoon was sufficiently intrigued by the idea to modify the concept to a two-class operation, business and economy. His thought was to dispense with the three-class structure that was becoming standard, by offering a business product that was as good as other people's first class. He also believed the budget product could be cheered up. (By 2000, the Upper Class/Premium Economy/Economy model resembled the mix on a typical 80s flight on other airlines, but with higher standards of comfort and inflight entertainment.)

The deciding factor for Branson was when he tried to phone the PEOPLExpress reservations line from his Oxford home, and found the line permanently busy. Either the Gatwick–Newark route was incredibly popular, he deduced, or the airline was incredibly badly run; whichever, Branson believed, there was clearly room for a new player doing something different from the existing competition. 'The problem with just being no frills is that another airline can subsidise an undercutting exercise and drive you out of business. That happened to Freddie Laker. To an extent that might have been what happened with PEOPLExpress.' Branson took solid advice from Laker: 'Freddie said that if you're economy only then you're vulnerable, because they [the competitors] can always cross-subsidise their economy fares with business passengers.' The record-company-boss-turned-airline-chief recruited staff from Laker Airways to run the company. Fields was sacked when the lawyer's eccentricities began to grate on senior executives; the New York lawyer almost grounded the maiden flight because he felt his pay-off was insufficient. Most significantly of all, Branson took on board Laker's instruction to sell himself along with the seats.

'I'd always taken my mum and dad's advice about keeping a low profile and keeping separate from the business,' says Branson. 'But when I had lunch with Freddie Laker and said that I was thinking of going into the airline business, he said, "You're up against Pan Am and TWA and British Caledonian and British Airways, and they've all got more money than you. So you've got to use your personality to promote your company, and milk it for all it's worth." And I've been doing that ever since. If you're a relatively small independent airline, advertising is extremely expensive, and you have to try to make yourself heard.' Despite the inevitable susceptibility to criticism that comes with entering the public domain, Branson found himself in the unexpected role of Britain's favourite entrepreneur, a post recently vacated by Laker. He passed the 'would you enjoy an evening in the pub with this man?' test, not least because of his celebrated non-aversion to alcohol.

Of the original competitors that Virgin Atlantic faced, only British Airways is still in business; BA swallowed up British Caledonian, Pan Am went bust three years after the Lockerbie disaster and American Airlines bought bankrupt TWA. But life is never easy for an infant airline. Not only was Branson, and his Virgin organisation, unfamiliar to many of the airline's prospective customers, so too was Newark, the New York airport to which the new airline would fly; PEOPLExpress had not put the New Jersey city on many people's maps. Newark was no further from Manhattan than JFK, and from a traveller's point of view a less depressing proposition, but it was the 'wrong' side of Hudson River and in a state – New Jersey – that many people regarded as a joke. Freddie Laker had managed to get access to the premier New York gateway of JFK. But the presence of British Caledonian on the Gatwick–JFK route meant that Virgin had to make do with an airport with which few UK travellers were familiar. Neither was the London end of the operation especially favoured. Gatwick, the welcome signs announced, was part of Crawley, 'a nuclear-free zone'. It was also 28 miles from the capital. And even among British travellers, few could correctly name the county it is in (West Sussex). Virgin Atlantic also faced huge problems in carving out a market between the UK and US. For legal reasons, the new airline could not advertise flights at all in America until it had a licence, which came through only the day before the launch departure. Yet buoyed up by the media launch, some residual affection for Laker and the fresh approach to aviation, the airline started making money almost at once. Indeed, it would be tough for any airline to lose cash across the Atlantic in summer. The tricky bit starts when the June-to-September high season ends and load factors dwindle. Which is why Branson diversified into no-frills aviation, quite possibly without realising it.

This highly significant aspect of the infant Virgin Atlantic fails to make it into both Branson's compendious autobiography, *Losing My Virginity* and the airline's official history. Shortly after launching Gatwick– Newark flights, the airline had started a route between the Sussex airport and the Dutch city of Maastricht. This was a classic no-frills operation that predated Ryanair, easyJet and Go by a decade.

The origins of this low-cost foray has its roots in the problems Virgin Atlantic faced in carving out a market between the UK and US. From Britain, there were already eight different airlines flying from London to New York, once the fifth-freedom carriers – Air India, El Al and Kuwait Airways – were counted. In summer, there was plenty of traffic to go around. In winter, everyone was trying to claw out whatever customers they could. So the Maastricht connection seemed like a good idea to set up at the end of the summer season. It was intended to connect with the Gatwick–New York service, to feed the route with traffic to and from continental Europe. Maastricht was splendidly placed at the south-east corner of Holland for travellers from Belgium and West Germany; these days, Ryanair might call it Aachen (West) or Liege (East). The idea was that, on quiet days, the flight would be operated by the Vickers Viscount, a small turbo-prop aircraft owned by British Air Ferries (BAF). The technical arrangement was that this was a 'damp lease': the pilots were from BAF, while the stewardesses were Virgin's (which, in the early days, always brought a laugh from some laddish quarters). But there was enough leeway built into the 747 schedule to allow, if demand was sufficient, for the jumbo inbound from New York to continue on from Gatwick to Maastricht.

The continental connection was not restricted to transatlantic passengers. British travellers had a new low-cost option to fly to Europe. It was the original cheap flight to the Continent, charging a flat £19 each way – far lower than the prevailing fares to Holland. Yet it was never the success that it was hoped to be, and as far as anyone can remember the 747 never once flew to Maastricht.

The reasons no-frills flying in Europe was initially abandoned are largely to do with Branson's having taken on Laker's advice, and developing a powerful marketing strategy to accompany Virgin Atlantic's launch. Attention was understandably focused on the more significant part of the operation, the London–New York link. The extraordinarily rapid build-up to the launch had generated vast amounts of media coverage. No record company had tried to set up an airline before, and speculation was rife about the rock stars passengers might find themselves sitting next to. Some of the gimmicks that never stayed the course – including the in-flight live entertainers, and a free economy ticket for every business-class passenger – proved highly newsworthy. Best of all was the Upper Class cabin, comprising just eight luxurious seats in the 'bubble', the upper deck of the Boeing 747. It caught the imagination both of the media and the passengers down below in economy class, which Branson had to be dissuaded from calling 'riff-raff'. With so much 'noise' being generated over the transatlantic route, it would have been counterproductive to muddle the message by dwelling on the new option that had opened up in Europe. Within five years, when the transatlantic operation had become established, the Maastricht connection was quietly abandoned. No one much noticed. Branson had other concerns.

1984 nearly became a nightmare project for the Virgin Group; the film of the George Orwell novel was as over-budget as it was overdue. But 1984 was also a nightmare year for British Airways because Virgin Atlantic got started. On 22 June 1984, the first Virgin Atlantic flight took off early in the morning from Maastricht to Gatwick, with no attention whatsoever. At 11 a.m., the first Virgin Atlantic transatlantic flight departed to Newark, with a huge amount of attention. The first flight was full – mostly with journalists and similar riff-raff – and ran out of champagne somewhere over Newfoundland. It set a pattern that has endured ever since (though with better-stocked drinks trolleys). Contrary to popular impression, Virgin flights have never been especially cheap. But they have always been fun. The launch flight of a new Virgin route has, ever since, been one of the most sought-after freebies in journalism.

There have been plenty to seek. Branson subsequently cherry-picked the most profitable US routes from London: Boston, Miami, Los Angeles, San Francisco, Washington. Once Virgin gained access to Heathrow, he

BRAND AWARENESS

The idea of a record company running an airline was absurd – but it worked. To have the logo of a record company on the tail made it comfortably familiar to the market of young travellers that Branson was keen to cultivate. And to be a record company that owned an airline did great things for the brand. 'An airline is a wonderful flagship for a company,' says Branson. 'The airline has put the Virgin name on the map, it's literally flying around the world, and we can use respect of the brand in tackling a lot of other industries that have similar faults to the airline industry when we went into that.' In 1984, when Virgin was mostly music, no other record label could boast that its logo flew each day between the two world capitals of music, London and New York.

secured rights for the other glittering prizes in aviation: Hong Kong, Johannesburg, Tokyo. In an industry that is notorious for helping people lose fortunes, owning an airline made Branson famously rich. He says now, 'Virgin Atlantic only cost us a million and a half pounds because we used some of the cash flow to get it going, and second-hand planes.'

British Airways, the dominant airline on his home turf, tried every trick in the book, and many that are not, to put him out of business. The 'dirty tricks' campaign involved BA staff hacking into the Virgin reservations computer and diverting prospective passengers with tall stories and free upgrades. Branson recalled Sir Freddie Laker's admonition to 'sue the bastards' and spent many years in litigation. Despite BA's best efforts, the airline survived, and fifteen years after the original flight – from Maastricht to Gatwick – Branson had sold a minority stake in Virgin Atlantic to Singapore Airlines for half a billion pounds.

One reason Branson cites for running a successful airline is listening to staff. He says this often involves flying with them, doling out meals with them, and going to their parties in the evenings. 'I think knowing how to party, being able to socialise with your staff – you know, if you fly somewhere, going out on the town with them – is more fun for you, more fun for them, and you'll be in touch with what's going on.' Branson's staff are joined in their appreciation of the Virgin boss by an aviation veteran living in the Bahamas. 'I love Richard. It's as simple as that. I think he has an incredible brain, I think he has done a wonderful job,' says Sir Freddie Laker; Branson says the feeling is mutual. But then Laker turns a little sentimental. 'We had LA and Miami, and we were about to get a round-the-world flight, Globetrain. Every route that Richard has we had or were going to get.'

I doubt the phrase 'Quit while you're ahead' is one that often finds its way into Branson's vocabulary. Part of the £500m that he earned with the sale of 49 per cent of Virgin Atlantic was sent to Brussels to shore up what was left of his next European no-frills operation, Virgin Express. And after 11 September, Branson found himself having to lay off hundreds of Virgin Atlantic staff, and delete his two cherished new routes to Chicago and Toronto. When I ask him about the difference between success and failure in aviation, he is precise: 'Very slim,' he says. 'A percentage above break-even can make you very profitable, a percentage below can lose you money very quickly.'

6. STANSTED, OR BUST

'Earlier in the programme, we referred to Michael O'Leary as chief executive of easyJet. He is, in fact, chief executive of Ryanair'

PM PROGRAMME, BBC RADIO 4, 3 OCTOBER 2001

'He's as tough as nails, a businessman through and through, no compromise'

SIR RICHARD BRANSON

'If I can get a £7 flight to somewhere within two hundred miles of Venice, well I'll fucking take it. Seven quid, I don't care where I fucking go!'

SIR BOB GELDOF

RYANAIR FLIGHT 203: STANSTED–DUBLIN

'Here you are, folks, a little late but safe and sound in foggy Dublin.' That is how the Ryanair captain announces our arrival in the Irish capital. His boss is less circumspect. 'Three dumb bastards decide they're not going to go to the gate on time.' It may sound like the start of a joke, but the lean 40-year-old Irishman with a chin as chiselled as Cape Clear is not laughing. I am running an hour behind schedule, and Michael O'Leary has made it his business to find out why.

If you are late for a meeting because your flight is delayed, try to make sure that your appointment is with the boss of the airline. But I suspect there are few chief executives who are so hands-on that they would greet you with a tirade against their own tardy customers. One week after the 11 September attack on America, the chief executive of Europe's leading no-frills airline is fuming at a trio of dawdling passengers. 'With all the extra security we're checking in two hundred bags a flight and it takes us twice as long to get their bags out of the hold.' O'Leary is taking it personally. 'They should be strung up.'

Lynching passengers is not part of the business plan at Ryanair, but O'Leary leaves few expletives undeleted as he talks about his success and others' failures. As I walk into his office, he is on the telephone explaining with some conviction that 'tourism in this country next year is fucked'. If whoever was at the other end of the phone was looking for a polite assessment of the prospects for tourism in Ireland in 2002, they asked the wrong man to provide it. O'Leary paces around an office larger than that of any of his European no-frills rivals, with a frown beneath thick eyebrows that indicates he is concentrating hard on his airline's interest in the Irish tourist trade. I know that he is not speaking to a radio station, as he often does, because on air he tempers his language to the ideal balance between being hard-hitting, controversial and consequently listened-to, and being so outrageous that he is never invited back. But in circumstances that can be regarded as private, even an event such as a meeting with stock-market analysts, the air is often peppered with expletives.

'I think it's interesting that Michael O'Leary has this image as a rough-and-tumble profane Irish farm boy,' says Barbara Cassani of Go. 'He's a trained accountant who went to one of the finest universities in Ireland.' Cassani is correct. The reason O'Leary was hired by the Ryan family to evaluate their small, independent and loss-making airline late in 1988 was his razor-sharp intellect and financial acumen. To be fair, O'Leary has respectable agricultural credentials: he lives on his farm an hour west of Dublin. 'I breed horses and cattle,' he says. 'It's the closest thing I get to a sex life.' But since taking over as Ryanair's chief executive on New Year's Day 1994, he has been concentrating less on the animals and more on running Europe's fastest-growing and most profitable airline.

The chief decoration in his first floor office is a poster from the *Evening Standard* announcing JUDGE BLASTS 'BA BASTARDS', an episode where even calling one of my newspaper stories as evidence failed to save British Airways from defeat at the hands of Ryanair.

Once our formal interview begins, the language is toned down but the robust sentiments remain. We are talking at a very sensitive time. Eight days earlier, the worst aviation disaster in history had seen two hijacked aircraft flown into the towers of the World Trade Center in New York, a third hitting the Pentagon in Washington DC, and a fourth deliberately crashed by its passengers in Pennsylvania to foil the hijackers' plan. The previous evening in Dublin, Aer Lingus had announced 1,600 job losses – a hundred more than the total number of people employed by Ryanair. Michael O'Leary, meanwhile, is in a good mood, wayward passengers excepted. His company's shares, like those of every other airline, had sunk in the aftermath of the attacks. But at close of business the previous night, Ryanair was valued by the markets at a higher capitalisation than either British Airways or American Airlines – an astonishing achievement for an airline that, a decade previously, was, to use O'Leary's succinct description from earlier, fucked.

Ten years earlier, says O'Leary, Ryanair 'was hovering on the verge of bankruptcy. In Spring 1991 I thought it would be a miracle if we were still in business three months later.' On 18 September 2001, Ryanair was more valuable than the biggest airline in the world. Handily for O'Leary, he owns 18 million shares in Ryanair, representing over 10 per cent of the airline.

Michael O'Leary spent much of the final three months of 2001 tussling with another airline multi-millionaire, Stelios of easyJet, to see who could get the most airtime. The media, including Radio 4's *Today* programme and BBC1's *Breakfast News*, developed a sudden interest in no-frills flying. The two men were confused in a report on Radio 4's *PM* programme that required an apology: 'Earlier in the programme, we referred to Michael O'Leary as chief executive of easyJet. He is, in fact, chief executive of Ryanair.' But quickly most listeners and viewers were well aware who was at the top of Europe's biggest no-frills airline. It was the man who, a decade earlier, had taken a basket-case airline and turned it into a carrier that flies to more European destinations from Stansted than British Airways does from Heathrow. 'We don't look upon ourselves as an Irish airline any more,' says O'Leary. 'We look upon ourselves as a European airline.'

So why isn't it called O'Learyair, then? Not because Ryanair is much easier for a Swede or an Italian to pronounce, but because the airline was the creation of an Irish businessman named Tony Ryan. He had been one of the leading figures in the establishment of Guinness Peat Aviation as a leading aircraft leasing company. (Dr Ryan's family still holds 15 per cent of Ryanair's stock, collectively comprising the largest shareholder.) In 1985, when aviation between Britain and Ireland was a straight carve-up between Aer Lingus and British Airways, Ryan saw an opportunity. He started an airline that flew between Waterford (where he is still director of a crystal firm) and London, using a single fifteen-seat Bandeirante aircraft, made in Brazil. The airline carried 5,000 people in its first year. In January 1986, Ryanair started flying on the Dublin–Luton route, charging £94.99 for an uncomfortable eighty-minute ride between the Irish and English capitals on ageing Hawker Siddeley 748 turbo-props. That fare compares very poorly with the lowest available today, but at the time it undercut the prevailing fare on British Airways and Aer Lingus from Heathrow. Even a promotional return cost £99. The airline rapidly expanded, with ATR 42 planes and the first BAC 1-11 jets taking it from 80,000 passengers in 1986 to 600,000 in 1989, and soon Ryanair was flying nineteen routes, including vaguely low-cost flights from Dublin to Paris and Munich. Partly because the fleet was such a muddle and the network so stretched, things were not going well. By 1989, Ryanair had lost £20m in four years. Tony Ryan covered the losses because, like many aviation entrepreneurs before him, he believed there was a profitable role for the airline bearing his name. Unlike most of his predecessors, he was correct – but first he had to change the direction, and the management, of Ryanair.

'We were trying to do what many other airlines were trying to do in Europe, which was to be a slightly lower fare "me too" carrier to Aer Lingus and British Airways,' says O'Leary, who joined Ryanair six weeks before the end of 1988. 'We had a business class and a frequent flyer club and all the rest of it, but the fares were about 20 per cent cheaper, which meant we just lost more money than they did.' BA and Aer Lingus were in a so-called 'pool' arrangement, an arcane affair which meant that all the earnings were split between the airlines. Neither had an incentive to be any better than the other across the Irish Sea, because any edge that either achieved would have to be split with the other.

Michael O'Leary progressed rapidly in Ryanair, becoming deputy chief executive in 1991. Who, exactly, suggested a trip to Texas is lost in the mists of Ryanair's corporate history. But a call was placed to Southwest Airlines, and Michael O'Leary flew to Dallas. 'Once we saw what Southwest was doing we thought this could be the way forward. We're imitating Southwest: selling at the lowest possible price to the maximum number of people. We've been replicating that successful formula now for the last twelve years with tremendous success.' Not *quite* the same formula as Herb Kelleher had created, though – most obviously by the mix of aircraft. While Southwest had stuck religiously to Boeing 737s, Ryanair began its born-again no-frills status using a fleet of six BAC 1-11 jets. All the propeller planes were pensioned off, along with all but five of Ryanair's routes. At the start of the 90s, the prospects for independent success were not encouraging. The Gulf War early in 1991 diminished the demand for air travel almost as dramatically as the 11 September terrorist attacks a decade later. Air Europe went bust trying to provide a with-frills service at low cost during aviation's worst-ever recession to date. In the same year, Ryanair cut fares on London–Dublin to £69 return, flew 700,000 people, and turned its first profit. Dan-Air collapsed in 1992, another UK airline that tried to offer low-cost flying and failed. British Airways, keen to capitalise on the opportunity for a ready-made short-haul operation based at Gatwick, picked up Dan-Air for £1.

Which is what a Ryanair flight may cost you in the first decade of the twenty-first century – though you'll pay at least ten times as much in taxes, fees and charges. The airline stands to earn less than the price of a cup of coffee from the relatively small number of passengers who pay such low fares, which is why you'll be encouraged to buy a hot drink aboard. Ryanair cashes in on peckish passengers. The airline's sales and marketing director, Tim Jeans, is more pragmatic about how Ryanair manages to generate impressive earnings: 'We sell the most expensive cheese sandwiches in Europe.' Thanks partly to the profitable catering (in-flight sales currently account for 7 per cent of revenue), but mostly to aggressive marketing, Ryanair's fortunes started to race ahead of its rivals in 1994. By this time it was carrying 1.5 million passengers and charging as little as £49 return between the English and Irish capitals. This was the year when Ryanair began replacing its elderly, noisy British-built jets with American Boeing 737s, the aircraft that Southwest relies upon. It chose the unusual technique, for a scheduled airline, of buying unwanted planes from a charter airline. Britannia Airways, then and now Britain's biggest charter carrier, wanted to upgrade its fleet, and sold its old Boeing 737s to Ryanair. Look closely at one of the Ryanair jets, and you may instead see traces of Lufthansa's insignia – the airline that O'Leary and Jeans love to hate. At the start of 2002, the average age of its Boeing 737-200 fleet was 21 years, a year longer than the useful life of the planes, as defined by the airline itself. Yet Ryanair also has a collection of fresh-out-of-the-box Boeing 737-800s, which are maintained by Lufthansa.

Ryanair used the 'new' aircraft to create a UK–Ireland network based at its headquarters in Dublin. Initially the strongest routes were from Gatwick and Luton to the Irish capital, but quickly a whole network of options was built up, from Bournemouth to Teesside. And crucially, Ryanair discovered Stansted.

As white elephants go, the Essex airport was outstanding. Actually, it was more of a shiny elephant, because of the prodigious amounts of glass and steel that went into Sir Norman Foster's beautiful but empty terminal. From opening day on 19 March 1991, the new Stansted was an extravagant embarrassment. A perfectly adequate small, regional airport had existed for decades, serving mostly cargo, charters and Air UK's network of domestic and European flights. To alleviate the shortage of space at London's other airports, it was decided to build a huge new terminal on the far side of the airfield. Regular travellers, used to the ease and simplicity of the previous terminal, found it infuriating to have to walk for miles or take a shuttle train to the gate. But what they couldn't complain about was overcrowding. Stansted was mostly empty, most of the time. The airlines, and hence the travelling public, shunned it in favour of Heathrow and Gatwick.

Within a year of its opening, an IRA bomb attack on the City of London had shown the vulnerability to terrorism of large steel and glass structures. Armed troops were detailed to protect it and, on some days, it seemed there were more people guarding the terminal than travelling through it. Except for the Air UK network, only a few off-piste airlines like Cubana (offering a weekly Ilyushin flight to Havana via Gander) served the airport. The place was ripe for a deal.

Ryanair initially wanted a cheaper alternative to Luton and Gatwick, and that was what Stansted provided. Dublin services were moved across from Luton to take advantage of the lower airport charges, and frequencies gradually increased. Not all the flights in the timetable actually flew, mind: 'I'm not going to deny that at one time in Ryanair's history, if fifty were booked on the 12 o'clock from Dublin to Stansted and there were fifty booked on the 1 o'clock, there would be a magical combination of those two flights,' says Tim Jeans. 'Consolidation' of departures in this manner is a useful tactic for airlines with precarious profitability, but aggravating for passengers. Jeans says Ryanair no longer cancels departures for commercial purposes.

In October 1995, Ryanair took the revolutionary step of opening a new *domestic* route in Britain, from Stansted to the Ayrshire airport of Prestwick. There is hardly any history of a nation allowing foreign carriers to operate domestic flights within its territory. Traditionally, this was partly to protect the national carrier, but equally important were the perceived risks if war broke out. Not only did a nation want to have a fleet of transport aircraft to call upon, it didn't necessarily relish having a potential enemy's planes parked on its runways. By the closing years of the twentieth century, Britain had decided that Ryanair did not pose a threat to national security, and was prepared to permit 'cabotage' – the freedom for a foreign airline to fly within the UK.

Britain is party to one of the most anti-competitive airline treaties anywhere, the Bermuda II agreement that restricts flights between the US and UK. But within Europe, it has been at the forefront of encouraging competition. Few other foreign airlines were tempted to start services; Lufthansa tried flying between Birmingham and New-castle, but soon gave up.

No one paid much attention to the start of flights between two of Britain's most underemployed airports, except Stelios – who was preparing to launch easyJet's first route from Luton to Glasgow the following month. If British Airways and British Midland (now BMI) even noticed the start of flights, they probably didn't regard it as competition. They operate from Heathrow to Glasgow's main airport, the prime business route between England's and Scotland's largest cities. Anyone using the Ryanair method to travel from the centre of London to the middle of Glasgow would have to cover at least seventy miles of the journey by road or rail. By 2002, though, the Stansted–Prestwick route had ten flights each way, every day, more than BMI between Heathrow and Glasgow.

Ryanair has not indulged in much more cabotage since then, perhaps because easyJet has overtaken it as the main domestic no-frills airline; Ryanair's only other UK domestic route is from Stansted to City of Derry airport, which effectively serves County Donegal in the Republic. Since its flotation in May 1997, the airline has been much more interested in starting routes to a bunch of places you never knew you wanted to go – or, more precisely, to a different place to the one to which you thought you were going.

Ryanair specialises in flying to 'secondary' airports. Passengers buy tickets to Stockholm (South), Oslo (South) and Brussels (South). In each case, 'South' is a euphemism for 'nowhere near', as the people enduring the sixty-mile bus transfer from Stockholm (South) to the Swedish capital itself will testify. Oslo (South) is either eighty or sixty miles south of the Norwegian capital, depending which line of the Ryanair press release you believe.

National borders prove no obstruction to Ryanair's assertions. In October 2001, Malmo in Sweden made an appearance masquerading as the Danish capital, Copenhagen. The Scandinavian airline, SAS, stopped flying between Stansted and Copenhagen, so Ryanair stepped smartly in, trumpeting Malmo as the new gateway to the Danish capital, thanks to a bus link. Low-cost airlines like low-cost airports, and in Ryanair's case that ideally means nothing more than a shed with a runway attached. And there are plenty more like that waiting to be discovered. 'There's all kinds of places in Scandinavia and down through Germany where NATO had bases during the cold war,' says O'Leary. 'Even in the UK there's dozens of airports.'

So how does Ryanair decide where to fly? 'Usually we make a decision based on that airport providing us with a very good package of facilities and they have to be efficient facilities, at low cost. Whichever airport provides us with the best package is the next new route we open.'

'Michael has a view that all you have to do is find an airport that will be given a discount or doesn't want to be paid at all,' says Stelios of easyJet. 'He says, "There's a desperate airport – I'm going to take advantage of it." ' Stelios says there is a problem with Ryanair's strategy. 'You end up flying from very small places, which means you end up flying at very low frequency, struggling to fit one flight a day, maybe two. Our strategy says, go to proper places – big catchment areas or big destinations – and blitz them on frequency.'

Some of the airports served by Ryanair give an approximation to the speed and ease of a private jet for a fraction of the price. Small airports have three obvious advantages for the traveller: quicker boarding and disembarkation; with fewer arrivals and departures, there is less chance of air traffic control delays; and quicker taxiing, meaning less time before take-off and after landing.

As Tim Jeans revealed, there is a fourth benefit, too, of which the traveller may not be aware: the flight may be subsidised by the airport, or the regional authority. 'The great advantage with secondary gateways over primary places like Barcelona, or even Bilbao, is that we matter to the people in Biarritz, in Alghero, Carcassonne, Pescara. Frankly I don't think Go matters to Florence or Naples or Prague. You're not on their radar. But in every city, town, village that we serve – we're on their radar, and that's the important thing.'

'We're talking with Ryanair about a hub,' says Maria Holbert, who works at the former US Air Force base of Hahn, on a plateau high above the Moselle Valley, close to the Luxembourg frontier. It is now known as Frankfurt, which happens to be the main aviation hub in Germany. That city is sixty miles east of here. But because the International Air Transport Association designated the airport as 'Frankfurt', rather than the more accurate Traben-Trarbach (the name of the nearest significant town), Hahn is building on its new identity. 'We're extending our terminal, so we will have a capacity of more than a million passengers a year. And we are just building new aprons, so we will be able to handle a hub. That would be very great for this region.'

So very great that the region is prepared to pay for it? Holbert will not say, and neither will Tim Jeans. But Ryanair's sales and marketing director freely admits that some airports on his airline's network turn the usual arrangement on its head. Instead of charging Ryanair for use of the runway and terminal, and the processing of passengers and baggage, they pay Ryanair for the privilege of working for it.

'We are talking in terms of marketing support,' says Jeans. 'It is very much part and parcel of any tourism and marketing activity and we simply are part of that budget.'

In 1998, Ryanair went into Rimini, on the Adriatic coast of Italy. The incentives offered by Aeradria, the airport authority, to Ryanair totalled a handy 1.25 billion lire – 'for tourist promotion plus other easements on airport costs', according to a local newspaper report at the time. 'Aeradria considers this an investment,' said the president of the authority. 'It will help us to receive new visitors at Rimini.' The airport was expecting around 60,000 extra passengers. In other words, the region was paying £400,000 – a subsidy of £7 per passenger.

Both Jeans and O'Leary are keen to condemn the way that other European airlines are supported by government aid, putting Ryanair at a competitive disadvantage. The airline has called for such subsidies to be outlawed. Yet the carrier is content to take cash from the municipalities it serves. 'Marketing support' may sound like a fairly innocent, marginal issue – except that marketing is a highly significant part of any no-frills airline's cost structure. It is a polite phrase for 'subsidy'. The people of Wallonia – the French-speaking part of Belgium, where Charleroi airport is located – or at least their regional government, are paying part of the fare of passengers using the local airport, or at least contributing directly to Ryanair's profits by meeting the airline's hotel bills. Doesn't this constitute an unfair subsidy?

'No,' says Jeans once more, choosing his words carefully. 'They are assisting in the development of their tourism infrastructure in exactly the same way as building a new roundabout to ease traffic exiting and entering the airport is an investment in access and egress from the region. It goes beyond the finance, it's a whole range of activities that assist Ryanair to make its presence felt, to make it a viable operation.'

After two years, Rimini's airport management changed and wanted to change the arrangement in its favour; Ryanair refused and pulled out. Michael Cawley, the commercial director, said, 'What they do not understand is that with ten existing airports [in Italy] and in excess of ten further airports seeking our business, Ryanair has more demands for its flights than it can supply for the forseeable future.' The airline soon started flying to nearby Forli (known as Bologna on Planet Ryanair) under what is believed to be a similar subsidy arrangement. If some airports are so desperate for the business that they are prepared to hand over hard cash, that appears to contradict the constant refrain from Ryanair and other no-frills airlines about unfair subsidies from governments to airlines. Surely, I suggest to Tim Jeans, you're in exactly the same game?

'Every airport, whether Manchester or Glasgow or Paris, will give an airline an incentive to start a new route. It's universal. The size of that incentive may be an issue. But it isn't state aid. It isn't a question of saying, "Write me out a cheque for 100m euros" or whatever. The amount of money you're talking about in state aid to European airlines is in the tens if not hundreds of millions of pounds. We're talking about a tiny fraction of that.'

Passengers benefit directly when they book on a new flight to or from Prestwick – free rail travel between the Ayrshire airport and any station in Scotland, which could mean a saving of up to £80. Prestwick makes the offer for the first six months of any new route. Glasgow's second airport is a classic no-frills destination. It is miles away from the city it is supposed to serve, which already has a perfectly good airport of its own. Prestwick was foisted upon Scotland by the post-war government, which wanted a reliable base for transatlantic flights: the weather on the coast north of Ayr is better than elsewhere in the country, with a much lower incidence of fog. While British Airways (and, before that, BOAC) was firmly under government control, it was easy for the Air Minister to demand a connection to New York. Even after that era ended, the government insisted that anyone who wanted to fly transatlantic to Scotland must land only at Prestwick. As soon as that stipulation was lifted, the airlines vanished to the more profitable pastures of Glasgow airport. For a time, the only presence was the ghost of Elvis, who touched down briefly for a refuelling stop on his way to serve in the US Army in Germany; Prestwick is the only piece of UK territory that Presley ever visited.

Sometimes a city's airport is so keen to join the network that it is prepared to be represented as a rival destination. Thomas Mann once observed, 'A great truth is a truth whose opposite is a great truth.' Perhaps Ryanair had the great writer's ambivalence in mind when, in 1999, it began flying to his home town, Lübeck. The airline described the handsome medieval city as 'Hamburg'.

This was a classic example of Ryanair's strategy. Find a destination with a significant population base and a 'secondary' airport that is eager for trade. Describe the airport as somewhere else, which already has a major airport and a flourishing business from London. And advertise fares that are not only unbeatable, but also unobtainable. When Ryanair promised 'London to Hamburg £19 return', the destination airport was more than forty miles away from Hamburg, and in an entirely different city. And the fare the passenger would pay was not £19 return, because a range of taxes and airport fees were not included. The passenger would pay a minimum of £50. The offer was still an excellent deal for anyone who knew they were not going to end up where the Beatles grew up, but in the birthplace of Mann.

The Advertising Standards Authority was getting fed up. The body that tries to ensure ads are legal, decent, honest and truthful felt that most passengers' main concerns about a flight are where it goes, and how much it costs. The ASA had already demanded that fares should include all pre-payable taxes. As a direct result of Ryanair's ambitious claims about airports and the cities they purport to serve, the advertising watchdog told airlines that the name of the destination airport must be made clear, and that headline prices must match what the passenger pays. Ryanair has repeatedly had its knuckles rapped by the ASA; the authority's spokesman, Steve Ballinger, told me the Irish carrier was 'the worst offender in the budget airline sector'. The authority has no legal powers, and Ryanair is quick to cite its Irish base as a reason why British rules should not apply. But on one occasion, Ryanair's perceived transgressions ended up in court.

EXPENSIVE BA----DS was how Ryanair chose to announce its six new routes for the summer of 1999. The ad, which appeared in London's Evening Standard in February of that year, accused British Airways of greed. It claimed that travellers could save hundreds of pounds flying Ryanair rather than BA. As you would expect, the Irish airline chose the departure days to suit its purpose: travelling out from the UK on a Monday or Tuesday, returning on a Wednesday or Thursday. Those had to be the exact dates; a day earlier or later, and Ryanair's fares went up; if a Saturday intervenes, then BA's prices fell sharply.

Ryanair also chose not to mention that its flights departed from Stansted, while BA's left from Gatwick and Heathrow – much more convenient for millions of travellers. BA's fares also included free meals and drinks, while on Ryanair you must pay for anything more substantial than water. Small considerations, you may think, since flying to Turin, for example, will cost you £119 on Ryanair and £462 on BA.

The problem, as I pointed out at the time in the *Independent*, was that BA doesn't fly to Turin. Instead, Ryanair quoted BA's fare to Milan, eighty miles away. It happened that BA's low-cost offshoot, Go, flew to Milan, too, with a no-frills service from Stansted. So why didn't Ryanair use the more valid comparison? Perhaps because Go charged only £100 return. The fares chart got stranger still. 'Ancona £129', boasted Ryanair, compared with £562 on British Airways. But BA's only destinations on the Italian Adriatic coast were Venice and Trieste, hundreds of miles away. The closest cities to Ancona to which BA actually flew were Rome and Bologna, each 125 miles distant. Ryanair chose Bologna: the BA fare there was higher than to Rome. Again, no mention of Go's fare of £100 return from Stansted to Rome or Bologna.

You're probably getting the pattern by now: 'Biarritz £99', against £534 on BA. No, British Airways did not fly to Biarritz. Ryanair contrasted its fare with BA's to Bordeaux, rather than that to Bilbao – even though the Spanish airport was nearer to Biarritz and cheaper to reach than Bordeaux.

Oddest of all was Dinard. Ryanair said BA charged £315, compared with its own fare of £99. BA has not flown to the Brittany resort since the 1960s. The airline did, though, offer a connection in Jersey to Air

Aurigny services, which could get you to Dinard for a maximum fare of £176 return – 45 per cent less than Ryanair claimed.

British Airways was furious. A complaint to the Advertising Standards Authority upheld that the headline 'was likely to cause serious or widespread offence'. Ryanair undertook not to repeat it. But BA took the case to the High Court, issuing a writ that claimed trademark infringement and malicious falsehood.

Rarely does a column for a newspaper travel section become evidence in a High Court trial. Yet BA felt the story I wrote about the Ryanair case would aid their cause. I had to sign a letter confirming that I had written the story, and that I stood by it. A lot of good it did BA. The airline's case was that Ryanair had failed to compare like with like. Its counsel took the example of London to Frankfurt, on which Ryanair claimed its fare of £45 saved £329 compared with a BA ticket. The barrister argued that its aircraft flew to the main airport in Frankfurt, while Ryanair uses Hahn, some sixty miles away. BA also offered some restricted tickets at lower fares than those shown in the advertisements, to passengers prepared to stay away a minumum of a Saturday night.

The Royal Courts of Justice on the Strand in central London were fairly empty when Mr Justice Jacob handed down his judgement to a chilly courtroom. One reason was that no one from British Airways had turned up to listen to his verdict; BA's legal team were on their own. In the Ryanair corner was Michael O'Leary, Tim Jeans, assorted photographers and journalists who had been tipped off about the judgement, and a retinue of public relations advisers. Ryanair could hardly have written a better script for the judgement, which effectively concluded that its mud-slinging was justified. Ryanair, said the judge, had not given the unfair impression that its fares were much lower. 'I suspect the real reason BA do not like it is precisely because it is true,' he said. Mr Justice Jacob rejected British Airways' claim of unfairness, saying, 'The average consumer would know BA was cheaper if one stayed over a Saturday.' He also said that conventional airlines like BA 'exploit the fact that in the case of short, mostly business trips, people want to go out and home for the weekend', and noted that many travellers resent the so-called 'Saturday night rule'.

The judge paraphrased BA's complaint thus: 'that Ryanair exaggerate in suggesting BA is five times more expensive because BA is only three times more expensive'. He added it was 'immature' for two large companies to be fighting such a dispute in court.

BA's expensive legal team scurried out leaving the field clear for O'Leary to milk the judgement for all it was worth. For a trained accountant, he has a way with words. Like Laker and Branson before him, the chief executive has mastered the sound bite that positions him as a David fighting on the traveller's behalf against the Goliath of British Airways. Outside the court, he accused BA of adopting 'bully-boy' tactics in taking the matter to court: 'Today's a victory for the small guy, it's a victory for Ryanair and it's a victory for the consumer.' He said that his airline might take advertising headlined 'Expensive buggers'. In fact, Ryanair steered clear of profanity, instead taking out ads reading IT'S OFFICIAL – BA ARE EXPENSIVE.

British Airways' response was muted. 'We're disappointed and we'll be studying the judgement to consider whether we appeal,' said a spokeswoman. The airline let the case rest. At one stage in the action, BA had earlier offered to settle with Ryanair if each side paid its own costs, but that had been rejected. The legal bill that BA faced was estimated to be at least £250,000. The damage to its image was considerably greater. The newspaper poster proclaiming JUDGE BLASTS 'BA BASTARDS' in O'Leary's office is an example of the PR disaster.

Ryanair proceeded to rub British Airways' corporate nose in the dirt. As Michael O'Leary directed his airline's apparently relentless expansion, he targeted two routes that BA served from Gatwick: Trieste and Salzburg. Within months of Ryanair starting flying, BA had withdrawn from each. The remaining new routes served a by-now predictable collection of secondary airports: Pescara in Italy, Esbjerg in Denmark, and Västerås in Sweden, described as Stockholm (West). The man charged with the task of persuading the travelling public to buy these flights is Tim Jeans – a genial Geordie whose language is more measured than O'Leary's, but who has the same propensity to speak his mind.

This helps to explain why he is reviled by much of Britain's mainstream travel industry. Jeans has presided over Ryanair's gradual disengagement from travel agencies, in the process feeling the wrath of almost the entire travel establishment. For a long time after Ryanair started reciting the low-fares mantra, it adhered to the accepted means of selling air travel: through agents. The agent accessed the flights on a computer reservations system (CRS) and booked the ticket. The agent picked up 9 per cent commission, the industry standard for international flights. On a typical £59 return flight from Manchester to Dublin, this earned the agent barely a fiver – only slightly more than the hosts of the CRS collected. But if a family of four was travelling, it was business worth transacting.

Unilaterally, Ryanair decided it would drop commission to 7.5 per cent, in line with the rate paid on domestic flights. Predictably, the agents howled, saying they were being asked to sell tickets at a loss. Ian Smith, then boss of Britain's biggest chain of travel agents, Lunn Poly, announced a boycott: his 800-plus Holiday Shops would no longer sell Ryanair. The Advantage consortium of agents said it would launch its own airline to Ireland to compete with Ryanair. (This venture has yet to come to fruition.) Some agents said that they would still book Ryanair flights, but needed to apply a service fee for so doing. Ryanair took them to court to stop them.

Next, Ryanair did a strange thing: it followed a British Airways initiative. In 1999, BA decided to show the passenger service charge (PSC) that it pays to airports as a separate 'tax' on tickets. This was a nonsense, since the PSC is a commercial fee levied by the airport and an element of an airline's costs like fuel for the plane and the crew's uniforms. Almost every other carrier followed BA's move, seeing it as a wheeze to convince passengers that the PSC was an official tax rather than just one of the many costs involved in running an airline. It was a handy back-door method to push through fares increases, or to reduce the amount paid to agents – traditionally, taxes do not earn commission. The Association of British Travel Agents fought the move, and a High Court judge accepted the agents' demand to earn commission on the PSC element of a fare. Airlines were faced with backdated commission payments. All paid up – apart from Ryanair. The sales and marketing director, Tim Jeans, became even more of a hate figure in the letters columns of the travel trade journals.

By 2001, at which point Ryanair was selling the vast majority of seats online, Jeans felt able to send out a letter to every agent in the country explaining that his airline would no longer sell through the trade from 1 November, summoning up all his not over-evident powers of diplomacy to describe it as the end of 'a fairly painful retrenchment of Ryanair amongst its travel agency partners'. On the day he saw the letter, Stephen Bath, president of ABTA, told me agents would not grieve unduly, and took the opportunity to rubbish the airline's prevailing offer of £9.99 flights to anywhere in Europe.

'All this talk of £10 flights is tosh as far as I can see. I got my secretary to check some flights on my favourite route to Dublin yesterday, and for me to go there and back tomorrow is £156, and the next day it's £189. I asked her to spend half an hour looking for a £10 ticket, and guess what? She couldn't find one. A lot of it is a figment of Mr O'Leary's imagination.'

I talked to Tim Jeans a few days later and put it to him that he was the least popular person in the travel industry at the moment. 'Judging from the amount of faxes coming in the office with four-letter words attached to them, I think you're probably right.' Yet such is his conviction about Ryanair's strategy that he cheerfully accepts industry speaking engagements in order to tell others where they are going wrong.

Jeans is a graduate of the London School of Economics. From there he took a traditional path into travel, working as marketing manager at P&O Ferries, the 'frilliest' of the Dover–Calais ferry operators, and then spending five years at Manchester airport in charge of business development: 'I learned how hopeless some airlines could be; on one route, the break-even load factor was 114 per cent'. He joined O'Leary, four years his junior, in 1995. Turning poacher, he reduced the number of Ryanair flights to Manchester airport after a row over charges. He still lives in the city, and commutes to both Dublin and Stansted to sell Ryanair's flights for whatever he thinks he can get.

One of the most prominent contemporary Irishmen is all in favour of Ryanair's policy of offloading 'distressed inventory' for a few pounds. 'If I can get a £7 flight to somewhere within two hundred miles of Venice, you know, destination unknown, magical mystical tour, well, I'll fucking take it,' said Sir Bob Geldof. 'Seven quid, I don't care where I fucking go!' The day before I flew to Dublin to see O'Leary, I had lunch with the Irish ambassador to London, Dáithí O'Ceallaigh, at which I discussed the same topic. He replied that he was not in favour of very low fares, because some passengers might think that the airline compromised on safety. Michael O'Leary was outraged when I repeated His Excellency's comments. 'An ambassador would say that, wouldn't he, given that he's hardly ever bought a fare with us anyway. You get this kind of nonsense from the people who don't have to pay for their own air fares.'

The most famous Ryanair passengers who did pay their way in 2001 were Tony Blair and his family. This episode was a double triumph for O'Leary's airline, since it got one over on both British Airways and easyJet. In June, a Downing Street spokesman had let it be known that the Prime Minister and his family would be travelling to their holiday chateau in south-west France on a no-frills airline. The *Daily Mirror* picked up the story, saying that the Blairs would be flying on easyJet for their French holiday in August. There was no official rebuttal, so easyJet plastered the roadsides of Britain with posters saying, 'Tony Blair got a bargain this summer – so can you.' Unfortunately for Stelios, there was never any intention at 10 Downing Street that the family would fly to easyJet's only French destination, Nice; it would be like flying to

Liverpool for a holiday in Yorkshire. The chateau was much closer to Toulouse, served by British Airways, and Carcassonne, where Ryanair flew. Ryanair got the business because, says O'Leary, 'The savings the Blair family made flying with us compared with flying British Airways to Toulouse were in excess of £2,000. Even for the most well-off people these are huge savings which simply can't be ignored.' BA was incensed that the first family chose to fly someone else's flag.

Where to next, Michael? We are standing outside his office, surveying his modest management kingdom, and looking at a map of Europe. 'You're now at the heart of our new route development strategy,' he says, not entirely in jest. Though the shape of the continent is familiar, the detail is not. It consists not of towns and cities, nor of physical features.

'Those dots are all airports,' says O'Leary. 'When you look at an ordinary map you think there's no more airports, in actual fact the place is absolutely awash with airports.'

They are the components with which O'Leary intends to realise his ambition. 'In five years' time we'll be double the size we are now, of the order of 20 million passengers. We'll go to half-a-dozen new destinations each year, two new bases every five years, unless we do something stupid like have a crash or join an alliance. There's a challenge every day in the airline industry not to do something stupid. Airlines are characterised by people who do something stupid.'

As O'Leary develops his theme, there are strong echoes of Herb Kelleher's mantra at Southwest: 'Too many airlines that have gotten it right for a certain amount of time have then suddenly started thinking they can walk on water, so they start buying hotels, or expanding into other businesses, or if you look at British Airways trying to serve every market you can from Britain.'

For the past week, the newspapers have been full of stories about the likely increase in fares and decrease in air travel. Within days, Virgin Atlantic and Continental had cut thousands of jobs and deleted numerous routes from the schedules. Intriguingly, the chairman of Ryanair, David Bonderman, is a tough-talking Texan who is also a director of Continental, which has suffered at the hands of O'Leary's role model, Southwest. British Airways and its fellow giants were examining how many thousands of workers would have to go, and how much more they would need to pay for increased security and insurance premiums. Reduced supply and increased costs inevitably mean higher fares, and entering the spiral of decline as passengers choose not to travel by air. O'Leary's mind is heading in a diametrically opposite direction from conventional wisdom.

'Somebody in the current market has to talk about expansion. A lot of the problems you see in the airline industry – let's take Aer Lingus as a classic example – they're not because of the awful incidents in the US. These had been coming for many months and possibly years. Some of Europe's flag-carrier airlines are still grossly overstaffed. They run at losses, they sell below cost, and they're incredibly inefficient. A massive restructuring of those airlines is twenty years overdue.' Since O'Leary heads the most profitable major airline in the world, his argument carries considerable weight. Within weeks, the airline that he regards as 'probably the greatest basket case in Europe' had gone bust. Sabena had lost money for almost all its history, even before Ryanair and Virgin Express parked their 737s on the Belgian lawn.

Surely, though, with less competition and higher costs fares must rise? 'That's always been the refrain of carriers around the world. We believe there'll be more opportunities over the next couple of years to charge people lower fares. Some costs will go up – clearly insurance is going to rise – but there are other costs that are going to fall. Clearly, aircraft values will fall significantly. Airport costs will certainly fall, because there's going to be a steep decline in traffic over the next year or two.'

O'Leary was one of the first to advance the now widely accepted notion that there will be a quick consolidation into three or four groupings of full-service airlines, with British Airways, Air France and Lufthansa in the forefront. How many no-frills airlines will there be room for?

'Over time there's probably going to be one or possibly two. If you go forward five years, all of the others will have disappeared, taken over, absorbed into somebody else.' The US market, he points out, is consolidating to three or four major traditional airlines, plus Southwest. No prizes for guessing who O'Leary thinks the winner will be in Europe. 'My money's on Ryanair. If there's two or three low-fares airlines, they rub up against each other.'

The rub has already started, even though the no-frills airlines still have minimal overlap with their route networks. O'Leary is disparaging about his rivals. 'I tend not to spend a lot of time talking to my counterpart chief executives of other airlines, mainly because they tend to congregate at conferences in Acapulco and Hong Kong.' Quoting Groucho Marx, he adds, 'I wouldn't want to be a member of any club like that which would have me as a member.'

Like a prizefighter, Michael O'Leary and his team seem intent on inflaming the coming conflict by needling the opposition at every turn. For example, after Ray Webster became chief executive of easyJet, the Irish airline decided to call its e-mail service Webster. When I tell Tim

Jeans that Webster (the man in charge of easyJet, not the e-mail service) had claimed he would own 300 aircraft within ten years, 'In that case we'll have 301, if that's what Ray says,' says Jeans. He knows where he will find them, too: 'There are clearly huge opportunities to pick up second-hand aircraft at very distressed rates, and I think that trend of being able to get aircraft at the bottom of the cycle will only benefit the cash-rich low-fare guys.' In the event, Ryanair placed the biggest order in no-frills history in 2002: 100 brand-new Boeing 737s.

What then, when those aircraft are put on routes that compete directly with the other big rival? 'There will be the most unholy scrap. There will be blood of unmerciful proportions spilt everywhere because quite clearly there will be a battle for supremacy on a particular route.'

The competition between the two biggest players continues when trying to hire staff: easyJet staged a pilot recruitment open day at Dublin airport. It is a safe bet that the aim was not to tempt back into business resting captains and first officers who had gone to grass in the Irish Republic. It was hoping to poach flight crew, partly from Aer Lingus but mostly from Ryanair.

The largest vat of vitriol is currently located at Enterprise House at Stansted airport, which Go shares with Ryanair. Considering senior executives from each airline are likely to bump into each other on the stairs or in the Gents, I am honestly surprised there have not been any fist fights. So far.

'They glorify making the experience as uncomfortable as possible,' says Go's Barbara Cassani, perhaps safe in the knowledge that she will not encounter Michael O'Leary or Tim Jeans in the Ladies. 'It's like a flying pub. Most of the time it's all right, though you invariably feel a bit dishevelled when you get off.' She says she disagrees profoundly with the way that Ryanair tries to cut costs. 'If a customer has a problem, they enjoy telling you to piss off. They believe that if customers aren't hurting, their costs aren't low enough.' Cassani develops her theme. 'Ryanair's profitable, but they don't have a good relationship with their people and they don't have a good relationship with their customers. They have good operational integrity. I'm sorry – two out of four ain't good enough for me.'

'Frankly we wouldn't lose five seconds of sleep over Go,' riposte O'Leary. 'They entered the Irish market offering to compete with Ryanair. What they seem to forget is that Ryanair loves competition. We have a very simple mission in all this: whatever fare Go charge, on whatever route, whatever day, we will undercut it by 50 per cent. Do we do it because of Go, or are we on some kind of mission to put Go out of business? No, we couldn't care less. The competition, and the low fares on the Dublin–Edinburgh and Glasgow routes will I think double, treble or quadruple the traffic this winter. We will be the largest carrier in all of that, we will out-carry both Go and Aer Lingus, and what happens to Go and Aer Lingus? Frankly, we don't care. They will never match or undercut our fares because we'll always lower our fares. It is a sine qua non of Ryanair's operation that nobody, but nobody, will match our airfares. And if they do, we'll simply lower ours straight-away.' In the event, Go retired from the Dublin routes after six months of substantial losses.

Sir Richard Branson, whose Brussels-based Virgin Express is in competition with Ryanair at Charleroi, is more charitable than Go's Cassani. Ryanair, he says, is 'willing to take on airports and governments to get the right deals. The quality of the product is not quite as good as easyJet, certainly not as good as Virgin Blue [Branson's Australian no-frills airline] but good enough for 95 per cent of people.' And he pays a qualified tribute to O'Leary. 'He's as tough as nails, a businessman through and through, no compromise. Arrogant but can get away with it because he's incredibly successful. He's not loved by his staff, but generally loved by the passengers for delivering fantastically low-cost travel.'

When I ask O'Leary what he is most proud of having achieved at Ryanair, he becomes positively evangelical. 'Saving European air travellers hundreds of millions of pounds every year over the airfares they would have paid to British Airways, and bringing air travel within the pocket or the budget of most ordinary people in Europe. Low-fare carriers like Ryanair, and to a lesser extent easyJet, have proven that you can carry people and make money at fares that are half those of the high-fare airlines.'

He says that the aviation industry has to ask itself. 'What the hell have we been doing for the last fifty years? We've been gouging the consumer, and putting the cost of air travel beyond the means of 80 or 90 per cent of the travelling public.' Those days are over, says O'Leary. His assertion is echoed by Maria Holbert of Hahn airport, the latest of the Irish airline's hubs: 'I am convinced that all the people travelling today would not be flying at all if it was not for Ryanair.'

What about the fact that British Airways is now aggressively targeting the European market? 'You're always going to be delayed. You'll get crap food, and a free drink worth £2 and you're going to pay £400 for it. The era of these rip-off airfares and horrible wine that you can't even drink are over.' (O'Leary is no match for the likes of Herb Kelleher of Southwest, and neither smokes nor drinks heavily.)

FLYING ADVERTISEMENTS

Even by the juvenile standards of no-frills airline design, Ryanair's logo is pretty mediocre. Michael O'Leary doesn't care what I think: 'We're not going to change the logo, we have no intention of changing the brand or redesigning the image or the rest of that old nonsense. In my ten years at this company, Aer Lingus has changed its branding three times, British Airways has changed it three times, we've changed it not once, and the virtue of what we've done has been proven. People don't fly with Ryanair because of our image or our brand, they fly because we guarantee them the lowest fares, when you get on the aircraft it's clean, it's bright, it's safe and reliable.'

The best-looking Boeings in the fleet are those where the old Southwest trick has been successfully replicated: using aircraft as flying advertisements. Kilkenny beer, Jaguar cars and the *Sun* newspaper have been plastered all over the 737-200s, in a sponsorship deal that is roughly equivalent to having one more passenger aboard every flight. Because the passengers only briefly look at the aircraft when boarding, there have been few objections – it's everyone else who has to look at the plane. But since airlines' logos are themselves nothing but advertising, there seems no good reason why Ryanair should not use its aircraft as poster sites. And it's better than having to look at that banal logo.

He has big plans for Ryanair. 'We're at ten years. Give us another twenty years and we will cover Europe. We intend to double from seven to fourteen million passengers in three years. We've got the same rate of growth as Southwest, 25 per cent per annum, so we should have thirty million passengers in ten years. We'll open half a dozen new destinations each year, two new bases every five years.'

Our interview is drawing to a close. Michael O'Leary has an airline to run, and not enough hours in each day to do so. But he loves it.

'This is not work to me. We're running the biggest, fastest-growing low-fares airline in Europe, revolutionising air travel. You can look at us as a small Irish company stuffing it to British Airways and Lufthansa and Air France. This is sheer fun at this stage. I'm only forty years of age, so I'll have at least another ten years here, antagonising and annoying other high-fares airlines around Europe, and probably everybody else as well.'

7. EASY: YOU DON'T NEED A TICKET

'It was 7 a.m., it was a wet, miserable, lousy day in Luton, and equally cold and miserable in Glasgow. I discovered very quickly that this was not going to be glamorous. The images of Branson and his rock stars, and everything else that I had associated with the launch of Virgin was just not going to be the case in our company'

STELIOS HAJI-IOANNOU, FOUNDER OF EASYJET

'The airline industry never has, and probably never will, produce a genius. Never has an airline devised a unique strategy to succeed. Most of what is needed is money'

FRANCO MANCASSOLA, FOUNDER OF DEBONAIR

EASYJET FLIGHT 11: LUTON–GLASGOW, 10 NOVEMBER 1995
When you walk into the headquarters of Britain's most successful low-cost airline, the first thing you notice is a tent – a small, two-person job, strung from the roof. The canvas accessory now resident in the foyer of easyLand in Luton was a powerful weapon in the war that a young Greek Cypriot has conducted on Europe's strongest airlines since a 'wet, miserable, lousy day in Luton' in 1995. Take one Greek shipping millionaire, two Boeing 737s normally used for British Airways flights and several gallons of orange paint, and you have a revolution in the skies. But industry watchers like myself were slow to realise the scale of the upheaval signified by the first flight of easyJet. When the aircraft had landed in the gloom and the captain had welcomed passengers to Glasgow, says Stelios Haji-Ioannou, 'I took the microphone and made a short speech – the first to my customers. I don't remember exactly, but I probably said, "This is a very important day for me, thank you for being on board, bye, have a nice day." And I got a round of applause and I thought, "Hey, they appreciate it! It doesn't matter that I've cut back on frills, on legroom, and the business class – they love it." ' Also on the flight was easyJet's sales and marketing director, Tony Anderson: 'I sat quietly at the back of the plane relieved to still be on board after a number of my colleagues had been offloaded at the last minute to make way for a film crew from BBC's *Money Programme*.' Stelios had learned early on that the best publicity was free publicity.

EZY flight 11 provided a great story because it was the first departure of an airline that had taken just five months from conception to first steps, far quicker than the normal gestation for an airline. As with Branson's Virgin Atlantic, the speedy birth did not, as existing carriers may fondly have assumed, lead to a premature demise. On the contrary:

easyJet has grown to become the biggest no-frills airline based in Britain, empowering travellers from its bases in the UK, France, Holland and Switzerland. The airline is starting to eclipse rivals who once rated its survival in days or weeks.

In June 1996, just after Nice was added to the easyJet route network, I was waiting in the departure lounge at the Cote d'Azur airport for the flight to Luton. A man, not in uniform, was chatting to the staff at the desk. He was lively and large rather than larger than life, with a grin as broad as the shoulders that were supporting an open shirt and a navy-blue blazer. His hair was dark and close cropped, his skin olive, his build tall and broad. You could imagine him lazing away his life on a yacht in the south of France or the Aegean – options that were, indeed, open to him. But he had chosen to make life difficult for himself. 'Stelios had none of the airs and graces you would perhaps assume from someone born with a silver spoon (more like a platinum ladel) in their mouth,' says Anderson. 'How many multimillionaires would give up the opportunity for a playboy lifestyle to work in a tin shack in Luton often into the early hours?'

Whatever your ambitions in life, and particularly if you want to start an airline, it helps to have a billionnaire Greek shipping magnate for a father. Since his birth in Cyprus on St Valentine's Day 1967, Stelios Haji-Ioannou believes he was groomed to take over his father's shipping line. 'I saw myself as a shipowner, and that was what I was trained to do,' says Stelios, as he likes to be called, in the manner of Madonna.

He studied at the London School of Economics, from which he graduated in 1987, and went on to take a Masters' degree at the City of London Business School. Throughout that time he was attending the London office that belonged to his father, Lucas Haji-Ioannou. By the age of 21 – when most students are still undergraduates – Stelios began working for the family firm. After four years, he decided to set up his own operation.

'At the age of twenty-five, somehow I convinced my father to trust me with a very large sum of money to go and start another shipping company,' he says.

A 'very large sum of money' meant $35m, at the time over £20m: 'enough to buy five or six tankers'. The announcement that Stelios was to resign from his father's company and start his own shipping venture made the front page of the Greek maritime journal: 'It's probably the first time I made the front page of a newspaper.' Stelmar, as the company is known (no prizes for guessing the derivation of the name), is listed on the New York stock exchange and is comfortably profitable. But within three years, Stelios realised that he was not the person to run it. He entrusted the firm to Peter Goodfellow, 'a safe pair of hands', says Stelios, and 'a much better executive than I am or ever want to be. He is more interested in the details, in the nuts and bolts, in running ships.' In April 2002, Stelios stood down as chairman at the Stelmar AGM. 'The cycle has been completed from idea, to profitable big company of six tankers, to listing on the NY stock exchange, to retiring from the board in ten years.'

'No Greek ship owner in my father's generation would have admitted that. They've always been very hands-on. So I made my mental shift, saying I'm not going to be running businesses in my life, I'm going to be starting businesses. I'm an entrepreneur.'

'The great thing about Stelios is that despite being a rich man's child, he's one of the few rich men's children who's done it with style and panache,' says another entrepreneur, Sir Richard Branson, who is something of a mentor for the easyJet founder. There are plenty of parallels between the chairmen of easyJet and Virgin – indeed, Sir Richard Branson says, 'I suppose I see a younger version of myself in him.' Stelios says, 'I've learnt in life that it's very difficult to have a single role model. Every person's individual anyway. So it's difficult to say, "I'm going to be like my father, or Richard Branson," or whatever.'

At the point where the Greek Cypriot began to take his hands off the Stelmar helm, he had not met Branson. But Stelios spent plenty of time shuttling between his two offices in Athens and London. Sometimes he flew on Virgin Atlantic; the airline had started up a franchise operation with a Greek company called South East European Airlines between London and Athens, which was finally abandoned in 2001. SEEA wanted to expand, and the airline invited Stelios to invest. 'I was thinking of just putting a million dollars into it, something very small. If nothing else, I was thinking I'll be flying from Athens to London for free, that was my motivation.' After studying the opportunities and the risks, and meeting Branson, Stelios decided against the investment. But by then, he says, he had contracted the virus that demands, 'I have to have an airline.'

In August 1994 he was invited to the Boeing headquarters in Seattle, thanks to a story in a Greek newspaper in June of that year. 'This article was saying, "Stelios, ship owner, son of Lucas, is thinking of starting an airline." The next morning there was a phone call from the Boeing group in Athens, saying, "Can I come and visit you and tell you what Boeing is all about?" That taught me that expressing your thoughts, going public about your intentions, is never a bad thing.' (Boeing's rival, Airbus, 'did not even pick up the phone and ask me to lunch until 1997,' says the man who has become a regular visitor to the 737 factory outside Seattle. Yet in 2002, he confirmed that he was considering an order for 75 Airbus jets in a deal worth £2.5 billion.) It was during the first visit, he says, that 'someone mentioned, "You have to try Southwest Airlines. You have to see how it works." And ever since then, in the year and a half that followed, I kept hearing rumours of how low-cost works in the States but it didn't work in Europe. But why would the Europeans be any different?'

Whether you rent them or buy them, Boeing 737s are more expensive than the oil tankers that Stelios's company was operating. He waited for the right moment to raise the subject of starting an airline with his father. It happened over dinner, in the family summer house south of Athens, in the summer of 1995.

Stelios recollects his opening gambit: 'If I set up a marketing organisation, and I don't buy the aircraft yet, I think I can make it take off with five million pounds. That's all I'm asking for at the moment. If it doesn't work, I'll pull the plug. We don't have to start an airline on the operational side. I have found a way of leasing planes, with pilots and everything else. I'll build a brand.' He had already been in negotiations with GB Airways about leasing aircraft. GB Airways is a franchisee of British Airways. That last point reassured Lucas on safety standards, and the magnate took out his cheque book. Stelios almost throws away the rest of the story: 'The airline started after my father gave me the go-ahead and the five million quid. I decided to call it easyJet.' Lucas made one stipulation about the venture: it must not be based in Athens. 'Probably the best piece of advice I ever took from my father,' says Stelios. 'It was a very valid point – a small and seasonal market at the end of Europe, it would have been a disaster.' In 1998, his airline started flying to the Greek capital, but it is an open secret that the service is far from easyJet's most profitable. Plans for a separate airline, EasyJet Greece, aimed at transforming the overpriced and underserved Greek domestic market, have never materialised.

The four obvious locations for starting a new airline were France, Germany, Italy and Britain, because these have the biggest populations in Europe. Stelios says the decision was based on language. 'I don't speak French so Paris was out of the question. Or German, or Italian. It would have to be the largest possible market in an English-speaking country, so London was the base.'

When people talk about 'London airport', they almost invariably mean Heathrow. It handles more passengers – 65m per year at the last count

– than all the rest of the capital's airports combined. And it is effectively full. Most additional scheduled traffic chooses Gatwick, which has room for perhaps 10 million more on top of the existing 30 million, but not at the times when most business travellers want to fly, at the morning and evening peaks. 'It was a process of elimination,' says Stelios. 'Basically the only two options were Stansted and Luton. I went to both and took the cheapest.'

If, in 1995, anyone had suggested that Luton airport would have scheduled flights to two dozen destinations, with six a day to Edinburgh and seven to Glasgow, they would have been politely asked to leave the departure lounge. The Bedfordshire airport was still suffering from the damage to its image wrought by television advertisements in which a fragrant beauty, standing on the balcony of her hotel, was asked by her admirer, 'Were you wafted here from Paradise?' to which her reply came in a broad Essex accent, 'Nah, mate, Luton airport.' Yet, thanks to easyJet, Luton has become one of the budget traveller's windows on the world.

Luton, like Gatwick, had helped to pioneer charter flights, which is why Britannia and Monarch still have their bases there. But Gatwick soon gained the upper hand, not least because the Sussex airport was easier to reach by most people in the capital. Getting to Luton airport from central London involved a half-hour train ride to the town's station followed by a fifteen-minute bus or cab ride. The main rail line from London passed close to the airport, but a much-needed airport station took another four years to open after easyJet started flying. Yet Luton had an overriding advantage for a fledgling airline: it was the cheapest of the airports that serve the biggest aviation market in Europe. 'It was purely cost driven,' says Stelios.

At the time, the man in charge of Luton was Richard Gooding. 'He was the first guy that realised there was some potential here,' says Stelios. 'He gave me the time of day, as a "paper airline", and sat down and drafted a contract that lasted for five years.' Looking back, Stelios says that the original contract read 'like science fiction'. It contained a clause that, if passenger numbers in a year exceeded two million, use of the airport would effectively be free. Gooding was not in fantasy land – he realised that a throughput of passengers on that scale would transform the airport.

In June 1995 Stelios visited the ugly modern offices of the Civil Aviation Authority on Kingsway in central London. The CAA regulates all British airlines' safety and financial standards. On 7 July he applied for an Air Travel Organiser's Licence (ATOL) that the CAA required him to have in order to protect passengers' payments. In the middle of

August, he signed the agreement to hire two GB Airways Boeing 737s, along with the services of the pilots and cabin crew – an arrangement known as a 'wet lease' (in contrast, a dry lease means the planes without the people).

GB Airways, whose main business is carrying passengers between London and the Mediterranean for British Airways, was surprised to be asked to supply planes and crew for an airline that, at the time, was still on the drawing board. But if GB Airways had declined the contract, someone else would have stepped in. In the words of the current managing director, John Patterson, 'If you're small you've got to take your chances. And that was an opportunity, there was obviously a return to be made, I understand it was quite profitable, it ensured that jobs were retained, and most people look back on it as a good thing.' Stelios was less than impressed with one unnamed executive at the airline when he outlined his plans. He had said, 'Look, this is my business plan. I'm going to reduce fares. And that's how we will make money.' The executive smiled conspiratorially, says Stelios, and said, 'Surely it must be a tax fiddle?'

The GB Airways deal was, says Stelios, 'a sea change for me' – not because he was dealing with aircraft rather than sea-going vessels, but because every Greek shipowner is normally to be found on his yacht in summer. 'No self-respecting Greek does any business in the middle of August, and here I was in the middle of London sweating in an office trying to sign a lease for two 737s.'

The office in question bears no relation to the garish orange shed in a corner of Luton airport where easyJet now resides. It was at his shipping company's premises at 35 Curzon Street in Mayfair, where property prices are of Monopoly proportions, that war was declared on Europe's traditional airlines.

On the evening that the deal was sealed, Stelios organised a celebration. He was conscious of the huge risk to which he, and his father's cash, were now committed. 'I said to my friends, "You know I'm starting an airline." And people laughed. It's not the sort of thing you drop into a dinner conversation seriously.' The guests reacted with sympathy, not excitement, as though Stelios had told them he had just been mugged.

Up to this point, Stelios's experience of aviation had been purely as a passenger. He was now chief of a nameless airline. 'Once I became serious about it, I moved out of 35 Curzon Street and went up to Luton.' The first, modest transformation at Luton was in a small prefabricated building some distance from the terminal, formerly the executive aviation terminal. It became the headquarters of Britain's newest airline. His first colleague was Nick Manoudakis, another son of a rich Greek magnate, who was appointed finance director. Stelios set up shop with one PC ('from Dixon's'), two desks and three phones. Plus 'a big round waste paper bin, with a note from me saying, "Scan documents, then throw them in the bin. This is a paperless office." '

One of the early recruits recalls that this theory did not work perfectly. 'In the airline's first few months the paperless office was implemented in its purest form. All employees had access to every document held within the airline. This inevitably gave rise to some problems, particularly when it was fairly easy to find out how much everyone was paid. If Stelios found paper on your desk it would be swept into the bin. Nick Manoudakis kept a hidden stash of documents in the ladies' toilets – the only place in the whole airline where they were safe from Stelios's eyes. The fact that his wife had become easyJet's administration manager meant that documents could safely be retrieved when required without questions being asked of Nick's use of the ladies' convenience.'

Besides being paperless, it was also a nameless office, because easyJet had yet to be christened. 'In the early days we went to an expensive brand consultancy,' says Stelios. 'They put together a contract for consultancy for £100,000 payable in three or four instalments.'

Phase One of the contract required the consultants to deliver a 'Mood Board' for £20,000. One month and £20,000 later, they came into the office with some magazine clippings stuck on to pieces of cardboard, saying, 'This is what the airline will look like.' Stelios said, 'These are just magazine clippings!' The consultants said, 'That's where you start from, that's how you start a branding exercise.' Stelios said, 'I don't think we can keep the cost down like this, thank you very much, that's the end of the contract.'

It is a matter of opinion whether Stelios was at this point £20,000 down or, more optimistically, £80,000 up. But with a month lost, the search for a name was increasingly urgent. As with Southwest and Virgin, it was a paper napkin that came to the rescue.

'I was jotting down names in Harry's Bar in Mayfair, and the word "easy" kept coming back again and again. So I decided that that was going to be the name.' The easy brand, like Virgin, has now been applied to everything from information technology to personal finance. 'He did model his company on Virgin,' says Sir Richard Branson. 'There aren't a lot of companies in the world that stretch their brand, he's attempting that, and he's got a very good brand name to do that with.'

The tricky part was, as Branson found with Virgin Records, to sell a new concept to a healthily cynical public. He employed headhunters to find a young, imaginative marketing guru, Tony Anderson, at the time working for the Thomas Cook conglomerate in European project development.

'I was approached by the agency Norman Broadbent,' recalls Anderson. 'They told me that someone was looking to create a European version of Southwest. I was sceptical, but interested. I had worked in the States for BA and Thomas Cook, so I believed it could work here. And it was the opportunity to get involved in something very exciting.' At the interview Stelios was charismatic, 'but not quite as confident and self-assured as he is today'. Anderson took the job as vice-president of sales and marketing – 'We tried the American titles for six months and it didn't work' – and started to formulate the marketing campaign. How do you start selling something which no one has the least idea about?

'I was trying to answer the question "What's the catch?" One of the biggest decisions we took before launching the airline was to go one hundred per cent direct and sell all our flights direct to our customers.' The new airline was the first in the world completely to insist that every passenger had to book direct by phone, and pay with a credit card. 'A number of trends were in our favour,' says Anderson. 'The UK had the world's highest penetration of credit cards outside North America, and there was an established culture of buying over the telephone with companies such as First Direct and Direct Line having blazed a trail for us to follow.'

Britain's travel agents found themselves in the uncomfortable position of being central to easyJet's marketing campaign. 'It gave us a fantastic marketing opportunity to position ourselves as the airline that cut out the middleman, a concept that our customers could readily understand. While travel agents weren't reviled by the great British public they weren't exactly loved. I dreamed up an ad with a cartoon of Stelios putting a stake through a cartoon travel agent's heart under the headline, "at easyJet we know how to deal with bloodsuckers" but I bottled out, not least because I'd spent the three years of my life prior to joining easyJet with Thomas Cook.' The airline still boasts that it is the only airline in the world that has never paid a penny in commission to a travel agent.

The brand was designed in a tiny design consultancy in Luton called White Knight ('I'd found them in the Yellow Pages,' says Anderson). The company was based on a grim industrial estate a few miles from the airport. 'It was in one of the sessions at White Knight that the telephone number on the side of the aeroplane and our original version of the easyJet cartoon plane was born.'

It was also where easyJet became orange, with Stelios sitting behind the operator of the Apple Mac directing operations. The results, according to one competitor, were 'sub-GCSE graphics'. But Stelios believes the unsophisticated design, based on the shade of orange known as Pantone 021C, works. 'It just happened. And ever since then I've been fighting creative people who want to change it.' The response is always the same: 'No, don't touch it. It has to be orange. Don't try and inject creativity into it, consistency's what builds us.'

Having procured the planes, the premises and the paint, the next problem was choosing some routes. This was the easy bit. The no-frills business model had been a long-term success only on domestic routes. The biggest markets from London for which air was a sensible alternative to road or rail were both in southern Scotland – so Glasgow and Edinburgh became the first easyJet destinations. 'I was trying to minimise risk,' says Stelios. 'All that had been proven to me up to now was that this thing works in a domestic environment.' With the routes and the start date planned, the press was let in on the secret. The first I knew about the new airline was when a scruffy fax turned up at the *Independent* office announcing the first flight of a carrier that was promising something different. New airlines that promise something different come and go at an alarming rate (one had gone out of business a few weeks earlier), and many of them never get off the ground at all. This one had a funny name, and a strange premise. It issued no tickets at all. Nor did it assign seats, or get involved with complications like frequent-flyer schemes. Enough journalists were interested in the project to provide a decent turnout at the media launch, which was held at Planet Hollywood in Leicester Square, London. Anderson recalls that, 'A litany of travel correspondents turned up to predict our demise.' Stelios says he had to handle a huge amount of scepticism: 'Is it safe? What sort of planes do you fly? Are they the little propeller planes with rubber bands? Where is Luton?'

Luton was where work was continuing, to get the planes in the air by the appointed date – accompanied by the kind of management upheavals that might have finished off other start-up companies. The chief executive, Peter Leishman, left abruptly. 'There was a clash of roles,' says Tony Anderson. 'Stelios wasn't expecting to be so hands-on, but he caught the bug and became de facto chief executive. And Peter was commuting back and forth from his home in Switzerland. I don't think it was ever going to work.' Leishman returned to Switzerland, where he became involved in Swiss World Airlines, which tried without success to operate a low-cost service to New York. Tragically, the chief operating officer, Dave McCulloch, fell seriously ill and died a few days later. Next easyJet was upstaged as the first no-frills airline between London and Scotland by Ryanair – at least according to Michael O'Leary, boss of the Irish airline: 'easyJet weren't the first low-cost airline between London and Glasgow. We started flying from Stansted to Prestwick in October 1995.'

Stelios disagrees about the nature of the Irish airline's flights. 'In those days Ryanair was just transforming itself into a low-cost carrier. In my mind, it was still essentially an ethnic carrier. They hadn't actually taken the low-cost model to the degree they have now. So it was still a conventional airline with tickets sold through travel agents, and I think you could still get free orange juice on board. They hadn't quite taken it to its logical conclusion, just bought some cheap aircraft from Britannia and that sort of thing. In my mind there was Southwest out there, no one was really doing it in Europe, and I had one chance of doing it.'

Ryanair's service to Prestwick, close to the port of Ayr, began in October. The only less-auspicious time to launch a new airline flying between an unfamiliar airport north of London and Scotland is the middle of November, which is when easyJet took off. 'That's when the aircraft was available,' says Stelios. 'It wasn't a matter of choice, and we probably paid for it in terms of losses in the first month, but that's neither here nor there. The point was to get it off the ground, and aircraft are cheaper in the winter than they are in the summer.' Once easyJet was off the ground, an ad attacking the opposition landed it in legal trouble. AYR MILES read the headline, explaining that easyJet flies from Glasgow International, not Prestwick, saving the 33-mile journey from Ayr. Ryanair did not object, says Tony Anderson: 'The response came from Air Miles [a subsidiary of British Airways] in the form of a lawyer's letter telling us that our use of the expression "Ayr Miles" was a phonetic infringement of their copyright.'

'Europe is not ready for the peanut airline,' was one rival's verdict after the easyJet launch, a nod at the Southwest image of offering fares for peanuts and only peanuts on board. Anderson says that 'easyJet's arrival was treated with scorn and derision by British Airways.' The load factors suggested the obituaries were premature: from the first day, easyJet was filling four out of five seats. Five days later, the Luton–Edinburgh run began with similar success. Predictably, the two much bigger rivals soon hit back with low fares. British Airways and British Midland (now BMI) suddenly found they were able to offer return flights

EASYJET'S FREQUENT-FLYER SCHEME

According to a survey carried out by the flight information company, OAG Worldwide, 98 per cent of business travellers collect frequent-flyer points assiduously. 'I've always considered Air Miles to be my biggest enemy,' says Stelios. He would warn his staff, 'It's not BA you are fighting, it's Air Miles.'

When he launched his third route, between Aberdeen and Luton, Stelios believed, 'These corporate executives would not consider flying with us because they were being bribed by BA.' So with a little inspiration from Southwest Airlines in the 70s, he invented his own frequent-flyer scheme. Anyone paying the highest fare, of £69, was entitled to collect a bottle of Scotch upon check-in at Aberdeen. Stelios insisted that, if the passenger's flight had been paid for by his company, the bottle had to be donated to the office Christmas party. There was, though, a catch. 'Our low-cost consciousness got the better of us,' says Tony Anderson. 'It was actually a half-bottle of whisky, which didn't go down too well with some of the passengers queuing up at the sales desk to collect their bribe.'

between London and Scotland for £58 – which just happened to be easyJet's return fare – with the added attractions of departures from Heathrow and on-board frills. Passengers who had been previously paying much higher fares were delighted, but easyJet's sales were dented. 'We were really hurting,' says Anderson. The strain took its toll on the airline boss, he says: 'Stelios was volatile and short-tempered in the first six months when things were looking difficult.'

'I realised very early on that the key to this is filling the plane – occupancy, driving demand and everything else will follow,' says Stelios. 'So I went to Nick [Manoudakis, easyJet's finance director] one day and I said, "What's our cash like?" And he said, "Well, about three and a half million, we've got through our first million." So I said, "Set aside another million for marketing. I'm going to spend a million pounds in the next three months." '

'Stelios opened his cheque book,' says Anderson. 'Our advertising budget was thrown out of the window. We bought almost every advertising slot we could find.' The world started to turn orange. There were full-page ads in the London *Evening Standard* and the Scottish press, wall-to-wall radio advertising and, incredibly, even a TV advertising campaign thrown together in a matter of days. Anderson describes 'one memorable meeting with Mike Hellens, the MD of our media buying agency' in which Stelios barked, 'Unless you spend a million pounds you're fired.' Conventional wisdom dictates it takes at least a month to create a television ad, but Stelios had insisted, 'I want to have an ad on television on Friday.'

'It was Tuesday,' recalls Anderson. 'Things like this just do not happen. We came up with someone holding a toy plane. It was truly awful, totally embarrassing. In fact some people told me they thought we'd deliberately made it that way. But the price message, Scotland for £29, was sufficiently strong that it had the desired effect of making the phones ring off the hooks.'

'A man possessed': that is Anderson's description of Stelios during the first six months of the airline's life. 'We were working seven days a week till late in the evening, our days peppered with crisis meetings and calls to action. Everything ratcheted up the stress. But it worked, sales rocketed and eventually BA got the message, Stelios had deep pockets and easyJet was here to stay.'

Cheekily, easyJet put up posters at Glasgow airport inviting passengers travelling on BA or British Midland to cash in their full-fare tickets, pay £29 for the easyJet flight and pocket the difference. Not everyone paid £29, though. After the initial launch, the word 'from' had crept in. Passengers found that £29 was merely the starting price, available to those who booked early for less-popular flights. Yield management, the technique of squeezing the maximum earnings from each planeload of people, pushed the fare up in £10 increments to £69. Some who took up the invitation found that the fare was considerably higher – and that they landed at a small, awkward-to-reach airport some distance from the centre of London. But they were still paying less than the full economy fare on British Airways.

While the marketeers were spending a million, Stelios was preparing for his next destination. To choose it, Stelios simply worked down the list. Next was Aberdeen, Scotland's third-largest city. Anderson says there was another important element: 'At the time Heathrow–Aberdeen was the route with the distinction of having the highest proportion of BA Gold Card holders anywhere on their network.' A few years previously, BA had successfully seen off a challenge from an unknown start-up called Aberdeen-London Express. 'I suspect they were looking forward to dishing out the same treatment to the next airline attempting to encroach on the pot of gold that the Aberdeen route represented,' says Anderson. By now the public was getting acquainted with the easyJet principle. So to maintain media interest, the airline started dreaming up stunts worthy of Southwest Airlines.

'We managed to secure a number of key advertising sites within the Aberdeen terminal,' says Anderson. 'These sites were strategically positioned around the BA check-in desk and above the luggage carousels where the "Fat Cats" collected their bags.' The airline's booking of the sites was viewed with some trepidation by the people responsible for granting advertising copy clearance, since the ads at Glasgow inviting BA and British Midland flyers to switch had already generated controversy. 'We were told in no uncertain terms that our copy would be subjected to close scrutiny prior to approval.' Sensing an opportunity, Anderson drew up the most outrageous copy he could think of, with the memorable tagline, 'Beware: thieves operate in this airport'. He knew there was no chance that it would gain approval, which was precisely the plan. When the anticipated rejection came in the form of a terse fax, a strategic leak to the media resulted in sensational headlines in the local press. NEW AIRLINE'S ADVERTS BANNED was the headline in the *Aberdeen Press and Journal*.

The first flight I took on an easyJet flight was to Aberdeen, a few days after the route began in January 1996. I actually wanted to go to Edinburgh, but a Rugby international was taking place in the Scottish capital that weekend, and basic yield management meant that the lowest fare being quoted for the one-hour hop from Luton was £59. In contrast, Aberdeen was still on sale at £29. So that was the one I took. My experience was just like that of millions of others since: it was extraordinarily ordinary. The plane was clean and comfortable enough for a one-hour hop. The staff were unusually dressed in a lurid shade of orange, but were polite and professional. I had to pay for coffee and biscuits, but that is the tradition on the trains I catch and the cafés I visit. I thumbed down the A90 to Edinburgh, and for the first time in a long hitch-hiking career got a lift in a Porsche. I arrived in the Scottish capital earlier and richer than if I had caught the newly privatised train. The first three routes proved a point that keeps cropping up in no-frills aviation: if new, low fares become available, the number of passengers increases by more than the extra capacity on the route. In other words, every airline finds it is flying more passengers. The problem for the existing carriers is that those passengers are paying lower average fares than before. By now, Stelios had persuaded British Telecom to allot him the number 0990 29 29 29, to remind people the base fare was £29. British Airways, which had for many years enjoyed a monopoly on flights between London and Scotland, was affected. But so too were two much smaller, independent airlines that, ironically, had paved the way for greater competition in aviation: Air UK and British Midland. Other competitors have proved resilient, notably Virgin – not one of the airlines, but the train company – and its railway competitor GNER. Twenty-nine pounds easily undercut the normal one-way fare on Virgin's west coast line from London to Glasgow, and GNER's east coast line to Edinburgh. Even with the tedious slog of reaching Luton, the journey between city centres by air was quicker. The train operators' opening price between London and Glasgow is coincidentally now £29, but that buys a return trip. One reason the rail companies can do that is because they receive subsidies from the Exchequer. In contrast, easyJet faced a new tax of up to 18 per cent on air travellers, which came into effect within six months of the first flight.

Kenneth Clarke, 'the best leader the Conservative Party never had', was widely regarded as a fair Chancellor. He was also concerned that air travellers benefited from the absence of tax on aviation fuel. No country had figured out a way to impose a tax on jet kerosene, because of an international understanding that it should be free of duty. So he imposed Air Passenger Duty of £5 on each European flight, thereby adding nearly one fifth to the typical easyJet fare of £29. It was a 'poll tax with wings', because of the way that it added a fiver to every fare. Accordingly, proportionately it penalised more heavily people who sought cheap flights. Business travellers paying £500 to fly to Athens would barely notice a 1 per cent hike, but it put the airlines in the price-driven low-cost sector at a huge disadvantage. 'I've always been very, very upset about the way the government has decided to tax the aviation industry,' says Stelios. But the Exchequer loved the simplicity – the airlines collected APD on its behalf – and the hundreds of millions of pounds it raised each year. So shortly before he lost office, Mr Clarke announced it would double. 'That really pissed me off,' says the easyJet chairman.

The incoming Labour chancellor, Gordon Brown, was disinclined to cancel the increase. On a £29 fare, that meant a tax of 35 per cent. Since then, the Chancellor has tweaked Air Passenger Duty so that one-way flights within Europe incur a tax of £5, which means that a return domestic trip stays at £10. To pay for this cut, he upped the tax for business- and first-class seats, but one bizarre loophole means that passengers on the world's most expensive aircraft, Concorde, pay just the same tax – £20 – on a flight from London to New York as easyJet passengers pay on the short haul from Luton to Zurich.

The tax did not upset Stelios so much that he could not bring himself to open new routes. Amsterdam was first, signalling easyJet's admission to the major league – because it had acquired its first wholly owned aircraft, and was flying into one of Europe's key hubs. Links from London Heathrow to Schiphol airport were great moneyspinners for BA, British Midland and the Dutch airline, KLM. The launch offer from easyJet – all seats for 39p on the first day – grabbed plenty of headlines. The PR stunt was to print coupons in the in-flight magazine addressed to the president of KLM complaining about the price of flights to and from Amsterdam. 'We turned up at their offices to personally deliver them to Mr Bouw. Needless to say we weren't granted an audience and only made it as far as the security gatehouse, though a representative did at least have the good grace to come down and collect them.' This made primetime news on all the Dutch TV channels.

The French city of Nice, convenient for Stelios's apartment in Monte Carlo, followed five weeks later, on 5 June 1996. To publicise the new route, he invited the press to fly out with him and watch the Monaco Grand Prix from his apartment. Starting with these routes, Stelios was able to demonstrate that the US no-frills model could work on international routes in Europe. The list of destinations from Luton expanded to include Barcelona, Palma and Madrid – in direct competition with another Luton-based airline, Debonair – plus Geneva and Zurich.

In March 1998, easyJet bought into an ailing Swiss airline, TEA, moved its base from Basel to Geneva, and rebranded it as easyJet Switzerland. The Swiss, who enjoy life outside the EU and its relatively open markets, had never seen anything like it. Swissair opposed easyJet's plans to fly to Barcelona, and insisted that the rival airline obeyed an obscure rule that its cheap flights must come with accommodation attached. Which is why visitors to easyLand in Luton are greeted by the sight of a two-person tent, dangling from the ceiling at reception. The easyJet tent was originally pitched on a site on a rocky hillside close to Spain's border with France, about a hundred miles north of Barcelona. A photograph of it appeared on the website. Anyone who booked a cheap flight from Geneva to the Catalan capital was actually buying a package holiday, but not one where they were expected to take up the accommodation portion. Eventually the Swiss relented, allowed easyJet to set fares as it wished, and the tent was moved to its present position, an example of the type of entrepreneurial marketing ploy that Stelios has become famous for – and the kind of passenger-friendly aggressive action people love to hear about.

The first day of July 1998 saw a classic easyJet launch on the new route to Athens – by far the longest flight on the network. The natural target for the publicity campaign that accompanies a new destination is the national airline. But Olympic Airways was, and is, in a dreadful mess already. 'There was no mileage to be had in picking on such a weak competitor,' says Anderson. Instead, the travel agents were targeted. A series of 'cut out the middleman' advertisements appeared in Greek newspapers, until the travel agents won a court injunction against them. 'We responded by painting the offending expression in ten-foot high letters on the side of one of our aeroplanes and flying it down to Athens,' says Anderson. 'The travel agents rose to the bait in style, launching a high-profile legal battle culminating in a court appearance in Athens by Stelios.'

The easyJet boss had ensured there would be plenty of cameras at the court by promising vouchers for free flights to London for anyone who turned out to support him at the trial. 'On emerging from the courtroom Stelios was greeted by a horde chanting his name, all anxious to get the vouchers,' says Anderson. Some of them were believed to be travel agents.

As new routes were added, the easyJet methodology became clear. On a perfect route map, every easyJet city would be linked with every other destination. This has benefits in terms of operational flexibility – planes and crews can be worked to the airline's maximum advantage – and in marketing. An ad that promises cheap fares from Amsterdam to one destination is as expensive as one that offers ten alternatives.

By now, easyJet was thriving. Stelios's new aircraft from Boeing meant that he was operating the youngest fleet in the UK. Ten days into 1999, a new base was established in Liverpool (Manchester proved too expensive and congested) with flights to Amsterdam, Barcelona, Geneva and Nice. The same week, the ascent of no-frills flying was paralleled by a television phenomenon, the 'fly-on-the-wall' documentary. It was inevitable that a low-cost airline and the docusoap should meet. *Airline* was the name of a documentary series made in the 70s about the daily life of British Airways. It was brought back by ITV as the title of a late-90s docusoap, this time featuring easyJet. There are plenty of casualties of 'warts and all' programmes in the travel industry: the country's biggest charter airline, Britannia, did not emerge well from its flirtation with the cameras, while depictions of the excesses of some of Unijet's overseas reps reinforced the image of debauchery in resorts. But ITV's *Airline*, the everyday story of easyFolk, is on its sixth series.

'I am a risk-taker by nature,' says Stelios, when I ask why any commercial organisation should expose its inner workings to primetime TV. 'I like risks, I can manage them. It's very easy to say with the benefit of hindsight, "you're famous anyway, why the hell subject yourself to that tormenting experience?" And the answer is that we weren't that famous back then in '97 when they first approached us. So it was a question of rolling the dice and thinking, "how can we make this company a household name in this country?" And it was the easiest, cheapest way of doing it. We took some risks, but I think people appreciate the openness. To put it bluntly, if that's the worst thing that can happen to you when you fly easyJet, you're probably all right.'

The airline's officials are permitted to watch the programme before transmission, but final editorial control rests with the production company, LWT. By the sixth series, the storylines are wearing thin, but there seems no limit to the public appetite for irate late arrivals, C-list celebrity passengers and overacting staff. Every time the primetime goes out, there is a visible rise in bookings for easyJet. 'OK, sometimes we're late, and sometimes the check-in desk closes before you arrive, but so what? It happens on every airline. And I think people do appreciate that we're entirely open, and we live with the cameras filming every aspect of our life. At least they remember the name, and they fly with you.'

Loyal viewers, of whom there are still several million, have witnessed an airline enjoying constant growth, with an owner who comes across as a genial godfather of no-frills flying – and personally goes to Seattle to kick the tyres of the new Boeings that he orders. The programme shows him working constantly on easyJet flights, talking to every single passenger – 'How did you book with us? What do you think of us?' – which, on the flights I have shared with Stelios, is typical. He is the airline magnate in his private life, too. 'When I walk into a room full of people, inevitably the discussion turns at some stage to aeroplanes. It is a subject people love to talk about, about defying gravity, flying and everything else. It's an industry people love to talk about – a very sexy industry.'

Sexy or not, since easyJet became an established part of the aviation scene, life has not always been easy for Stelios's airline. It offers the most generous delay-compensation system of any carrier: after an hour's delay in departure, passengers can cancel without penalty or re-book on another date. After four hours, everyone on the plane travels free, having their fare refunded. But at the very end of 2000, severe wintry weather at Luton and Liverpool combined with a shortage of de-icing fluid to cause massive disruption to operations. Thousands of passengers had to abandon their New Year journeys, while many others spent long hours waiting for their flights. Few were compensated. Luckily, perhaps, the camera crew had taken time off and were not around for the full fury.

A happier story, which rarely gets reflected in *Airline*, is the extraordinary success that easyJet and its rivals have had in attracting Internet business. In early 1998, about the time filming began, easyJet had a very basic website that effectively told people to ring the call centre. 'Stelios was himself initially sceptical, setting a limited budget for us to build our first site,' says Tony Anderson. As is customary in telesales marketing, a different number was assigned so that its reach could be tracked. At a marketing meeting, Stelios says that he noticed that many more callers were dialling the number they saw on the site. 'So that's what convinced me to invest a little bit more money to make the website interactive so it can take bookings.' The airline made its first Internet sale a few months later and has never looked back: nine out of ten easyJet seats are sold via the Internet, a far higher proportion than its counterparts elsewhere in the world. 'My contribution to this industry has been the web discount,' says Stelios. 'You incentivise the consumer to behave in a way that saves money and saves you money, so you've aligned interest.' Another sophistication is what is called the 'rolling window'. The easyJet rule is book early and you will (usually) get the best price. The catch for technophobes is that telephone bookings are allowed only for people flying in the next two months. 'So the people who are keen to get the best prices are forced to go on the net,' says Stelios. 'That's what pushed easyJet from zero to 90 per cent in two years.'

With buoyant sales, and a web of bases at Luton, Liverpool, Amsterdam, and Geneva, easyJet was beginning to look a lot like the cherished Southwest Airlines. Which meant that it was time for Stelios to leave the limelight. 'I'm not interested in running anything – ships or planes. I'm interested in having ideas, implementing them, working very hard on them and handing them over to executives to do the job properly.' The beneficiary was Ray Webster, a New Zealander who had begun working in aviation before Stelios was born. Besides vast amounts of experience, he handily possesses a razor-sharp intellect. He had been appointed as chief executive after an interview of only twenty minutes, as Stelios relates: 'On a phone call from New Zealand, Ray said, "I want the job." And I said, "Are you really interested? Are you keen?" And he said, "Yeah." So I said, "Come over for an interview, but you have to pay for your own ticket from New Zealand." The conversation was on Thursday and he was in Luton on Saturday morning, from New Zealand. It was really a very quick affair.'

I first encountered the former engineer in a car park opposite Guy's Hospital in a particularly unsalubrious part of south-east London. Ray

Webster, with 35 years experience in aviation, had accompanied Stelios to the launch of easyRentacar; the chairman seems to have a knack of starting ventures on grey, miserable days. Stelios unveiled easyRentacar, which aimed to strip away the costs of car rental, and brought along the man who was taking over the easyJet reins. You could rent a car from Stelios for as little as £9 a day. Not any old banger, either: from easyRentacar you can hire any kind of car you like, as long as it's a brand-new Mercedes A-class. You could book only on the Internet, but Stelios Haji-Ioannou would rent you a terminal, too, at one of his easyEverything emporia. (Later, a regular easyJet passenger to Barcelona told me an interesting story about Stelios. He had met her on a flight, and urged her to book an easyRentacar next time she went to Spain. When she arrived at the Avis check-in, she found a familiar figure in the queue ahead of her – none other than Stelios.)

Webster was a strategic planner for Air New Zealand who had been given the task of exploring the opportunities for a low-cost airline. 'The company unfortunately took the other option of buying Ansett, and the rest is history,' he said. That history was that Air New Zealand closed down its loss-making subsidiary, Ansett, within hours of the terrorist attack on America on 11 September 2001. At the time, Webster was at his desk, 10,000 miles away in Luton, in a very crowded and very orange easyLand; perhaps a blessing in such an orange environment, Webster is colour-blind.

Unlike all the other airlines' chief executives to whom I talked for this book, Webster has no separate office. 'One of the problems with today's traditional airlines is that they've got used to all these luxurious environments and very comfortable existences for the executives,' he says. 'They're not challenged in their work: "I've got my office, and a secretary to bring me my tea . . . and I've got a driver to take me to lunch." ' His desk is in the middle of an open-plan (at least, I assume there's a plan) office close to Toby Nicol, the airline's PR guru. 'We have to make sure that people feel part of the business,' says Webster, 'and that executives are not shut away from the business, but they're all part of it.' Despite half a lifetime of experience in aviation, he realises that the airline he is presently piloting is on a journey into the unknown. 'There's no road map to what we're doing, this is adventuring almost, we have to be very quick on our feet, we have to be very quick to seize opportunities very quickly.'

As if to underline the point, he has just taken a call from BAA Gatwick and is about to head around the M25 to the Sussex airport to discuss using the slots made available by the post-11 September aviation slump.

Webster has a calm, cheery demeanour. But if you want to see the relaxed smile disappear, you could always try talking about head-to-head competition.

'We will certainly not tolerate that. We think the market in Europe is immense: that's absolutely no reason at all why a low-cost airline has to start stamping on the patch of an existing one. There's a big sandpit here and plenty of space. Recently when Go announced services out of Belfast into Scotland, a day after we announced ours, we quite rightfully sent a very clear message saying this is not going to be tolerated. They will find it very, very difficult to make profits on those routes. We have a very good cost base and a very strong brand. As if that wasn't enough, they tried to take on Ryanair by flying into Dublin. These guys are on a suicide mission.'

That might not have been an ideal choice of phrase so soon after the terrorist attack on 11 September, but the tragedy did little to dent easyJet's fortunes. By the end of October 2001, easyJet's share price had doubled in a single year relative to the European aviation sector as a whole. The airline announced profits almost doubled to £40m on turnover of £357m, made from 7.1m passengers. In other words, each passenger flown contributed an average profit of £5.50. Six out of seven seats were sold on the Internet. The airline confirmed it would almost double its fleet size to 48.

A good moment for Stelios to cash in some of his chips, to sell 18.5 million shares, worth £69m on the day he made the announcement. The cash would be handy to find with easyEverything, easyRentacar and a price-comparison website called easyValue, which allows consumers to compare rates on everything from MP3 players to flights to Glasgow. But Stelios still believes passionately in his creation – and his ambition has not dimmed. 'In this market the lowest cost producer will win. Nothing else matters. Safety's important, and punctuality's important, but once you take those as a given, nothing else matters – not the colour of the plane, not the designer outfits of the cabin crew, not the quality of the sandwiches, not even which airport you fly from.'

Stelios is not just popular with travellers; he is also well regarded by most of his counterparts in the industry. 'He's a very pleasant sort of person,' says Sir Richard Branson; 'If there was a vote amongst his staff against Michael O'Leary's staff, he'd win it hands down.' Barbara Cassani of Go says simply, 'He's a brilliant guy.' One of the few other women prominent in the travel industry, Martha Lane Fox of LastMinute.com, says, 'I think Stelios is fantastic,' to which Stelios replies, 'I think she's great, too.' Tim Jeans of Ryanair says, 'Stelios has done the low-fares

WHAT WENT WRONG WITH THE TONY BLAIR HOLIDAY?
In summer 2001, the *Mirror* ran a story that Tony Blair and his family would be flying off for their summer holiday on easyJet. A Downing Street lobby briefing confirmed the report. Immediately, the posters started going up: EVEN TONY BLAIR GOT A BARGAIN THIS SUMMER. But it turned out that the Prime Minister never had any intention of travelling on Britain's leading no-frills airline.

'The spin doctor, Alistair Campbell, was too fast to say he was flying easyJet to the south-west of France, because we do not fly to the south-west of France,' says Stelios. 'And I worked it out backwards after the event, and he was going on holiday to his friend's chateau in the south-west of France. So why on earth would he fly to Nice [easyJet's only French destination]? So I think it was the spin doctor getting it wrong in the first place, and us perhaps, prematurely, relying on it for our advertising campaign. They corrected their mistake, and said, "Actually, we're flying Ryanair." So good luck to them.'

industry a huge favour; [easyJet] is a well-managed airline.' Even Franco Mancassola, boss of Debonair – the Luton-based low-cost airline that failed to survive – can summon up some faint words of praise: 'Stelios is a brave man. Of course it's easy to be financially brave when you've got plenty of money. Bless him.'

8. LOW COST EQUALS LOW SAFETY?

'Five ninety-two needs immediate return to Miami . . . we're on fire, we're on fire'
COCKPIT VOICE RECORDER OF VALUJET FLIGHT 592, MIAMI–ATLANTA

'For those of you who haven't been in a car for the past thirty years, this is how to fasten a seat belt'
SAFETY ANNOUNCEMENT BY NORTHWEST FLIGHT ATTENDANT

'We never anticipate a sudden change in air pressure; if we did, I'd get another job'
SAFETY ANNOUNCEMENT BY SOUTHWEST FLIGHT ATTENDANT

'Welcome to the Flight 592 Memorial.' So begins one of the more tragic pages you are likely to find on the Internet. 'This Memorial is dedicated to those who lost their lives in the senseless and unnecessary air disaster of May 11, 1996, and to the families and friends who must endure the pain of their loss forever.'

'It's something else,' promises a slogan for AirTran. The Florida-based no-frills airline certainly is, at least in name. At the time that flight 592 departed from Miami, destination Atlanta, on 11 May 1996, the carrier was known as ValuJet. The website contains a gallery of smiling faces, the people who paid a few dollars less for the flight from Miami to Atlanta, and ended up paying with their lives. One of them was Dana Lyn Nelson-Lane, who had married her husband, Roger, six months earlier. On the website, her father writes, 'Some people are followers, only a very few are leaders . . . Dana was our leader. Who will lead us now? *Dana was a giver . . . right up until the time our daughter was taken.* Besides the virtual memorial, there is a monument in black and red granite at Woodlawn Park Cemetery in south-west Miami.

The McDonnell-Douglas DC-9 took off on an easterly runway, flew over the city and turned to head north-west. Almost immediately, a fire broke out in a cargo hold. Within six minutes, smoke and flames had spread to the passenger cabin and the cockpit. Fifteen miles west of Miami airport, the plane plunged almost vertically into the swamps of the Everglades. Accident investigators were unable to determine if the crash happened because of a mechanical loss of control or because the crew – commanded by the first American woman captain to lose her life in an accident – were incapacitated by the fire.

The cargo hold contained a consignment of oxygen generators – aircraft parts used to deliver oxygen to passengers and crew if an aircraft is holed and loses pressure. On this occasion, these safety devices brought down the plane. They are regarded as hazardous material, yet were not labelled as such and had not been properly boxed. They were stored in a hold that had neither a smoke detector nor a fire extinguisher. Along with the aircraft, all 105 passengers and five crew, some travellers' confidence in no-frills aviation was destroyed that day. 'That was difficult for the whole industry, but especially for the low-fares airlines,' says Greg Wells, who is vice-president for safety and security for the world's biggest low-cost airline, Southwest. 'Theirs was directly related to a mechanical issue, a failure apparently with the maintenance department.'

The subsequent National Transportation Safety Board investigation blamed three organisations: ValuJet, for poor maintenance practices; SabreTech, the firm that supplied the generators; and the Federal Aviation Authority, for failing to give proper oversight. ValuJet's licence was revoked, and the airline stopped flying.

By the time the airline was allowed in the air again – offering a Boston–Philadelphia hop for just $42 – its name had changed to AirTran. The airline has not had a crash since, which is what statisticians would expect from an airline that has operated relatively few flights in its new identity. Fatal accident rates in Europe and North America run at one in every million or two departures.

At this point, please read a health warning about the available data on aviation disasters: fatal aircraft accidents are, thankfully, so rare that it is tricky and potentially misleading to attach words like 'dangerous' or 'safe' to individual planes or airlines. In July 2000, an Air France Concorde crashed a few minutes after take-off from Charles de Gaulle airport in Paris, killing 113 people. Some people insist that the fact that Concorde can crash must make it even more likely that other, cheaper airlines will fall to earth, killing everyone on board and possibly some unfortunate souls on the ground. With the £9,000 price tag for a transatlantic round-trip – by far the most expensive plane ticket in the world – surely passengers are buying the best safety possible? If no-frills airlines are obsessed with cutting costs, might they cut corners on safety?

A theoretical argument can be made for a rational consumer accepting a higher degree of risk in return for low fares. After all, cost/risk trade-offs are made all the time on the ground. Motorists often know that the brakes really need adjusting, or the tyres need changing, but they postpone the investment; local government engineers may decide not to invest in a segregated cycle lane, but to spend the cash on something else. In both cases, there is (or should be) an awareness that they are assuming a higher risk of a fatal skid or a dead cyclist, possibly both at the same time.

By their nature, no-frills airlines are much younger and less experienced than traditional carriers with a long history. Some passengers may deduce that, accordingly, they lack the depth of knowledge that traditional, more established airlines may have.

Low-cost airlines agree on hardly anything. But the one topic on which all are unanimous is safety. In particular, they refute any suggestion that buying a cheap flight is a risk. 'Some people may draw that conclusion,' concedes Tim Jeans of Ryanair, but he insists 'there are no cost compromises on safety'. Indeed, avoiding crashes is even more crucial to no-frills operators than traditional airlines, Jeans contends. He turns the economic argument – that low cost somehow implies low safety – on its head. No-frills airlines, he says, should actually be safer than traditional airlines. 'Safety standards have to be as good, or better than, the full-service competition because clearly the downside to an accident for a low-fares carrier would be considerably greater than if it hit a full-service carrier. We're only too well aware of that.'

'Is the aircraft safe?'

Vladimir Raitz says that was one of the first questions he was asked when he introduced charter flights to Corsica in 1950. Then and now, some people assume there is a catch with every cheap flight. When easyJet started up in 1995, it used a cartoon plane in its advertising. The marketing director at the time, Tony Anderson, soon changed that image: 'At a focus group, a number of the participants thought we flew old propeller-driven aircraft.' The airline's chairman, Stelios says, 'Up until a couple of years ago, I still had to defend myself against questions like "Are the planes safe?" ' He believes that the public is gradually getting the message that no-frills airlines have even younger fleets than their traditional rivals.

The arrival of Go to the no-frills market helped perceptions, because people associated safety with British Airways, the company that was very visibly behind Barbara Cassani's airline. And British Airways is closely associated – in bed, some would say – with Qantas, which many people believe to be the safest airline in the world.

> Charlie Babbitt (played by Tom Cruise): Ray, all airlines have crashed at one time or another, that doesn't mean they are not safe.
> Raymond Babbitt (played by Dustin Hoffman): Qantas. Qantas never crashed.

This piece of dialogue, in Barry Levinson's 1988 film *Rain Man*, helped him win the Oscar for best director and movie, and Hoffman the award for best actor. But it set back the cause of rational discussion of air safety by years. Movie-goers concluded that Qantas was the only airline in the world never to have suffered a crash. In fact, the Australian airline has had plenty of accidents, but thankfully has always managed to crash gently, without loss of life. Cruise's assertion that 'all airlines have crashed at one time or another' was even more damaging. Plenty of carriers, from Air China via Emirates to Virgin Atlantic, have never suffered a fatal accident. Many now-defunct operators, including Laker Airways and Canada 3000, went through their whole careers without a crash. But misapprehension characterises fear of flying. 'Air travel is such a different form of travel still,' says Greg Wells of Southwest. 'It's very sensational when a 110,000 lb aeroplane for some reason falls out of the sky, and sometimes two hundred people can die. That doesn't happen in an automobile, it doesn't happen in a train.'

A train. That is what I need right now. I am at Salinas station in California, just inland from Monterey, hoping to travel north to San José. This is John Steinbeck country, and considerable wrath has been visited on the shabby, flyblown railroad station. I am waiting for the Coast Starlight, the train that is supposed to get me to San Jose in time to connect with a flight to Seattle. It is a dark, starless night. I ask the ticket clerk when the train might get here.

'That depends what else is on the line.'

Things like freight trains, I speculate.

'Uh huh, and animals, and kids, abandoned cars, that sort of thing.'

When the miscellany of trackside impediments is finally cleared, I reach San Jose just in time to catch the next-flight-north-but-one to Seattle. The aircraft used for the shuttle between Silicon Valley and the home of Microsoft is an MD-83 belonging to the semi-low-cost Alaska Airlines; on the last day of January 2000, an identical aircraft crashed into the sea off the coast of Los Angeles, with the loss of 88 lives. Upon our safe arrival in Seattle, I learn that Alanis Morissette is performing. Her first hit, Ironic, includes a description of a nervous flyer ('Mr Play-it-safe') dying in a plane crash. Ironically, I am here to meet the man who probably knows more about air safety than anyone else on the planet: Dr Todd Curtis.

In 1995, Curtis was employed by Boeing as an aviation safety analyst. He realised the public had a profound interest in the subject of which planes crash, who operates them, and how likely passengers are to die. But accessible information on which to make rational decisions was often cloaked in jargon. 'At parties, I never had people saying, "The hull-loss rate of that aircraft really worries me," or "Gee, the breakdown rate that doesn't lead to fatal injury of this aircraft concerns me." They were worried about events where people ended up dead.' At the time it was difficult even for people within the aviation industry to gather that information in a form where sensible comparisons and judgements could be made. Curtis crunched the numbers and put together a website to address travellers' concerns.

AirSafe.com answers basic questions like 'Has this airline ever had an accident? What's the safety record of this aircraft?' The site allows users to dig deeper to find out the circumstances of the hundreds of aviation disasters that have taken place in the past three decades. The subtext throughout the traveller's clicks is 'So am I going to be killed or not?'

Curtis directs his attention towards that fundamental human concern: 'I had a very simple rule: if a passenger had got on the aircraft with the intent of going someplace and they died of other than natural causes, that's a fatal event. I didn't look at crew, not because I don't believe their lives are not valuable, but simply because the paying passenger worries about the paying passenger. They don't worry about the crew. As far as they're concerned that's a workplace hazard, not a travel hazard.' He is keen to stress that his site never says an airline or aircraft is either safe or unsafe. 'In my opinion, that is a subjective judgement call that is up to the individual. No matter how expert I am in some issues, I can't say that something is safe or unsafe. That's like saying this is beautiful or this isn't beautiful. I give you the data, you make the decision.'

The basic currency of the site is the Fatal Event Rate, a measure of the number of accidents per million flights. Way ahead of the pack is Cubana. Not only is Cuba's national airline almost totally devoid of frills (but without the usual accompaniment of low fares), it is also a serial crasher. Since 1970, one departure in 52,000 has, on average, ended in a fatal crash. In contrast, almost all the no-frills airlines have a perfect record: easyJet, Ryanair, Go, Buzz and Virgin Express; Spirit and Vanguard in the US; WestJet in Canada; GOL of Brazil. But all are relatively young. Ryanair has flown more than its European rivals, but is still a long way short of a million missions.

In a numbers game where one fatal accident every two million or so flights is a good average, one airline is way ahead of the game: Southwest has flown 10 million flights without losing an aircraft in a fatal accident. How does the airline stay aloft? 'I wish I could bottle their secret and pass it around to everyone in the world,' says Curtis. 'From the very beginning they've had a very hard-nosed attitude towards operational safety. Southwest is rather well known for its marketing campaigns, in the early days for the hot pants-wearing flight attendants. But behind all that they have a very solid operation, run by a very straightforward group of people.'

It helps that the airline has only ever flown one kind of aircraft, the Boeing 737. 'They have a very intimate understanding of how to fly that aircraft. Also, for most of their history, they have flown in places that were not overwhelmed with other airlines – so for example they don't fly into Atlanta, they don't fly into JFK.' Some in the industry maintain that this means there is less danger of involvement in a collision caused by an error on the part of another pilot, such as the one that destroyed an SAS aircraft at Milan in October 2001. They argue that big, busy airports with a large number of small carriers are riskier. A more universally accepted benefit is that, at airports where Southwest is the dominant carrier, crews gain a lot of experience. Curtis says the nature of the operation enhances Southwest's safety. 'Very few of their flights are over a couple of hours in length. If you do shorter flights there are certain things that you're not going to be exposed to that will happen on longer flights. They don't fly over water. So they do a particular kind of flying, they do it very well, they do it very frequently, and they have a very thorough understanding of the aircraft and how it flies.'

Consequently, Southwest is the one big US airline where the flight attendants can afford to joke their way through the safety demonstration. Duane Redmond embellishes his announcement by saying, 'We never anticipate a sudden change in air pressure; if we did, I'd get another job.' Another favourite of crews is to indulge in theatrical sighs when the plane touches down: 'Phew . . . we made it!' is typical. But the airline is careful never to boast about its safety record.

'It's not something we use in our advertising,' says Greg Wells, who is the man responsible for safety at Southwest. He attributes the awesome record to Southwest's people: 'We're owners of the airline with the profit-share program, everybody has a piece of this company, there's a tremendous amount of pride in what we do. It really goes all the way down from our pilots to our baggage handlers. I can't see that you can be oversafe. We take every measure to make sure we operate a safe airline. The age of our fleet is young. The way that we grow, the speed at which we grow and retire airplanes. With that in mind, of course, we have less mechanical issues.'

None of the Boeing 737s flown by Southwest has crashed, but more than fifty others have. The loss of an Air Philippines 737 in a crash in April 1999, in which 124 people died, marked a significant moment. The 737 had equalled the number of crashes sustained by the Boeing 727. Within two months, another accident in India meant that the 737 had suffered more fatal crashes than any other commercial airplane. But that does not mean you should avoid flying on the plane. The aircraft chosen by almost all the no-frills cheapies is easily the most widely flown jet. All other things being equal, you would expect it to suffer more accidents than the rest. The accident rates for Airbus are slightly less favourable, though still extremely good. It would be nonsensical for a passenger to adopt the policy revealed on one of the top-selling items at the Boeing Everett Tour Center near Seattle – a bumper sticker reading, 'If it ain't a Boeing, I'm not going'.

The construction process is monitored fastidiously. Behind the engineers comes a platoon of inspectors, who go to the extent of using dental mirrors to peer into tight corners to check that a bolt has been correctly lacquered. Even before a new Boeing 737 takes off on its maiden flight, it thinks it has been flown five times. To test the pressurisation, each aircraft undergoes a simulation of a flight at 91,000 feet, which is 50,000 feet higher than the normal maximum altitude.

Of the 5,000 737s that have been made, about one in a hundred has been lost in an accident. But that gives a fatal event rate of one loss every 2.2 million departures, thirty times better than Concorde. After the supersonic aircraft crashed, some observers insisted that Concorde had previously held the best safety record worldwide. They argued that, because it had not suffered a fatal accident after more than twenty years in service, the supersonic jet was safer than anything else in the skies. But the Boeing 717 and 777, and Airbus's A330 and A340, have flown far more missions without incident. And Todd Curtis points out that 'the Boeing 737 series has more flight operations in ten days than the Concorde has had over its entire fleet history. No one would dare remark that the 737 has a remarkable safety record because it has not had a fatal crash this month.'

Aviation safety is based upon a series of disasters. Planes started crashing even before the Wright brothers first got off the ground in 1903. From every accident, investigators learn lessons. Steps are implemented to minimise the chances of repetition: to design out unforeseen risks or sloppy practices, or to develop systems that change convention for the better. Take the flight dispatcher: often 'people think we're the people on the ground with the paddles,' complains Steve Hozdulick, who runs the Dispatch control centre for Southwest. The dispatcher's job was created when it was deemed that the captain needed someone to watch over them. There had been cases where, for example, a pilot decided to take a chance with the weather in order to get home that night, but came unstuck. Like the pilot, the dispatcher is highly trained and strictly licensed. He or she helps plan and follow every journey. With an extra pair of eyes, the chances of making an imperfect decision are reduced. These days, if a warning light comes on in the flight deck of a Southwest plane at Los Angeles, the captain will talk to his opposite number at Dispatch in Dallas. Between them, they will decide the best course of action.

Accidents still happen, though not to Southwest. Some disasters lead directly to action that affects upstart airlines. After the ValuJet crash in 1996, the rules tightened: the FAA began to monitor the infrastructure, management and standards of all new airlines for five years after they enter the market.

A school of thought among some travellers is that 'lightning doesn't strike twice'. The theory runs that the safest time to fly on an airline is immediately after it has suffered a crash, because 'in the aftermath of an accident suddenly everyone remembers exactly what it is that they're supposed to do,' says a pilot. But the evidence of the world's most crash-prone airline, Cubana, suggests otherwise. In the final fortnight of 1999, the Cuban national airline suffered two fatal accidents within five days.

The final few months of 2001 made grim reading for prospective passengers. Between 11 September and 21 November, seven commercial flights were lost with all souls. Four of them were hijacked by suicidal terrorists in the US on 11 September; a fifth came down just after take-off from JFK airport in New York; another was shot down accidentally by the Ukranian military over the Black Sea; and the seventh was the SAS aircraft that hit a stray business jet at Milan. To this already scary total, the assiduous Dr Curtis adds three more fatal events: the Crossair crash at Zurich where most of those on board a regional jet died; a Brazilian flight in which an engine exploded and broke two windows, and one passenger was sucked out in the sudden depressurisation; and a tourist charter flight that crashed moments after take-off from Chichen Itza in Mexico, killing all on board.

If ten flights can crash in as many weeks, surely any sane person would be mad to fly?

Actually, no. The perception of risk is magnified hugely by many airline passengers. In fact, as practised by airlines in North America, Europe and Australasia, flying is very safe. Looking globally, a plane crash is a one-in-a-million chance, though figures vary dramatically between airlines and regions. Among US airlines, the average is around one crash for every two million departures. European carriers suffer around one per million flights. The numbers get worse elsewhere in the world, with Asia, Latin America and Africa incurring more frequent rates, though there are some airlines in these regions with excellent records. Overall, people who say 'there's a one-in-a-million chance of this plane crashing' are about right (unless, I hear you say, the plane belongs to Cubana).

There are steps you can take, besides consulting AirSafe.com, that will help to enhance your safety. The single most useful step to reduce your exposure to risk is to find an airline that flies non-stop on your chosen route – if necessary, pay extra for the privilege. Most accidents occur during the take-off, climb, descent and landing phases of flight. An intermediate stop doubles the risky parts of the trip. Jets have a better record than propeller planes, so you may wish to choose them over small commuter aircraft.

'We ask you for your complete attention for just a few moments, while the cabin crew point out some of the safety features on board this aircraft, a Boeing 737.' The mandatory safety demonstration to every passenger aboard an aircraft does not help calm nerves. It actually exacerbates anxiety, suggesting flying is prone to danger. Airlines are legally required explicitly to describe procedures when things go awry. In fact, most other forms of transport are more dangerous per mile or even per trip, but only aviation is required explicitly to describe procedures in the event of an incident.

The briefing on every Ryanair flight continues: 'To inflate your life jacket, pull down sharply on the right toggle. Do not inflate your life jacket inside the cabin as to do so may impede your exit. Your life jacket is equipped with a light to attract attention.' And a lot of use that is going to be in a storm-ravaged North Sea. By now, many frequent travellers believe the whole safety demonstration is laughably archaic. They will chuckle at the flight attendant on Northwest Airlines whose briefing begins, 'For those of you who haven't been in a car for the past thirty years, this is how to fasten a seat belt'. But among nervous travellers, who perhaps travel infrequently or have never even flown before, anxiety can escalate. A lot of worried flyers prepare themselves for the journey by aiming to be as calm as possible at the time boarding begins. If there is a delay, that process is interrupted. It makes matters worse if bad weather or mechanical problems are blamed for the wait: the uncalm passenger may deduce that a storm is likely to assail the plane, or that it has a fundamental flaw. If ground staff give the impression that they don't know what's going on, fearful flyers are likely to have even less confidence in the flight crew.

'A stress reaction is a primitive, mortal fear that something is going to happen to you,' says Dr Steve Ray, a clinical physiologist at Oxford

Brookes University. 'If the people that you perceive to be in control keep you waiting, even if it's only for five minutes, that in itself can cause exasperation.' Passengers may turn to drink, and then turn nasty. Their fears about flying may begin to be self-fulfilling, as anxiety and alcohol start to mix. And, for Todd Curtis, that is a problem that is potentially as dangerous as a hijacking, but far more easily preventable: 'Many air-rage events are associated with passengers who came on board intoxicated. It's clear that is one risk that can be taken away.'

On an average day, three or four flights on UK airlines are affected by disruptive passengers. Most are relatively minor infringements, such as arguing with others or complaining vociferously about the service. But every five days, on average, there is a more serious episode. 'Serious' means passengers starting fires in the toilet when smoking illicitly, becoming violent to crew or passengers, or damaging the aircraft. Men are three times more likely to be troublemakers than are women. Two thirds of offenders are in their twenties and thirties. Only one out of four incidents involves someone travelling alone. So you can understand why airlines are concerned when groups of young men get aboard.

The usual triggers for air rage are the three Ss: stress, smoking and spirits – too much stress, not enough nicotine, and an excess of vodka or whisky. Airlines such as Saudia, which ban alcohol, report low levels of air rage. British World Airlines, which often charters planes on an ad-hoc basis to Ryanair and other no-frills operators, has an even tougher policy when transporting oil workers around Scotland: 'Each passenger must go through a full security check and body search before boarding the aircraft. Any passenger suspected of having alcohol in their bloodstream may be breathalysed.'

Back in the commercial world, where airlines cannot be quite so strict with their passengers, you can look upon the typical flight as a big psychological experiment. The subjects comprise a group of people who have had a stressful few hours between leaving homes or offices and reaching the airport. Some of them are anxious about the prospect of flying; a proportion of passengers is being deprived of the drug on which they depend – nicotine; another group of people is being fuelled with free alcohol; and often those groups intersect. A smoker who is also an anxious flyer may drink heavily to try to alleviate the stress caused by nicotine deprivation and fear. No wonder many of the normal rules of civilised behaviour change, even among frequent flyers. The writer Jonathan Glancey sums up the pressures on passengers: 'If you put lots of people into a small cylinder and put them thirty thousand feet up in the air they suffer from claustrophobia, they get bored and frustrated.

Also, they're strapped in for much of the time and if you restrain people, they get angry. I get angry when I travel on aeroplanes, secretly and quietly, as I don't like to be restrained and I don't like being told what to do.' Add unlimited free alcohol, as many traditional airlines do, and you have a rather less appetising cocktail than the G&Ts or Bloody Marys that the passenger has been throwing down her or (more likely) his neck. Todd Curtis warns that, 'Unless something very dramatic happens, unless a drunken passenger results in a crashed airplane, you will still have this controllable risk up there in the sky.'

The no-frills airlines do not go to the extremes of British World Airways' oil charters, and breath-test passengers, but they report relatively low levels of disruption. Two reasons no-frills airlines are relatively unaffected: they sell, rather than give away alcohol; and they benefit from the fact that a flight of an hour gives less scope for boredom, frustration or nicotine deprivation than a transatlantic crossing. The air-rage triggers are minimised.

You might imagine that the terrorist hijacks would dampen the incidence of disruptive passengers. You would be wrong. 'We haven't had any more or any less than before 11 September,' says Greg Wells of Southwest. 'Air rage hasn't changed, it's not going to change, people are people.' The difference now is that passengers and crew are much more alert to the dangers of someone interfering with the safety of the aircraft. 'The passengers are coming to our aid quite a bit,' says Wells. Many captains, in their pre-flight announcement, tell the passengers that if they are concerned about the behaviour of any other passenger, they should take steps to tackle the passenger. 'Throw things at him, throw your purse, throw your shoes, and several of you get together and subdue him,' is a typical instruction from the flight deck.

The panic on the flight deck of ValuJet 592 is palpable from the transcript of the cockpit voice recorder. 'Five ninety-two needs immediate return to Miami . . . we're on fire, we're on fire.' The National Transportation Safety Board report describes the consequences tersely as 'in-flight collision with terrain/water'. The final chapter of the accident took place in December 2001. Earlier, murder and manslaughter charges – one of each for every victim – had been laid against the owners of SabreTech, which had supplied the oxygen generators. It was the first time that a commercial company had been so charged after a crash. In return for dropping the 220 charges, the company agreed to pay half a million dollars to charity, which works out at $4,500 (£3,000) for each life lost. Half the money went to the National Air Disaster Alliance and Foundation, which lobbies for increased safety.

THE PARTY QUESTION

I asked Todd Curtis what people ask him when, at a party, they discover what he does.

'A primary concern is, "Well, if the airplane crashes, will I die? Is it 100 per cent certain that I'll just be dead?" My answer to that is, well let's look at the numbers from around the world. More than half the time where there's a fatal event involving an airline, there are survivors. In fact most of the accidents are going to kill fewer than ten of the passengers. Some of them are very dramatic, but it's rare that you have one that kills everyone on board. Most accidents will be relatively minor – no injuries, no deaths. A very small number involve passenger fatalities.

'Another question that comes up over and over again is, "Where's the safest place to sit on an aeroplane?" I've looked at all kinds of data, asking, "Is there a pattern around the world of people surviving in certain parts of the aircraft if there's a serious accident?" And the answer is, if it's such a serious accident that a good number of people are killed, there is no rhyme or reason about what area of the aeroplane has the most survivors. It depends on the accident, and it depends on the aircraft.

'If you can tell me what kind of airplane you're flying in and what kind of accident you're going to be in, I can tell you the safest seat on the airplane to sit. In fact if you can tell me the second piece of information, I'd tell you not to fly at all. So that's a question that doesn't have an answer. It's impossible to know ahead of time the safest place to be.

'Some people ask about the safest days of the week, whether male or female pilots are better, etc. Only a few of these sorts of questions are answerable. You can look at the day-of-the-week question and try and figure out if one day is more prone than another. Well, weekdays are because more flights are happening then, but as far as flights per million take-offs are concerned there's no pattern. The male/female pilot question is one that can be answered. But, as with many other questions in aviation safety, there are certain political or social ramifications of even asking the question, that could put one in very dangerous waters. Some years back when I was at Boeing, that question did come up in conversation one day. I went off into a corner, and I thought how would I answer this? I had to figure out how many female pilots are flying. That was the most difficult part. The other part was how many female pilots have been involved in very serious accidents with jet aircraft, and that was actually very easy. And the answer I got was no pattern there either.'

The cash will help, says Dr Todd Curtis, but there are limits to how perfect any machine can be. 'There is a variety of complex technologies on the planet – power plants, spaceships, commercial aircraft – where, as sophisticated as they may be, as well trained as the operators may be, accidents still happen, sometimes due to combinations of events that no one could have foretold ahead of time. That problem has not been resolved in any area of high technology.' Curtis is doing his bit to increase safety and understanding of risk, yet he is not a serene flyer. 'I'm just the kind of person who would much rather be in the cockpit flying the aeroplane than in the back seat not knowing what's going on. It's a total control issue. It's not logical at all. It's emotional.'

For nervous flyers, here's something to think about while you're gripping the armrests on your next no-frills trip: why are flights that go direct from A to B called 'non-stop', since they all stop once, when they reach B? Or, at least, you hope they do.

9. SEX AND THE BUS

'I really love this idea of having your cake and eating it too – finding a way of giving people something that was just that little bit more but still very true to being low cost'

BARBARA CASSANI, CHIEF EXECUTIVE, GO

GO FLIGHT 901: STANSTED–ROME

Go's first-ever flight took place one sunny May morning in 1998. Along with the usual crowd of airline high-ups, excited travellers and seen-it-all-before journalists, there was something strange about seven of the passengers in the queue. They stood out at check-in at Stansted because all, including a large, Mediterranean-looking gentleman, were wearing orange boiler suits. Stelios of easyJet wanted to make sure that Go's inaugural flight was anything but easy. In the tough environment of the no-frills airlines, heaping scorn upon your rivals is standard practice. But this action was different; why had Go aroused so much anger from easyJet?

'The low-cost airline from British Airways,' as Go called itself, has had a short but eventful life. It was created in a controversial conception, experienced a noisy birth and, in its own words, became 'the teenager that flew the nest'. But some critics say it was born with a silver in-flight spoon in its mouth, funded by a rich parent with the express intention of squeezing rivals out of business. Their anger is focused on one woman: Barbara Cassani, the stylish and – say some friends and foes alike – sexy woman who brought Go into existence.

As far as I can tell, she is the only female chief executive of an airline in the world. In the almost exclusively male higher echelons of aviation, Barbara Cassani is a striking exception – not least because her background is so different from most airline executives. She is first-generation American, born to an Italian father and Irish mother in Boston in July 1960, in the heady summer days when the city was the hub of the Kennedy campaign for the US presidency. Cassani could have been a diplomat. She graduated from the New England college of Mount Holyoke in 1982, with a degree in International Relations, which she followed up with a Masters' in Public Affairs at Princeton, the Ivy League university in New Jersey. 'Your education either teaches you how to think, how to look at things critically, or it doesn't. And sadly I think for some people it doesn't. But I was lucky and those were the skills that I took out of my education.'

Cassani headed for Washington DC. But instead of taking her diplomacy expertise to the State Department, she joined Coopers & Lybrand (now PricewaterhouseCoopers) as a management consultant in its international division.

'I worked in a number of different businesses to help them make the right decisions about what was the right thing to do commercially, in terms of expanding their business, contracting it, going into new markets. I think that was a very helpful way of training my brain to think of different business problems.' But by 1987, Cassani had had enough. 'I was frustrated with coming up with what I thought were great ideas, and then have these idiots that were called the management implementing them.'

So she joined British Airways – at the time, emerging from privatisation and keen to import American expertise to rejuvenate an airline that had hitherto been regarded by some of its staff as a particularly comfortable branch of the civil service. The arrangement was that she would come in as an internal business consultant for BA, and in due course would move into line management. She shudders when she recalls some of the projects she was asked to work on: 'I had to investigate why one US tour brochure cost $10,000 to produce yet it only generated ten seats. Aaaahh!' There was culture shock on both sides. The existing BA management team was overwhelmingly male, middle-aged, conservative – and British. When Cassani walked in and started to challenge the status quo, besides being young and attractive, she had to be tough. 'Cassani was one of the first people who was around the place with an American accent,' says an insider who followed her progress from within BA. 'She came in and was fairly quiet at first, but she suddenly seemed to have a meteoric rise and managed to attach herself to the top people. Wherever Cassani was tended to be on the inside.'

In the decade that she spent with the airline before starting Go, Cassani had seven jobs. She says she was called in when her bosses were uncertain about a project. 'We really don't know what to do here, so we'll ask Cassani to do it.' She was well regarded by Michael Levin. He was a New Yorker brought in during the mid-80s as personal adviser to the then-chief executive, Colin Marshall, in a bid to shake up a complacent management in the painful process that culminated in privatisation. 'There was a revolution going on,' says one insider. He describes Levin as 'an unbelievably intimidating character who would pitch into a department, observe it and undermine the managers. He thought the only way was the "kick-ass" American way. While the public face of BA was improving, inside the company it was just a bloodbath.'

Cassani particularly impressed Bob Ayling, who was at the time legal adviser but later chief executive of BA. 'She always struck me as someone who stood out from others because she's got courage, personal courage. She doesn't say things because they are the party line, she says them because she believes in them.' One of the things Cassani believed was that a job to which she had been assigned should be abolished.

'I was head of sales in the southern part of the UK – it was massive, I could have been Queen, it was huge. But I didn't feel that was the way the business was generated. So I was part of a team that reorganised the sales force, and I got rid of my job. I was very happy doing that. Some people think it's nuts, like, "Why on earth do you want to get rid of your own job?" But I just didn't want to be doing a job that is useless.'

One of the tasks she was asked to do led her to making an appearance in Martyn Gregory's book *Dirty Tricks: BA's secret war against Virgin Atlantic*. The writer asserts that Cassani analysed sales and punctuality statistics from Branson's airline. These had secretly been taken from the BA reservations computer that hosted Virgin's flight information. 'I was a manager in the sales department at the time,' she later said, 'analysing information that I subsequently found out had been obtained through Virgin systems. That became one of the areas of interest in the case. It was a bit part, but it was a very sad time in BA's history. There were things going on within the company I didn't know about. I could vouch for my own behaviour as being proper, but there were question marks around the company.'

What turned out to be Barbara Cassani's last line-management job in BA was in the airline's most crucial battleground, the US. What she discovered at the New York headquarters of BA alarmed her, not least the airline's pay agreements. The call centre staff, for example, earned more than any other telephone salespeople in the US. 'It wasn't because the management were stupid and it wasn't because the unions were evil, or because the people were lazy,' says Cassani. 'It was a series of things that happened over years and years and years. The true objectives of remaining competitive in the market, but not ahead of the market, were lost. Some of the management I worked with were very negative about unions, but my view is that it takes two to tango. The unions didn't put these wages up, the management did. Obviously I did play with the cards I was dealt when I was in that job, but I didn't feel comfortable with it.'

During her time in New York, Cassani met a British investment banker, Guy Davis. They married, and have a daughter and son. A less promising relationship was the one that BA had at the time with US Air (now US Airways). British Airways had been courting United as a strategic partner. That deal fell through, precipitating the 'Black Friday' crash in London and Wall Street of 1989. BA settled instead for a substantial stake in US Air, an ailing second-string carrier. 'It was a very good financial relationship for BA – they got pots of money out of it,' says Cassani. But the alliance fell apart amid considerable acrimony. 'There wasn't enough win-win on both sides. BA was winning and US Air didn't feel on a day-to-day basis that they were. BA quite rightly said, "Hey, we coughed up a couple of hundred million bucks and we kept you in business when nobody wanted to talk to you." But it's amazing that as time goes on, a new chief executive comes in place, US Air said, "What have you done for me today?" '

Even before the tempestuous corporate divorce had been completed, British Airways had set its sights on bigger fish. The airline drafted in Cassani as part of the negotiating team for the proposed strategic alliance with the giant American Airlines. As it had tried with United and US Air, BA wanted to team up with an American carrier to offer joint services and marketing, a shared frequent-flyer scheme and 'seamless' travel to customers. Cassani spent a year in discussions that foundered in a morass of legal challenges over competition issues. By the end of that stint, Cassani was through with BA. 'I loved the company in the sense that I had received an enormous amount of personal opportunities. I had a wonderful time and worked with really good people, but I really needed to do something different.' She told Bob Ayling, 'The only thing I really want to do is to run my own business.'

It so happened that the BA bosses needed the right person to head up a new no-frills operation. Bob Ayling had been studying the low-cost sector for some years: 'We had talks with Ryanair about a possible investment by BA but for various reasons this was not proceeded with. There was then an approach by easyJet to British Airways, which we responded to, but those discussions did not proceed to a conclusion. So if there wasn't to be a vehicle in which we could invest, the third route for BA was to establish a business of its own.' Ayling concluded it would be impossible to create a fully fledged no-frills brand within the BA empire: 'Unless you have something which is wholly outside the existing structure, costs leech across. The functional organisations within a mother company are powerful enough to capture and kill a radical new thing like this.'

A new operation required a tough new boss. 'If a low-cost airline set up by British Airways was going to be successful, it had to be run by somebody who had the stamina to take on the rest of the company.' Just as there would be objections from outside, predicted Ayling, there would be jealousy and opposition within BA. 'You had to have someone who had the personality who could cope with that.' Barbara Cassani was the woman. In 1997, she was offered the chance to start her own business.

'I was completely taken aback,' she says. 'It's like that expression, "Be careful about what you ask for, you just might get it." ' Her family were happily settled in New York; her husband, Guy, had not even been to America before they met, but was now ensconced in a good financial job in Manhattan. 'I called him up and he said, "You just have to do it! You do!" So I said "Thank you. Bye." And I scooted off to London and started working on the business plan.' The family remained in America for five months, while Cassani commuted between New York and London. She soon discovered that Ayling's concern about internal pressures was well founded. 'In some ways it was a hindrance being part of the BA group because they were people with very strong views of how they thought things should be done, and we had to fight those off.'

When 'Operation Blue Sky', which led ultimately to Go, was launched in November 1997, Cassani was given a relatively free rein in drafting the business plan, though Ayling made three key stipulations: 'It was going to be tagged, for some time, as "the low-cost airline from British Airways". Therefore anything that went wrong at Go was going to come back on BA itself. The safety systems that were put in at Go were put in under the very close supervision of the BA safety managers. That was an area I wouldn't compromise on. Barbara just had to live with that.' The second area was customer service. Even though it was a completely different proposition, 'If people were really fed up they would equally be fed up with British Airways. So the customer proposition had to be an honest one which we knew could be satisfied.' The third issue comprised the trade unions that had given BA's chief executive a fair amount of grief. Bob Ayling had experienced a damaging and expensive industrial battle with cabin crew, which culminated in a three-day strike: 'I made it clear to Barbara from the very beginning that this was not going to be a non-union business. That had no future. It had to be a unionised business, but with the relationship between the management and the unions, from Day One, set up on a completely different and new basis.'

As a number of US airlines have painfully found with their own low-cost offshoots, it is far better to start from scratch than to try to squeeze significant savings from an existing airline operation. Barbara Cassani had discovered this five years earlier.

In 1992, Dan-Air was heading for a corporate crash. The Gatwick-based charter airline had diversified into a network of scheduled flights at an inopportune time. In the financial gloom that followed the Gulf War it was bleeding cash. As Dan-Air teetered on the brink, British Airways bought the scheduled part of the failing airline for a pound. The buyer gained a ready-made European route network, and a large number of staff whose pay and conditions were different from those at BA. Cassani was brought into the team charged with bringing the two operations together.

Bizarre as it may sound, British Airways has always struggled to make money at Gatwick. The basic problem is that BA's costs at the Sussex airport are almost as high as at Heathrow, yet passengers are not prepared to pay as much for flights. The usual rule, on otherwise identical routes, is that revenues are 20 per cent higher from Heathrow than Gatwick. BA's repertoire from Gatwick has always been a bit of a ragbag. When the airline amalgamated its existing network with that of British Caledonian – Freddie Laker's old business – it was left with an untidy mix of routes: an unwieldy collection of domestic, European and long-haul flights that collectively served as a pretty good definition for the word 'motley'. They had grown up in an arbitrary manner, with no sense of underlying strategy. You could fly in from Jersey and transfer to Genoa or Atlanta, but for anything more ambitious it was usually necessary to travel around the M25 to Heathrow. To succeed, the Sussex airport needed more routes and a lower cost base. That was what the young American and her team were told to construct from the remains of Dan-Air.

One reason BA had rescued the company was the prospect of acquiring flight crews with whom it could drive a hard bargain and thereby reduce costs in line with the lower yields that could be achieved at Gatwick. But the takeover of Dan-Air ignored the human dimension. As Cassani says, employees were not thrilled to be told, 'You should be really happy you have jobs, because your company was just about to go out of business, and by the way, you'll be wearing BA uniforms and we're going to cut your pay by 20 per cent, and that's just life.' Shortly after the takeover, I flew from Gatwick to Vienna on a former Dan-Air jet with ex-Dan-Air crew. Unprompted, the lead stewardess spent half the flight telling me how bitter she and her colleagues felt about their treatment by the new owners. Today, Cassani recognises the problem in telling staff, 'You have to deliver the same service, you have to work just as hard as the people at Heathrow, but tough luck. You're down at Gatwick.' Ill feeling prevailed for some time, but BA relented on its original plan and raised pay for its short-haul crew based at Gatwick.

Cassani now says, 'As I went through my career, there were a number of experiences where I thought, "If I had the chance to start something, I would never do it this way."'

She got the chance to do it her way five years later.

'The thing that excited me was the opportunity to start up a low-cost airline – that had really, really, really low costs.' But Barbara Cassani was far from certain she would succeed. She told herself, 'I'm not going to waste my time on a business that isn't worthwhile. If I don't think you can make money on it, I'm not going to set up another basket-case airline that is always going to need to be bailed out.' But two months into the operation, Cassani was convinced it would work. She had settled on Stansted as the base for the operation (the airline still cheekily makes the claim that the Essex terminal is the most convenient airport for the City of London). She had begun headhunting. 'I had a very profound sense that I could find the right people to do this well, to be safe and secure, to have operational robustness.' Cassani brought in a senior management team that bore little resemblance to a traditional airline – except operationally, where she (and Ayling) demanded blue-chip candidates; Ed Winter, the chief operating officer, is a former captain with a vast amount of experience. For a no-frills airline, an absolutely key position is the sales and marketing director. Cynical prospective customers (and a sceptical press) have to be convinced about a new carrier's proposition. The position was filled by a first-generation Anglo-Italian named David Magliano, who was at the time masterminding the Ford advertising account.

Most of the established no-frills airlines chorused disapproval at the new arrival. Leading the barrage of condemnation was Stelios of easyJet, though his version of events is starkly at odds with that of BA's chief executive:

Bob Ayling, says Stelios, 'was the first executive to believe in us'. One year after easyJet's maiden flight, he says, the two airline bosses met at an aviation conference in New York. 'I wasn't speaking, I was only attending,' says Stelios. 'Who would invite me to speak in those days?' Ayling was one of the speakers. After the presentation, Stelios approached him, and asked if he had heard of easyJet. 'He said, "Of course I've heard of you! You run a great company. Come over for a cup of coffee."' Back in Britain, says Stelios, he arranged an appointment at British Airways' headquarters, at the time a grim 60s office block next to Hatton Cross Tube station called Speedbird House. His account is that the meeting lasted an hour. Stelios says, 'His parting shot was, "Do you think BA and your company can do something together?" So like what? "Like invest in it, because we believe it's a separate sector. And I believe that you've cracked it." ' The rest, says Stelios, is history. BA sent people into easyJet to take a look at the operation, as any firm considering a big investment would do. Three months later, Stelios says he received a letter saying that the giant airline was no longer interested. 'And Go was invented.'

Bob Ayling has a radically different recollection of events: 'Yes, I did meet Stelios in New York, fleetingly, and yes I had admiration for what he was doing in the industry, but the idea of an investment was theirs. They approached British Airways. I can't remember if it was direct or through an intermediary. Anyway, one of my colleagues had some very preliminary discussions with them, which we decided not to proceed with. That's the end of the story. It's rather a dull one.'

Stelios called Go 'a photocopy of the easyJet business plan'. No one can copyright a concept like no-frills airlines. But the easyJet boss was incensed that British Airways, the dominant force in UK aviation, was able to sponsor a subsidiary that could attack the rest of the field. He believed the airline was using the BA connection to get favourable terms on financing aircraft, yet protesting its independence from the parent company. 'Go has been given permission by BA to lose £29 million,' Stelios asserted, 'and then close in three years having put its rivals out of business.'

The Godfather of low-cost flying had urged legal action in a telephone call. 'The phone rang in our downmarket Luton office,' says Stelios. 'I picked it up. "Hello, my name is Freddie Laker, and I just wanted to tell you, that you're doing a great job and you should sue the bastards." I was chuffed. I arranged to meet him immediately, at a hotel in Victoria.'

Encouraged by Sir Freddie, Stelios accused BA of using its commercial muscle to support Go in a bid to drive competitors out of business. Bob Ayling calls that argument 'silly', comparing the £25 million investment with other industries. 'Look at any other sector – motor car manufacturing, or software development or new media businesses – there, the seed capital's enormous. Twenty-five million quid is a drop in the ocean.' And Cassani is equally vituperative. 'Did easyJet benefit by being owned by a guy with a shipping company? Yeah, they probably did. So did we benefit from BA backing? Yeah, sure we did. The question that was debated in the various lawsuits from easyJet was that cross-subsidisation was unfair. I have been very happy to defend Go's activities, and therefore BA's, at any time. And I think it was very marked that easyJet's lawsuit against BA with respect to Go – while I think it's still pending – has basically been made redundant since Go began making money on its own account. We're now profitable. So it's a dead issue from my perspective.' Five months after the Go launch, Stelios flew to Brussels to meet European competition officials to argue his case that Go constituted unfair competition aboard a specially prepared easyJet aircraft with STOP BA STOP GO emblazoned on the side, like the NO WAY BA/AA message on Virgin Atlantic planes. 'None of these complaints made any headway,' says Ayling. 'Presumably if there had been any merit in them they would have done.' Stelios still believes the legal action warned BA as to its future conduct in supporting its low-cost offspring. Ryanair's view of the new arrival was more benign than easyJet's. 'Go did the industry a favour because it was the love child of BA,' say Tim Jeans. Hitherto, he says, 'It was basically the Paddies and the Greeks playing at the low fares game, before BA turned up and gave it some respectability. So it gave it that stamp of credibility that the industry needed.'

'We were a completely separate team,' says Barbara Cassani, though resources from BA were brought in – some of them on the insistence of Bob Ayling, who says, 'The safety systems that were put in at Go were put in under the very close supervision of the BA safety managers.' The cabin crew were recruited by BA personnel staff, and trained at the BA facility at Cranebank, near Heathrow. But, says Cassani, 'We didn't take anything from BA and simply adapt it for Go. Nothing.'

Cassani was spending a lot of time and energy thinking about easyJet, too. But unlike Stelios, she conducted focus groups.

'At the time easyJet was perceived to be too orange for most people. They've really moved on – as everyone has – and become a lot more acceptable to everyone in the marketplace. Five years ago it wasn't. I can remember doing focus groups when customers said, "I really don't want to fly on an aircraft that has a phone number on it." And it really seems ludicrous in today's day and age when we whack our URL on everything but at the time it wasn't. So I thought, "There's something going on, customers are trying to tell us something they can't articulate." '

As well as in the UK, market research was conducted in all the prospective destination countries around Europe. Cassani says that each nationality had its own concerns. 'In Germany, them saying "I find the orange thing very disconcerting" meant "I don't want it to fall out of the sky." In Italy, the response to credit card bookings was, "I don't want to give you my credit card because then the man down the street can sell the number." '

One result of the research was that Go decided to break the no-frills tradition, from Southwest to easyJet, of spending as little as possible on design. Instead of a colour scheme and a logo that looks like a failed first-year graphic art project, Cassani invested heavily in a brand that demonstrated no-frills planes need not look awful. 'I did not want my cabin crew wearing a jacket that said, "I'm an easy crew member". That is anathema to what we're about. Our people are professionals. We wanted to create a brand that was modern and simple and inviting. And a service style that was friendly and not stuffy but professional.' Pointedly, the airline's publicity promised, 'We are a different proposition from the other low-cost airlines. Our cabin staff are trained to the highest standard and our food is better. Customers have to pay for it but instead of being given a can of fizzy pop and a bag of crisps, they can have real coffee from a cafetière and a selection of excellent pastries.' It was this emphasis that led Tim Jeans of Ryanair to observe that, 'Go is the low-cost airline for the middle classes.' Cassani ripostes: 'In some ways it's a good description of why we appeal to virtually everyone. The only aspect is that in Britain when you describe people as part of a class, some are excluded. In an American definition, everyone from the richest businessman to the poorest describes themselves as middle class.'

Choosing a middle-class name took time. The working title, Blue Sky, had been acquired along with British Caledonian in 1988. For a while, the favourite was The Bus, which has echoes of Sir Freddie Laker's mission to make a transatlantic flight as easy as getting on a train. But Cassani did not wish to be known as 'chief executive of the bus', and the name did not research as positively as the shortest airline name the world has ever known: Go.

It took three years of lobbying before the airline could procure the two-letter code; before that, it was OG, which led to confusion in Copenhagen because in Danish 'og' means 'no'. But the airline managed to acquire a catchy phone number in the same way as easyJet had done: 0845 60 54321. After the 0845 prefix denoting a local-rate call, the next two digits are intended to look like GO, before the 5-4-3-2-1 countdown that suggests launch is imminent.

Throughout the development of the airline, Cassani was so hands-on that she even wrote the announcements that you hear when boarding a Go flight. 'I don't want any airline language, I don't want any disembarking. When do you disembark in your life? You get off things, you get out of your car, off a train.' She believes that the jargon generated around airlines 'is there to develop a barrier between employees and customers. And employees quite like it, one of the reasons they like uniforms and language is to keep people at a distance. I wanted to get rid of that, I wanted our employees to look at our cabin like their living room, as if inviting guests in. Therefore you want people to hit the call button, you want people to ask you things because that means you've created an environment where people feel comfortable enough to do that.' The people who would be answering the call button were drawn from a wide range of businesses: insurance call centres, shops, schools. A significant number had previous experience with long-haul flying, which they had given up after starting families. One of the original applicants for cabin crew was Luke Deals, a thirty-year-old radio journalist, keen to shake off office politics. 'They were interviewing hundreds of people. We were all gathered in Enterprise House on a Sunday afternoon.' The selectors, he says, were looking for people who were 'Outgoing, competent and confident'. He clearly was, because he was called the following day, invited back for a second interview and given the job. 'The pay was dire, but I thought that if it all went tits up I'm sure I could go back to journalism.' (Which he has subsequently done.)

The training course was, he says, 'Intense but fun. It was done by British Airways, so you knew you were going to get a good grounding. We had to drag bodies around in the swimming pool, and we were put on the chutes of the 767 simulator. You have to know about heart disease, pregnancy, how to deal with an irate passenger. But nothing prepares you for the day you're faced with 148 rugby fans going up to Edinburgh.'

Initially, he says, the atmosphere was 'like a big family'. When the first 737 arrived, 'everyone was excited by it'. So were some people over at Luton airport. When the first three destinations, and the date of the maiden flight, were announced, Go's most vocal rival felt comfortable enough to block-book ten seats on the first Go flight, from Stansted to Rome. Any airline boss cherishes its maiden flight: just ask Branson or Stelios. Some people have likened the first departure to an act of sexual consummation at the end of an intense courtship. Certainly, one executive described the moment the wheels lift from the tarmac as 'orgasmic – no, actually it was better than sex'. It is the sort of moment that needs to be celebrated with people to whom you are close, which is why Barbara Cassani invited her husband, Guy, and five-year-old daughter, Lauren, on board. She did not invite Stelios and his staff. But he gatecrashed the party anyway, and Cassani was expecting him.

'I'm convinced that if Stelios hadn't such a distinctive name, we would have taken them by surprise,' says Tony Anderson, the easyJet executive who bought the flights. 'I booked the seats in three separate calls. The itinerary for Stelios's booking came back with a handwritten note from Barbara Cassani saying, "looking forward to seeing you on board".'

There is no law against buying a seat on a rival's inaugural flight, yet some of the easyJet staff were uneasy. 'The day before the first flight,' says Stelios, 'we had a marketing meeting in the office and half the people defected. They said, "No, you're going to be arrested. It's not possible to go on somebody else's inaugural flight." So I said, "If people don't want to come, fine." We ended up with seven people on board and three defections.' When they planned the details of the public relations assault, Stelios made two rules: 'We have to be light-hearted and we have to be giving some things away. So we put on the orange boiler suits so we were making a fool of ourselves, and appeared non-threatening, and gave away free tickets, which always works.'

Across at Stansted, Barbara Cassani was anxious. 'We realised there was a group of easyJet people quite early on. I guess it was inevitable. My first consideration was I don't want them to do anything that was unsafe. I was concerned about what they would do. Once I was convinced that was fine, I thought I'd put on a big smile and play with them.'

The mood on board was surprisingly friendly, considering that the previous week easyJet had sought an injunction against Go's plans, arguing that British Airways was abusing its dominant position in the market. Once Go was airborne, the other airlines took their gloves off, too. The immediate response from Debonair was to undercut Go's fare to Rome by £1; Richard Branson's Virgin Express sliced off a fiver, though passengers had to change planes at Brussels. The same pattern emerged at Milan: KLM UK knocked £1 off the Go fare, while Virgin Express again undercut the new airline by £5. More seriously, the large Scandinavian airline SAS weighed in with a £99 ticket to Copenhagen, including meals and drinks. When the Stansted–Munich route was launched, Lufthansa started its own service from the Essex airport – and undercut Go's fare by £2, while still offering all the frills. At this point, it was time for the no-frills airline's lawyers to complain about predatory pricing. When that action failed, Go abandoned the Munich route, though it has since returned to the network and Lufthansa has pulled out.

Go's initial route structure was aimed at destinations that could support a good mix of business and leisure travel. These markets have different characteristics, and when one is weak the other tends to be strong. Milan and Copenhagen had previously been off the no-frills map; Rome was served from Luton by Debonair, but often only after a stop en route. Go's routes to Bologna and Naples serve Italian destinations some distance away from the Ryanair airports in Italy, while its Venice flights go direct to the city's main Marco Polo airport rather than the more distant Treviso. Munich and Lyon are business destinations that also served numerous ski resorts. Interestingly, all Go's routes were already served from Heathrow or Gatwick by British Airways.

The first casualty of Go's expansion was KLM UK (formerly Air UK), which for years had been the only substantial airline serving Stansted. Loyalty and perseverance counted for nothing; once Go started flying from the Essex airport to Glasgow and Edinburgh, the full-service airline retired hurt from all its Anglo-Scottish routes. It now flies from Stansted only to Amsterdam, as a feeder service for its parent, KLM; other routes have been abandoned or transferred to the no-frills Buzz operation.

In July 1998, Go strayed into territory occupied by another low-cost carrier. It began flying from Stansted to Lisbon, a route already flown from Gatwick by AB Airlines. Within a few months, the competition had gone out of business. And soon after that, Go abandoned the route to its parent British Airways and Air Portugal. Debonair, damaged by the new competition on its flight to Rome, followed AB Airlines in closing down shortly afterwards. By early in 2000, Bob Ayling had parted company with BA; the airline's board allowed him the honour of presiding over the opening of the British Airways London Eye (the 'Millennium Wheel'), his lasting legacy for London, and removed him the following day.

Down at Gatwick, meanwhile, the structure that Cassani had painfully tried to put together after the Dan-Air takeover was unravelling. Ayling's successor as BA's chief executive, Rod Eddington, lost little time in reversing the decision to treat Gatwick as a hub airport. One of his first decisions was to cut back services from the Sussex airport savagely, to reduce the duplication of routes from Heathrow. Looking back, says Cassani, 'It was probably a failed strategy. BA bought Dan-Air in order to gain short-haul routes there, to create a hub down at Gatwick. And that's being pulled apart now.'

Go, too, would have to go, said the new BA boss. The airline had lost £20m in each of its first two years, but was moving smartly into profit. So why would British Airways want to put its high-achieving corporate child up for adoption? Why, especially, when Stelios had pronounced that 'In ten years' time, all aviation in Europe will be no frills'? While Bob Ayling had seen Go as an essential long-term investment to ensure that British Airways was strongly represented in the no-frills sector, his successor thought otherwise. 'Go is an excellent airline with a fine management and workforce,' said Eddington. 'As a no-frills operator, however, it simply does not fit in our full-service strategy.'

Few tears were shed at Waterside, the palatial new headquarters of British Airways. Barbara Cassani had made plenty of enemies within BA. Flight crew were alarmed that her cost-savings would be replicated at the parent airline. Marketing people responsible for selling Europe saw Go eating away at their earnings. BA had enjoyed a monopoly of the London–Naples route until its no-frills subsidiary came along and slashed fares. To Milan, BA's full economy fare was £443, while Go came in with fares at a flat £100 return. Plenty of BA staff saw 'cannibalisation' of the parent's passengers as an inevitable conclusion: the parent airline would fill fewer seats and earn a lower average fare for each ticket that it did sell. 'We were pouring money into a company that was stealing our customers and reducing our yields,' says one insider. 'It was mad. Go had to be closed down or sold.' With some estimates that Go was worth half a billion pounds, Eddington chose the latter course.

No one had sold a prospering low-cost airline in Britain before, so valuing the company properly was a tricky business. Initially, the City believed Go would fetch at least £300m. 'Bad PR management by BA,' says Cassani. 'We hadn't even announced our first profit figures. They left that impression.'

For a time, there was talk that easyJet would take over Go. After months of negotiations, Go was sold to the venture capitalists, 3i, for £100 million. This was, as it turned out, just enough to save British Airways from incurring a loss in BA's first post-11 September financial results. 'We were able to extricate Go from the BA network with relative ease,' says Cassani, 'as a result of the way we set up the company, which made it very easy to separate.' The ink was barely dry on the deal before the no-frills upstart began biting the hand that had nurtured it, by pouring scorn on BA's latest round of World Offers. Go abruptly stopped advertising its connection with BA, then publicly rubbished the value of those deals. Other connections were quickly broken; the free flight privileges Go's staff enjoyed from British Airways were soon cancelled. A hitherto-unbroken no-frills rule was transgressed, too. In the final few years of the twentieth century, there had been plenty of room for expansion for the large no-frills carriers, Go, easyJet, and Ryanair. Airlines did not need to trespass on each other's turf. Then Go decided to start flying to Nice, one of the most established destinations on the easyJet network. 'We've been flying to Nice for five and a half years,' said Stelios, 'and in that time we've seen a number of competitors come and go. I don't know how long Go will last on that route.'

Cassani is confident it will be a long time. 'Could easyJet be making more money if we didn't fly to Nice? Maybe. But that's what competition's about. If there's a distinct market between Stansted and Nice, it's my job to fill it. It isn't my job to see if it offends easyJet's sensibilities.' In the slanging match that ensued, Go made much of the extent to which Luton–Nice fares on easyJet could rise. Michael O'Leary of Ryanair watched from the sidelines. 'It's ridiculous – like two Jack Russells fighting over a bone,' he told me. 'They're having a row over who had the highest low fares.' His airline claims to be the only one to guarantee to have the lowest fares, though since Ryanair's nearest destination to Nice was Genoa across in Italy, this was immaterial. 'Who charges the highest low fares?' O'Leary asked me, rhetorically. 'Who cares?' But when Go announced flights to Dublin, the home base of its biggest rival, Ryanair, O'Leary reacted with more than mockery – and the new financial backers of Go suddenly found they were caught up in the mother of all no-frills fares wars.

Cassani had no intention of competing directly with Ryanair on its seven daily services from Stansted to the Irish capital. At the time, though, the main airports for Scotland's two biggest cities were linked to Dublin only by Aer Lingus. Sensing an opportunity, Go announced flights from Edinburgh and Glasgow. But if Cassani thought Ryanair would sit back and let Go move into its territory without a fight, she was sorely mistaken. Not only did Ryanair immediately cut fares on the existing Dublin–Prestwick service, which served Glasgow; it also launched flights from Edinburgh, which previously was off the Ryanair map.

Tim Jeans, sales and marketing director for Ryanair, says he was amazed at Go's move. 'I could lie awake for hours at night and wonder why they did that. Imagine the scenario: you're just newly enfranchised, the umbilical has been cut from your BA parent, you have £100 million worth of 3i's cash in your wallet, and what's the first thing you do, you go and blow X many millions, having a head to head with the biggest, baddest, boldest bully on the block. It beggars belief really that they would do that. I think they thought that we would have a fight from a distance in Prestwick and not follow them into Edinburgh. They were wrong.'

For three months in the autumn of 2001, the fare between Dublin and Scotland fell as low as £10 including taxes and charges, which meant the no-frills rivals were selling every seat at a loss. Aer Lingus, which was sinking ever deeper into a financial morass and saw its monopoly on a couple of handy routes smashed, was dismayed. Cassani was not. 'For all these routes – and any route we've been flying for over a year – where we're flying against another low-cost airline we're making money. And at the end of the day, that's what we're here to do. There will be some instances where we double up and it doesn't work. But it's very difficult to predict. It's only when you start observing customer behaviour and whether or not your competitors are behaving rationally that you know whether it makes sense.' Rational or not, Ryanair's behaviour forced Go out of Dublin in March 2002, after six months of losses.

The planes that previously flew to the Irish capital had to be moved somewhere. Cassani and her team decided to open a third UK base, at a venue where no-frills competition was absent: East Midlands, the airport serving Nottingham, Derby and Leicester. Well, there was no competition when Go announced the move – but within weeks a brand-new rival emerged. The local travelling public had waited years for a no-frills airline, and then two came along at once. East Midlands has long been the home of BMI, formerly British Midland. Like other traditional airlines, BMI had been financially hit by no-frills flying. Suddenly, its home base – at which it held a near-monopoly of scheduled flying – was to see competition move in with high-frequency, low-cost flights. BMI responded by deploying some of the excess capacity that had lain idle since 11 September to start up a new no-frills airline, BMIbaby. Its route network was remarkably close to the Mediterranean destinations that Go was targeting. The airline said it had been planning the move for a year, and that its announcement so close to that of Go's was purely coincidental. But as she faces up to yet another scrap, Cassani remains confident and cheerful.

She is working twelve hours a day for one of Europe's fastest-growing airlines, and loving it. 'The reason I like the airline business is because the problems and opportunities are more interesting than anywhere else I can think of. You've got huge assets to manage with your aircraft. You've got huge groups of people to manage, and then finally you've got this wonderful consumer marketing challenge. It's a business everyone can relate to. And I think you either enjoy that, or it wears you down and you exit to selling widgets or something.' She is genuinely evangelical about her company, which she rates as a cut above the competition: 'I really love this idea of having your cake and eating it too – the idea that you could find a way of giving people something that was just that little bit more, but still very true to being low cost and being safe and secure. In Go terms that means, "You're not putting your life and your savings at risk by booking or travelling with us." We have our good days and bad days, but I think we achieve that more than most airlines do, and I'm very proud of that. But I think the second we think we're doing it well, and we stop trying – forget it, we'll have lost it.'

And that launch flight?

'I'll be forever grateful for Stelios,' insists Cassani. 'Ironically we ended up with far more publicity than we would have got otherwise. And one of the orange boiler-suit wearers is now working for us.'

10. 'IT'LL NEVER FLY HERE'

'Any new airline has an automatic advantage over any old airline'

TONY WHEELER, FOUNDER OF LONELY PLANET

'You cannot form a low-fare airline simply by spray-painting your planes yellow. Buzz just aren't at the races'

TIM JEANS, RYANAIR

BUZZ FLIGHT 2584: STANSTED–VIENNA

'Three people had an idea,' went the original Buzz slogan. It was intended to convey the idea that a trio of three imaginative souls had dreamed up an airline that would deliver what others did not. But was it a good idea? There is plenty of time to consider that question while I wait for Buzz flight 2584 from Stansted to Vienna, on what asserts itself to be 'the low-cost airline that gives you more'. With no-frills airlines like Southwest, easyJet and Ryanair showing how successful the concept can be, it is no surprise that entrepreneurs around the world have been tempted to set up low-cost airlines – with varying degrees of success. But Buzz was the invention of necessity.

From the departure gate where I am sitting, on the patch of terminal turf that KLM UK used to call its own, I have almost enough fingers and toes to count the passengers for this morning's flight. Twenty-one, all told, barely enough to fill one in five of the seats on the BAe 146 – the same type of aircraft that Franco Mancassola calls 'a mistaken choice', which helped bring about the downfall of his airline, Debonair.

If everyone has paid the same as me – £40 for the one-way hop – the grand total of revenue doesn't even reach a grand: £840. The Chancellor of the Exchequer immediately trousers £105 in Air Passenger Duty without the need to get out of bed at around 4 a.m., which is what the rest of us have had to do. The airport authorities at Vienna are set to collect even more, probably half the remaining total. There is precious little for much else, such as the wage bill for the two pilots and three cabin crew, whose workload for the day involves just this gentle trip from Stansted to Vienna and back.

KLM UK, son of Air UK, son of Air Anglia, son of Norfolk Airways, began flying from Stansted to Scotland decades ago (the airline's latest incarnation is unable to say just how long). It had stoically provided a scheduled airline presence at the Essex airport through the years when no one much else apart from Cubana wanted to fly there. The customers, most of them from the northern and eastern fringes of London, Essex and East Anglia, were loyal. Air UK was an innovative third force in scheduled European flight, behind British Airways and British Midland, now BMI. By 1997 the airline had built up a flourishing network of flights from Stansted to all the leading European business centres – Paris, Brussels, Frankfurt, Milan – plus domestic links to Aberdeen, Edinburgh, Glasgow and Inverness.

The Dutch airline, KLM, bought up Air UK and superimposed its initials. It wanted to secure feeder services to its hub in Amsterdam, and benefit from the sizeable domestic earnings. So popular were the airline's Anglo-Scottish flights that KLM UK began flying to the two largest Scottish cities from London City airport.

Then some strangers showed up and started throwing their 737s around. Ryanair had begun its British low-cost operations in Luton, but the Essex airport provided a better deal and had plenty of room to expand, the only other significant tenant being KLM UK. The incumbent was further squeezed when a new neighbour, Go, arrived at Stansted. Go moved into the suite of offices opposite Ryanair in Stansted's Enterprise House and began flying in May 1998. While the new arrival's first tranche of routes seemed aimed at the heart of Debonair, once domestic flights began KLM UK was in the firing line, with its lucrative services to Glasgow and Edinburgh under attack. Virgin Express, Richard Branson's European air operation, briefly helped to eat away at the customer base. The Dutch-owned airline was also hit by easyJet's cut-price flights from nearby Luton to Aberdeen and Inverness. Soon, not a single service to Scotland remained; KLM UK had thrown in the tartan towel. On the services to Paris and Brussels, increased competition from Eurostar trains depleted passenger numbers. And if that was not bad enough, an alliance with Alitalia went sour after a few angry months of cohabitation. The airline had been forced into a corner. As the KLM UK network diminished, and it became clear the new no-frills competition could not be beaten, the company decided to join them.

Buzz was felt to be the best hope for the future. The new airline was unveiled four weeks to the day after Debonair collapsed. Cheap flights were promised to six destinations in Germany, France, Italy and Austria, starting on the third day of the year 2000. Some loyal KLM UK passengers were not impressed. They saw what was happening as a mere rebranding of existing routes like Paris, Milan and Frankfurt as no-frills flights. They would no longer get the hot breakfasts and frequent-flyer points to which they had become accustomed.

The existing low-cost airlines lined up to offer a barrage of hostile spin to greet the launch of Buzz. Tim Jeans of Ryanair said, 'It sounds like Debonair mark two, flying to the wrong airports with the wrong kind of aircraft.' Even the names of the airline's restricted and flexible products, 'Done Deal' and 'Open Deal' respectively, attracted criticism. 'They're a joke,' said one rival. 'Punters are going to think "I've been done", and others are going to assume that Open Deal means it's an open ticket they can change without penalty or get a refund, which they can't. Some people might even think they haven't got a reservation.' A year on, Buzz had abandoned the 'deals' policy in favour of the easyJet one-way pricing system. At the same time, I was discussing route opportunities with a marketing man, who was very keen on the possibilities for south-west France. At one point I said, 'But Buzz already flies to Poitiers.'

'They do at the moment,' he smiled.

Tony Comacho, commercial director of Buzz, has one of the sharpest brains in the airline business. He also has some of the bluntest planes: the British Aerospace 146 is small, fat and slow. 'Is the 146 the right one? No, in the long term.' He didn't order the eight in his fleet: they were what was left when KLM stripped out the unwanted routes. But he says that the aircraft's small size means Buzz can develop routes that would not be feasible for an all-737 operation. His aim is to 'use what we have sensibly'. Besides the eight 146s, he has two 737s. The advantage that the former have is the ability to land on runways too short for most planes. The summer 2002 programme saw flights to small airports like Limoges and La Rochelle, and two flights a day to the Normandy city of Rouen – a level of service that is easier to sustain with a small aircraft than with a 737. But these are just some of the latest routes and tactics that Buzz has tried in its brief life.

'We will never suggest that all our seats are available at the very lowest price,' said Comacho when Buzz was launched. 'We will always show both the lowest and highest prices available.' Three people might have had that bright idea, but the pledge did not last long. Neither did most of the new routes: Hamburg, Lyon, Helsinki and Vienna have come and gone, leaving a rump of German business destinations plus a French and Spanish network based almost entirely around secondary airports; the exceptions are Paris Charles de Gaulle, Marseilles and Bordeaux.

'Final call for Buzz flight 2430 to Berlin. Would passenger Clemence proceed immediately to gate 37, where your aircraft is fully boarded and awaiting your arrival.' If the aircraft is fully boarded, that implies Mr or Ms Clemence is already on board. At least the Buzz ground staff show some respect for the language of the country to which they are flying. The Spanish city of Jerez is pronounced, meticulously, as he-RETH; were Ryanair to fly there, I daresay one or two of their staff might pronounce the destination as DJErezz, doing no favours for the Spanish passengers.

Still no sign of any action on the Vienna flight. Meanwhile, boarding begins for KLM UK's flight 2000 to Amsterdam. For their extra cash, passengers get to use a jetway to board without further exposure to the elements. The Amsterdam service is the last vestige of KLM UK at Stansted. The route is seen as sufficiently high-yield to justify retaining the breakfasts and frequent-flyer points. Michael O'Leary of Ryanair believes that 'KLM UK is one of those airlines that has been taking everyone for a ride for far too long.'

I wish I could be taken for a ride. The Vienna flight number shares the same two-letter prefix – UK – as the Amsterdam departure, but, so far, it does not appear to have the benefit of an aircraft to operate it. 'Very last and final boarding call for KLM UK flight 2000,' which has apparently also fully boarded and is awaiting immediate departure.

Unlike us. About twenty minutes after the departure time for Vienna, we are finally invited to board. There is not too much of a crush getting on to the aircraft. It has seen many better days. The decor is a bilious combination of purple, yellow and lime green. The carpet is scuffed and worn, as on Ryanair's elderly Boeings, the ones bought second-hand from Lufthansa and Britannia. Just as with those aircraft, there is a sense of confusion about which airline, exactly, I am about to fly with. The same staff purport to work for two separate companies. One of the cabin crew is wearing a KLM UK lapel badge and has 'Buzz' embroidered on a pocket.

'You cannot form a low-fare airline simply by spray painting your planes yellow, and keeping everything else the same,' says Ryanair's Tim Jeans. 'Same crew, same pilot agreements, same airports, fundamentally the same cost base. They're just not at the races.' Barbara Cassani of Go says, 'They created a low-cost airline by creating a new brand name. It may be better than what was there previously. It's not a sustainable business model.'

'I would call this a medium-cost airline,' counters Comacho, adding – with some understatement – that 'Our first year was more difficult than we expected.'

When I first boarded a Buzz flight to Vienna, two months after the airline began, the BAe146 got only as far as Belgium, at which point the pilots were so worried by a technical problem that the jet turned around and flew back to Stansted. Eighteen months and several unanswered letters to Buzz customer relations later, I paid up again and booked on the same flight. Barbara Cassani was urging others to sign up for the route to Vienna, too: 'It's the biggest public service they are doing, subsidising people to a monopoly airport, flying them there for £40 return when at least half of that is going to the airport.' This time, the aircraft is set to go the distance. By the time I tucked into my chicken with pasta and poured the first cup of coffee from a cafetière, we were already over Germany. The navigation charges, which each country levies for its air traffic control systems, were eating into the revenue for the flight even more quickly than I was devouring the pasta.

'On Vienna and Lyon we overestimated the potential for attracting business travel,' says Buzz's Camacho. To make matters (much) worse, both Ryanair and Go were piling on capacity with new planes and new routes, many of them taking traffic that Buzz might have expected to enjoy. 'The landscape has changed so much since January 2000,' says Comacho, but he maintains 2001 was 'a very good year' and that it put Buzz 'back on expectations'. (The parent company, KLM, does not reveal in its accounts the performance of the no-frills subsidiary.) In the summer of 2001, says Comacho, the French routes were achieving load factors in the mid-70s – in other words, selling three out of every four seats. For the third year of the airline's existence, the Buzz fleet has remained basically the same, but a new collection of destinations has been introduced. The unfamiliar French cities of Brest and Toulon find themselves on the route network, and Buzz is also operating domestic services from them – the first no-frills flights within France.

The French traveller's gain is the Austrian's loss. It is an historic moment for Vienna. In half-an-hour's time, the Austrian capital will lose its only no-frills flight, and join the 35 per cent of Europe's population that has no easy access to low-cost aviation. Of the remainder, 55 per cent can fly only to London. Only one in ten European citizens is within easy reach of an airport with multiple destinations on no-frills flights. When the flight touches down at Schwechat airport, no one seems to be remotely concerned. Buzz's daily flight was of little consequence to the airport authorities. They have a handy near-monopoly of aviation in the region; Bratislava, across the border in Slovakia, has so little air traffic that many Slovakians travel by bus to Vienna airport to fly from there. Even travellers from Budapest are bused to the Austrian capital's airport. The closest any no-frills airline gets is Ryanair's flight to Salzburg, but that city is a four-hour rail journey away at the other end of Austria.

No-frills flying is concentrated on airlines based in North America and the British Isles. You might be tempted to ask, if no-frills is so good,

'I discovered very quickly this was not going to be glamorous' – Stelios Haji-Ioannou, chairman of easyJet

Above Taking the message to the skies: easyJet protests about British Airways' decision to start up a no-frills subsidiary, Go

Right The Raitz stuff: Vladimir Raitz, inventor of the package holiday, relaxes on the Med between charter flights

Right 'Hard work and luck' – how Barbara Cassani got where she is today, chief executive of Go

Below Sir Freddie Laker, founder of Skytrain and Travel Personality of the Year for five straight years from 1977

Sir Richard Branson christens the first Australian Virgin Blue 737

'We were very, very, very close to making it' – Franco Mancassola, chairman of Debonair

Each Boeing 737 costs around $30m, plus extra for the seats and toilets

bmibaby.com
the airline with tiny fares

Above Another no-frills airline, another name that shuns capital letters

Herb Kelleher of Southwest. Daddy of them all.

'Nobody, but nobody, will match our airfares. And, if they do, we'll simply lower ours straight away' – Michael O'Leary, chief executive of Ryanair

Left Ryanair's response to the trauma of 11 September: one million seats at under £10 (plus taxes, fees and charges)

Right Buzz's response to the no-frills competition: a summer 2002 schedule that includes nine new routes from Stansted to France

why has it not taken hold in every region of the planet, not least continental Europe? The answer is that some have tried, with limited success. KLM has a low-key operation called Basiq Air, based in Amsterdam, in addition to its investment in Buzz.

Buzz was forced into existence by the new competition. But on St George's Day 1996, no one coerced Richard Branson into buying a majority stake of an ailing airline, EuroBelgian Airlines, which soon became Virgin Express. Buzz's tribulations are mild compared with the traumas endured by the surviving staff of Virgin Express. With a hub at Brussels, the airline aims to offer a high-frequency, low-fare service. When I first tried Virgin Express, it was a no-frequency service. In October 1998, I turned up at Heathrow for the dawn flight to Brussels. At check-in, I was offered an afternoon train from Waterloo to the Belgian capital, which was not quite what I had in mind. Virgin Express, it transpired, was chronically short of aircraft. Those that were still airborne were being used to fly some desperate Sabena passengers to Brussels; Virgin Express had the contract to operate the Belgian airline's services from Heathrow. Most of the passengers were travelling on from there to elsewhere in Europe, or Africa or Asia, and their connections were looking fragile. I made my excuses and came back the next morning. There was an aircraft, and I was able to check in for it, but after a few more hours in the departure gate – a wait made more entertaining by the arrival of a British Airways crew and passengers expecting to use the same gate for a flight to Berlin – I abandoned the mission. Some weeks later, when I tried again, I made it to Brussels and back nearly on schedule but my bicycle, which I had checked in, set off on its own little tour of Europe.

'It was a mistake,' says Sir Richard Branson. 'We should have actually set it up in the UK.' He had originally considered establishing a no-frills airline in Britain, but concluded that the Virgin Atlantic brand in the UK could be muddled if another Virgin airline were to start up. Besides, the Gatwick–Maastricht route, in Virgin Atlantic colours, had been allowed to lapse. Shortly before the collapse in 1992 of Dan-Air, the charter airline that developed a scheduled network, there were rumours that Virgin would buy the European routes. Nothing came of it, or the UK-based no-frills operation.

'Instead, we bought a small company in Brussels with all the adherent problems, and the cost base was far higher than most low-cost carriers. I think Virgin Express was an example of what not to do.' It looked, no doubt, like a good idea at the time, not least because of a vague plan to share aircraft with Branson's new European package holiday operation,

Virgin Sun. But Virgin Sun obtained its own planes, and anyway the whole Mediterranean holiday operation was sold off to First Choice within a few years. There were problems with aircraft, with staff, and with management, for which a military solution was eventually found.

Neil Burrows is an RAF man. He studied at the aeronautical college at Cranwell, and spent eleven years in the Air Force, 'Before I came to the conclusion that they probably weren't going to make me an air marshal. And so I left and went into civil aviation.' Burrows rapidly scaled the flight deck career ladder from co-pilot to senior training captain, and worked as an inspector for the Civil Aviation Authority. He flew for the ruler of Abu Dhabi for eighteen months, and then became part of the team starting the charter carrier Air 2000. In 2000 (the year, not the airline), he joined Virgin Express as operations director. 'We had a really terrible year,' he says, 'with the tripling of fuel prices, the 30 per cent fall of the euro against the dollar, and overcapacity. This company lost a lot of money.' The page in Virgin Express's annual report entitled 'Year 2000 at a Glance' shows exactly how bloody it was. The airline lost Euro45.5m on its operations – representing a loss of £10 for every passenger on its scheduled flights. It got rid of half of its planes, closed its Irish affiliate and shut down bases at Shannon, Gatwick and Berlin, adding another Euro20m to the loss for the year.

To add to the problems, Swissair had taken a 49.5 per cent interest in the Belgian national carrier, Sabena, and was in the process of doubling capacity at Brussels – 'hammering the market', as Burrows puts it. The VEX code that Virgin Express uses looked ominously appropriate.

Virgin Express's relationship with Sabena was tricky because it had contracts to fly the prime routes to London Heathrow, Barcelona and Rome. That meant Virgin Express had to offer a two-class service with more legroom (and fewer seats), which no low-cost start-up would countenance, in order to match the standards that Sabena passengers had come to expect. In addition, passengers are given meals on all Virgin Express flights. And Virgin Express operates between high-cost, primary airports. In 1998 it made an excursion into traditional no-frills territory at Stansted, but Burrows says, 'The airline went in too late, when other low-cost airlines had got a toehold in there. To have all these low-cost airlines fighting for the same patch meant that you were going to have to stay in there losing quite a lot of money to develop. We didn't have that sort of money to throw at that sort of battle so we beat a retreat.'

The airline's incumbent managing director beat a retreat from Virgin Express; he got a job at Ryanair, which was establishing a hub in Charleroi, south of Brussels. (To try to stymie the new operation, Virgin

Express offered any Irish citizen whose last name was Ryan a free flight to Gatwick.) When Burrows took over in November 2000, and started wielding the hatchet, he was determined that Virgin Express should concentrate on the Belgian market – a difficult proposition, even with the Branson marque. 'It's one of the most valuable assets, to have the Virgin brand on the aircraft. We try to live up to it.'

Some people in aviation don't believe the airline has. Burrows's counterpart at Go, Barbara Cassani, agrees that 'Brussels is a tough place to launch a low-cost airline', but contends that Branson's short-haul operation 'has been an embarrassment to the Virgin Group'. Some passengers boarded Virgin Express jets expecting similar standards to those prevailing on Virgin Atlantic; when these were not forthcoming, a number of unfavourable comments were carried by the media.

Burrows is the man who has to turn around those opinions, along with Virgin Express's finances, helped by a £20m injection from Branson. 'It's very difficult, but not impossible, for us to be low fare – which we are. And the only way we can be low fare, is to be more efficient in the management of our costs to reduce our overheads.' Tim Jeans of Ryanair believes it is a hopeless task: 'They have a vastly high-cost hub in Brussels, a very expensive operation, leased aircraft, and they're trying to get by on some business-class products, some economy traffic, messing around with transfer traffic from London to Copenhagen via Brussels for £49. Even our yields don't sustain that kind of pricing. So they're a long way off salvation in my view.'

Strangely, salvation could come partly thanks to Ryanair, whose Charleroi operation is helping to overcome a perception problem about what no-frills airlines are all about. 'We're a continental airline, not a UK airline, and I'm not sure that the continental public yet understands it,' says Burrows. What the Belgian public certainly understands is that the national airline, Sabena, went spectacularly bust in October 2001. Swissair refused to pump any more cash into it – and the European Commission outlawed the Belgian government propping up an airline that had failed to make money in any of its eighty years of existence.

'We were competing with a company that had no interest in profit,' says Branson. Once Sabena folded, he says, there was 'a fantastic opportunity for Virgin Express to step into their shoes, lower cost-base or lower fares on lots of routes, but the Belgian prime minister decided that they just had to have a state airline. So they basically went and twisted the arms of a couple of hundred businessmen in Belgium, to fund an airline called DAT, which was part of Sabena and was losing an absolute fortune.' DAT began branding itself as 're-connecting Brussels', saying, 'Belgium once again has an airline.' Virgin Express was furious, since it had, de facto, become the national carrier. Furthermore it had lost a lot of money when Sabena collapsed, because its was no longer being paid for the majority of seats on its routes to Heathrow, Rome and Barcelona, which it had operated on behalf of the erstwhile airline. Three days before the end of 2001, Virgin Express revealed it was talking to DAT about setting up a new, business-focused airline for Belgium. Along with the low-cost principles, it appeared that the Virgin Express name would become just another also-flew in the annals of aviation history – one of the many casualties of 2001.

Sir Richard Branson is hoping for better things in Australia. The launch of Virgin Atlantic in June 1984 was a complete success in terms of coverage from the British media. But the launch of Virgin Blue in November 1999 had us completely flummoxed. The cream of Britain's travel journalists – and the rest of us who make up the non-fat milk of that trade – were in the right country at the right time, having assembled in Australia for the Association of British Travel Agents' annual convention at Cairns, in the far north of Queensland. The first any of us heard about Richard Branson's launch of a new airline for Australia was when our news desks in London started calling mobile telephones, demanding to know why we hadn't filed stories about the new airline. No one is quite sure what the collective noun for travel journalists should be (an overbooking?) but it became clear that Branson was 1,500 miles south of us, announcing the birth of his latest venture, an Australian domestic airline known as Virgin Blue – livery: red and white; slogan: 'You're just buying the flying'.

'An enormous country, where everyone has to fly' is what attracted Branson to Australia. The new airline had an uncomfortable birth, with the aircraft sitting on the tarmac at Brisbane airport for several weeks while licensing issues were straightened out. This allowed another airline, the former charter and freight operator, Impulse, to get in ahead and proclaim itself as Australia's third airline. Given that the majority of Australia's population resides in Sydney, Melbourne and the region between them, and that the third-biggest airline market in the world is Melbourne–Sydney, it was in any case an interesting decision to base the new airline in the Queensland capital, Brisbane. Once it was allowed to take off, Virgin Blue had to compete with Impulse as well as the old incumbents of Qantas and Ansett. The Qantas chairman, Geoff Dixon, sniffily dismissed Branson as 'Richard somebody-or-other' on ABC television.

For most of their lives, the two recognised national carriers had enjoyed a comfortable duopoly with only temporary intrusions from short-lived companies such as East-West Airlines. The public loved the sudden outbreak of competition that Virgin Blue and Impulse brought. Fares fell as low as A$39 (about £15) on routes that previously would have cost a minimum of five times as much. When he announced this on the Sydney–Brisbane route in March 2001, Gerry McGowan, the executive chairman of Impulse, promised his airline would 'not allow anyone to interfere with the mission to become the domestic airline price leader and price innovator'. He talked of his 'long-term strategy to ensure the carrier forever breaks the domestic airline duopoly'. Two months later, Impulse was taken over by Qantas, and was effectively shut down less than a year after services began.

One of Australia's most frequent travellers, Tony Wheeler, founder of the guidebook publisher, Lonely Planet, believes the Branson effect has been less than earth-shattering. 'Has Virgin Blue transformed aviation in Australia? Not that I've noticed.' During 2001 he flew domestically on Ansett, Qantas, Virgin Blue and Impulse. 'They were all nice shiny planes, they all got you from A to B without any hassle.'

By the end of that year, the choice was reduced to two carriers. Ansett, Australia's second airline, went bust within hours of the attack on the World Trade Center on 11 September, leaving Virgin Blue as the new number two Australian airline. The Star Alliance (in which Virgin Atlantic's part owner, Singapore Airlines, has a high profile) found itself with a large Australia-sized gap, and there are all kinds of moves to allow a reformed Ansett to take to the skies. 'People are not willing to let go basically,' says Branson. 'Even if Ansett get going again, they're not going to have as low a cost base. We've got the airline with the lowest cost base in the world.'

Lonely Planet's Wheeler is not surprised that Virgin Blue should be prospering where Ansett failed: 'Any new airline has an automatic advantage over any old airline in that they're making new employment agreements which are always better (from the airline viewpoint) than old ones.' These, he says, date back to the days 'when airline pilots were gods (not glorified bus drivers) and flight attendants goddesses (not fast-food servers).'

Branson calls Virgin Blue 'the best investment ever, a startlingly magnificent brand', and believes that 'Virgin Blue will be around in thirty, forty, fifty years. We saved the Australian travelling public A$250 million in the first year – and we made a profit.' Virgin Blue reported strong earnings in February 2002, but also revealed it was in talks with the born-again Ansett management.

Cassani often cites Canada's WestJet as an example of how to do things right. It was started by an Englishman, Clive Beddoe, and three other entrepreneurs based in Calgary. When the airline began operations in 1996 – three months after easyJet launched – it had the by-now-traditional three aircraft. Now it has around thirty, serving twenty destinations across Canada. The airline's manifesto bears plenty of evidence of Beddoe's experience at Southwest: 'At WestJet we keep the spirit alive by:

- Being successful in the air.
- Being successful on the ground.
- Celebrating new markets.
- Providing legendary service.
- Experiencing legendary growth.
- Creating internal "magic" and external "wow".
- We are TEAM WESTJET!'

The Southwest tricks work north of the 49th parallel dividing the US and Canada; in 2000, the only North American airline that was more profitable than WestJet was Southwest.

At the time, Air Canada – which dominates the country's aviation – was busy taking over the number-two carrier, Canadian Airlines. By November 2001, it was ready to take on the competition, and launched a new discount offshoot called Tango in November 2001. Like Go's birth in Britain, the new airline was set up by a national carrier in direct competition with the no-frills upstart and itself; unlike Go, Tango went one stage further and flew on identical routes between major airports. Some Canadian travellers say it put the final nail in the coffin of the biggest independent, Canada 3000, which promptly went bust three weeks later. 'Fares increased the moment Canada 3000 disappeared,' says the Montreal-based travel writer, Cleo Paskal.

Tango goes further than other airlines in playing up the safety concerns among passengers. 'The consumer benefits from a world-class safety record,' says the airline. Air Canada's president and CEO, Robert Milton, emphasises the airline's 'high operational standards' – with the implication that this was something other low-cost operators could not offer. Tango also makes an unusual claim to offer a 'unique "all extras are optional" pricing policy, including a menu selection of in-flight snacks and refreshments at reasonable prices,' which sounds exactly like every other no-frills airline. More ominously for WestJet, Milton says, 'We continue to plan for the launch of a Western Canada-based, short haul, low-fare airline that will be operated as a wholly owned subsidiary and that will provide employment opportunities for some of our surplus staff.'

ONLY JOKING

'Last time I went down to Australia, we were under enormous pressure to sell out Virgin Blue to Air New Zealand [owner of Ansett, and keen to dampen domestic competition]. Twelve months in, they sent me over a cheque for A$250m [nearly £100m]. Virgin's always spending before we've actually got money so it's always tempting to take it. So we called a press conference for 12 o'clock, in front of one of our planes, and we got up in front of cameras and the press and I said, "It's a sad day for the Australian aviation industry but we've decided to sell. We have saved people all this money and it's been a great year, a great start." And there was this deafening hush and I hadn't realised that some of the staff were standing just behind bursting into tears at this stage. I looked into the camera and said, "Only joking" and ripped up the cheque.

'Ansett had been saying to me right up to the last minute, "Look if you don't sell out, we're going to throw hundreds of millions into this and we're going to drive you out of the market." And then only about three days later, Ansett announced that they were bankrupt.' – Sir Richard Branson.

Sir Richard Branson believes his Virgin Blue experience can work elsewhere in the world, and is actively looking at opportunities in Africa and Latin America. He had better move fast: South America's largest country, Brazil, has a new no-frills airline called GOL – pun on the Portuguese word for 'goal' intended. It is running a successful operation between its base in Sao Paulo (the biggest city in the continent), the capital, Brasilia, and Rio. The latter service arrives at Santos Dumont airport, whose name honours the Brazilian aviation hero who, many locals believe, pioneered powered flight before the Wright Brothers.

11. LOSS LEADERS

'My wife said, "You've got nothing left to mortgage but the dogs"'

FRANCO MANCASSOLA, FOUNDER OF DEBONAIR

'Scotland's travel agents told us we'd never sell a flight in Scotland without them. Several million flights later they're looking pretty stupid now'.

TONY ANDERSON, EASYJET'S FIRST MARKETING DIRECTOR

'Low-cost airlines are doing for the scheduled market what we've always been doing in the charter market'

JOHN DE VIAL, THOMSON

DEBONAIR FLIGHT 092: LUTON–PERUGIA–ROME

May Day 1999 is not a happy time to be at Gatwick airport. It is the first day of the summer charter season. At the start of May, the whole package-holiday industry lurches from the undemanding schedule of winter into the peak season, in which everyone and everything is worked to the maximum. To add to the confusion this particular year, British Midland has launched a new handling operation on behalf of charter airlines such as Monarch. There are teething problems. Basically, the whole check-in and baggage system appears to be running at quarter-speed. The concourse of the South Terminal is heaving with increasingly fractious children, their parents, and implausible mounds of luggage. As my early morning flight to Pisa on Monarch gets shifted later and later, I reflect on the irony of taking a charter flight to cover a story about a no-frills scheduled airline.

Franco's coming home. One of aviation's most colourful and respected characters, Franco Mancassola, is about to start flying to his home city, Perugia. But I have to get there before he does, so that the city-break story – '48 Hours in Perugia' – can appear in the *Independent* just before Debonair's scheduled flights from Luton begin. From the research I have done so far, the Umbrian capital sounds a marvellous place – three-dimensional in every sense, with art and history concealed within a maze of streets perched high on a hill. Just the sort of destination you'd like to go for a weekend.

All of Britain's newspapers owe thanks to the no-frills airlines for an almost endless sequence of new destinations that can refresh the travel pages: Moenchengladbach, Cergy-Pontoise and now the Umbrian capital, Perugia. And those were just the routes started by Franco Mancassola, founder of Debonair.

Perugia airport is among the most beautifully located in the world. It occupies one of the few flat pieces of land in central Italy, straddling a narrow plain midway between the Umbrian capital itself and the hub of the St Francis industry, Assisi. The tall, stern columns at the airport entrance look all the more out of place because of the way they are planted amid languid agricultural land surrounded by craggy hills. But they correlate closely with the fascist architecture favoured by Mussolini. Beyond them, a long, triumphal drive leads to a terminal building that is in the final stages of renovation, with someone attaching a sign above the new car-rental desk. These are exciting times for the airport: it is about to become linked with Europe's biggest city, thanks to a man who left Perugia nearly four decades earlier. Sometime later, I met him at Gatwick airport. He is now running an Italian aircraft supply company, Avia Interiors, which makes seats for airlines. With a handsomely sculpted face, dark hair and alert eyes, he is energetic and expressive, just as he was when he appeared in Debonair's ads. But he looks more relaxed now that he is out of the no-frills business. He told me how he had got caught up in the business of flying people for less.

Early in 1995, Mancassola was living happily in Hawaii. To that point he had enjoyed a lively career working for a range of airlines. 'I fell into aviation when I came to England in the early 60s,' he says. 'I found a temporary job at Monarch, and from there I decided that was what I wanted to do.' Given the delays and uncertainties about the Monarch flight to Pisa, it would have been handy if he had stayed; his reputation is of a highly effective and inspirational manager. He caught the attention of a US-based airline, Continental. In the late 60s, he moved to California.

'It was, at the time, a domestic carrier. I told the chairman that, in a global economy, an airline like Continental should at least be exploring the possibility of some international routes. He said "Can you do it?" I said "Sure." Two years later we were flying into Mexico.' Continental has since expanded all across Latin America, and is one of the British budget travellers' favourites for cheap, reliable travel.

Shortly after the expansion, the airline decided to move to Houston, to take advantage of the Sunbelt's low costs and booming economy. It was in Texas's largest city that Continental was to try to suppress Southwest, now the biggest no-frills airline of all. But while California can, in places, do a pretty good impression of Umbria, Texas cannot. 'I decided I wanted to stay in California,' says Mancassola. 'So I moved to World Airways.'

At the time, World Airways was a with-a-few-frills airline that was suffering from being a relative minnow in the US, and was trying to turn around its fortunes and break into international aviation. As with so many other airlines, from Laker to American, it started transatlantic flights at Gatwick using DC-10 aircraft. World Airways soon established a successful link from the Sussex airport to Baltimore-Washington International, with fast connections to the West Coast. Once again the prevailing certainties about the origins of no-frills flying are questioned – this time, about who thought of low-cost flights between the US and the UK.

'World Airways was doing it before Freddie Laker. World Airways was the airline that started affordable but comfortable transatlantic flights. They were inexpensive but the passenger had dignity. They had a good seat pitch, 34 inches, and good service. I've never been a believer that cheap must mean shoddy. In a way I carried that little idea, if you will, into Debonair.' World Airways' improving fortunes meant that the stock that Mancassola says he was planning 'to plaster my bathroom with', turned into good money.

At this point, many people might have taken the cash and flown off into the sunset to enjoy it; Mancassola headed west, but not to relax. 'I decided to go to Hawaii and start my own airline, Discovery.'

In theory, the Hawaiian archipelago is ideal territory for a low-cost airline, with strong year-round demand from both leisure and business passengers, and no effective competition from other modes of transport. But Mancassola says he was squeezed by the existing airlines and political interests in the same manner that Sir Freddie Laker suffered in the early 80s. At the point where it seemed all was lost, he says, 'My wife said, "You've got nothing left to mortgage but the dogs."' Against the odds, the airline was revived and the dogs survived. Discovery found a buyer who was prepared to pay a reasonable price – enough for Mancassola to live on, and to make him want to try again.

'You can take a man out of Luton,' as the saying nearly goes, 'but you can't take Luton out of a man.' Franco Mancassola decided to move to Britain, specifically to the Bedfordshire airport.

'Deregulation was beginning to take hold in Europe,' he explains. 'At the back of my mind I always knew that Europe was ripe for a low-cost airline. So I packed my bag, and I said to my wife, "Right, off we go," and on the door of my house in Hawaii there's still my wife's fingertips when I . . .' At this point, Mancassola makes a very Italian scraping noise. '. . . when I drag her away. We came over here and we started Debonair.' His philosophy was a model of clarity: 'Think of the passenger. Keep it simple, keep it affordable, keep it safe, keep it reliable. By providing good and friendly service the passenger will realise that cheap does not mean shoddy. If an airline can achieve these objectives, it will win the loyalty of passengers, it will prosper and it will be satisfying a demand which will grow in the years to come. And, who knows? It may even be profitable.'

The man from Perugia was not the only southern European who, in 1995, was keen to start a low-cost airline. Stelios Haji-Ioannou was already looking for opportunities, and eventually reached the same conclusion: that Luton was the place to begin. The difference was that easyJet earned all the publicity that comes with being the first mover, launching something demonstrably different.

'Stelios beat us by five months. Of course he had his own money, while I had to go around and raise it.' That proved difficult. 'We put together a business plan, and I began to canvass financial institutions, banks, potential investors.' Mancassola soon found that 'Everyone's got tons of money until it's time to put it on the table. It went on for about a year, and I was getting disheartened.' Eventually he went back to the US, and talked to a merchant bank in Phoenix. 'They liked the plan, and by the time I landed in London the half-million dollars was already wired, so I put in my bit.' This was estimated to be around $1m. 'We did a second offering, and raised another $6m, and did a third offering, and raised another $4m.' Then he went to Greece, the home of Stelios. 'I walked into a room full of about two hundred investors and said, "Ladies and gentlemen, I'm here for one reason and one reason only. I want your money." We raised another $4m.'

The airline was still less well funded than Mancassola had hoped, which he blames on Europe's rules about airline ownership, which limit non-EU holdings in member states' airlines. 'If I could have gone and raised capital in Hong Kong, I could have probably raised $20m and the airline would have been saved. But that law prevented me. It's an absurd law.'

Mancassola feels that legislation sought to confound him at every turn. One of the Civil Aviation Authority tests for new airlines is sufficient cash reserves to survive for three months with no cash coming in. 'It's an absurdity,' says Mancassola. 'No airline can survive for three months with no income. It's the bureaucracy that keeps you on the ground, burning cash, while bureaucrats have ninety days to respond. A horrid, horrid system.'

Despite the obstacles, Debonair took to the air in 1996, within seven months of Mancassola sealing the funding. The airline's first flight was on 16 June, remarkably close to the date, twelve years earlier, when Virgin Atlantic had taken off. Early summer is a good time to launch an airline, since it should ensure strong earnings during the peak season.

But Mancassola is clearly regretful that Stelios beat him; I calculate by seven months, rather than Mancassola's figure of five. But while Stelios had concentrated on Anglo-Scottish routes initially, Debonair was focused on an entirely different market: continental Europe. 'Moenchengladbach in western Germany, also known as Dusseldorf Express airport; Copenhagen in Denmark; and Barcelona in Spain,' recites Mancassola. 'We expanded to Madrid, and Munich, Newcastle, Rome.' It was a brave move to fly to so many destinations so quickly. 'We had to expand very rapidly to keep up with the market. And the problem is when you expand, you put an airplane on a route, from day one that airplane costs you X. Before you fill it up, you maybe have to bleed for two, three, four months.'

It also helps if the plane doesn't keep breaking down. The shortage of capital meant that Mancassola had opted for British Aerospace 146s rather than the no-frills industry standard Boeing 737. With hindsight, Mancassola would have chosen differently. 'It was a choice dictated by our lack of finance. At the time, they were available, they were parked in the desert. It turned out to be a poor decision on my part, and I take full responsibility for that.' The aircraft proved to be unreliable, and in worse condition than anticipated. Not only were Debonair's operations disrupted in the all-important summer launch period, but 'we had to spend tons of money to put it right. It was simply a mistaken choice made by yours very truly.'

What there was no mistake about, he says, was the level of service offered. Of all Europe's no-frills airlines, Debonair came closest to matching the Southwest Airlines product. Passengers could book through travel agents without penalty, or direct. A modicum of free refreshment was available on board – coffee and a muffin – with alcohol available for sale. Seat pitch (the distance between the front of one seat and the front of the next) was a comfortable 32 inches, which is better than many long-haul airlines. 'Comfort is not a class privilege, everyone should fly comfortably,' says Mancassola. Connections were allowed, and some flights operated multi-sector. And there was a simple but effective frequent-flyer programme, where after ten return flights you got a free trip. Mancassola also aimed to keep fares simple: 'One of the key elements of a successful price policy is to keep it simple. Passengers for too long have been confronted by a mass of incomprehensible figures and letters when trying to ascertain how much it will cost them to fly between point A and point B.'

With the no-frills industry in its infancy, and low-cost competition only slowly encroaching, Debonair made it through the first year. April

1997 saw the completion of the so-called third package of the liberalisation of the civil aviation market, and the introduction of total cabotage. In simple terms, any European airline could fly anywhere it wished within the EU. 'We were the very first to start pan-European services,' says Mancassola. 'We flew as a domestic airline in Germany, and that went straight up the nose of Lufthansa.'

How did they react? 'Oh, appallingly. They tried every trick in the book to ground us. Anyway, two years later we became almost partners, we were doing some flying for them.'

Plenty of other people saw what Stelios, Mancassola and Ryanair's O'Leary were doing, and believed there was cash to be made. Autumn 1997 saw a so-called 'pathfinder' flight from Hurn airport in Bournemouth to Glasgow. Conveniently soon after the devolution vote, a new airline called Euroscot Express blazed a trail between England's south coast and Scotland's largest city. The words 'doomed to failure' reluctantly but, as it turned out, accurately, attached themselves to my report at the time. The market may have been there – as Ryanair may yet demonstrate with a Bournemouth to Prestwick service – but the aircraft (small propeller planes and 1-11s), the marketing and the fare-cuts were insufficient to attract it.

Back home in Luton, Franco Mancassola's gleaming Alfa Romeo was still receiving admiring glances, but life was becoming tougher. Within Debonair's first year, stage whispers were circulating about the financial health of the airline. When rumours take root about the fortunes of a carrier – even if they have no basis in reality – they have an unfortunate habit of becoming self-fulfilling. Individual passengers are reluctant to risk cash in the event of an airline failure, while businesses cannot afford the prospect of executives being stranded. Travel agents certainly want to avoid getting involved in cancelled flights, refunds and unpaid bills. In other words, it is to the benefit of rivals if a competitor is thought of as shaky.

Financial problems can be exacerbated in a more proactive (and morally dubious) manner by the practice of short-selling, though everyone's lawyers should be happy to note that I know of no evidence of this having happened in Debonair's case. The idea of short-selling depends on the settlement date for a share trade falling some time ahead – in other words, you can buy or sell without having to fulfil the bargain. An individual might sell stock in a rival company even though he or she does not (yet) own the shares. The sale itself helps to depress the share price, so the rival can buy the necessary stock for less than they sold it and satisfy the original transaction. He or she happily turns a profit on the transaction, as well as depressing the financial form of the target company. Even if anyone had thought to try this with Debonair, they would have found that the company's shares were not being traded in sufficient quantities to make short-selling feasible; if there are few buyers and sellers, the trick is hard to pull off.

When Go began life in May 1998, two of its first three routes were to Debonair destinations: Rome and Copenhagen. Both tempted people across to Stansted from Mancassola's base at Luton, not least because on some of Debonair's flights it was necessary to stop en route in Germany. Later, Go attacked Mancassola – and Stelios's easyJet – on the Barcelona route. Also, Ryanair increased its presence in Italy, which stole market share from Debonair. And in July 1998, AB Airlines started flying from Gatwick to Nice, with a lead-in fare of £109 return (cheap in those days, but now well above the lowest widely available fare of around £60). A route that Debonair had started in competition with only British Airways and Air France was now carved up between seven airlines: the new players were easyJet, AB Airlines, British Midland (now BMI, flying on behalf of Air France) and Virgin Express from Gatwick, Heathrow and Stansted via Brussels.

Soon, to protect its share of the market and to help expand its route network, Debonair established an alliance with the newcomer, AB Airlines, on routes to Barcelona, Berlin and Shannon. AB, based in Gatwick, was a third incarnation of something that had started off as a sensible and profitable entity: Air Bristol. It was a charter-based airline that had a lucrative contract to shuttle between the British Aerospace facility at Filton, north of Bristol, and the main Airbus factory at Toulouse in south-west France. Every day, a BAC 1-11 would fly there and back purely for the staff of Airbus and BAe. Air Bristol saw the opportunity for liberalisation to open a new route from Gatwick to Shannon. Since Air Bristol would be a confusing name for an airline flying between London and the west of Ireland, the name was changed to AB Shannon. Gradually, other routes emerged – from Gatwick to Nice, and Lisbon in Portugal. A new non-specific name was needed, and AB Airlines did the trick. But Tim Jeans of Ryanair says the carrier was at the wrong place at the wrong time: 'They focused on Gatwick, at a time when Gatwick was being pumped full of British Airways capacity.'

At the same time, Luton was becoming increasingly orange, with easyJet imagery obscuring the neatly designed livery of Debonair. Mancassola had to do something. You might remember the distinctive Debonair advertisements that appeared in the press and on the London Underground, featuring the airline chairman. 'Stelios came out with a very clever idea – "as cheap as a pair of jeans". That was very distinctive, and putting his number on his airplane, I take my hat off to him. So we wanted a spokesperson who said, "Hey, I'm in charge, I take responsibility, you can trust me." They suggested that giving a face to the airline was a good idea. I wasn't very keen, actually, but in the end I said, "If it's a good idea, for the sake of the airline, I'll do it". It put the airline on the map.' So Mancassola joined Laker (and, much later, Stelios) in presenting the advertisements.

The tag line of the ads was, 'My finance director tells me I'm mad,' for charging low fares while giving more. Franco proclaimed the many virtues of Debonair, next to details of cheap flights from Luton to Europe. The ads were prophetic. Traditionally, travel companies in Britain that are in difficulties fail on Fridays in September. So it proved for Mancassola. 'We were faced with mounting debts, but we had the option to get out with style.' On the last day of September, 1999, Debonair stopped flying.

'We were very close,' says Mancassola, adding, for emphasis, 'very, very, very, very close to making it. But it was not to be. We simply ran out of cash.' Tim Jeans of Ryanair is harsher. 'Debonair tried to be all things to all men: business, leisure, primary airports, secondary airports, hubs, point-to-points, transit traffic.' Mancassola again: 'Debonair had very high loads. Our downfall was rapid expansion. We started off with six aircraft, we finished with sixteen.'

Jeans: 'They just didn't frankly have the direction that was required to succeed.'

Mancassola: 'We had 70 per cent load factors. Our fares were right, our quality was right, we were giving more than the others.'

Jeans: 'They basically floundered around until they put themselves out of their own misery.'

Mancassola: 'On 30 September we paid all the employees, we paid everyone. We simply closed the door.'

Anyone who expected a period of calm reflection among the no-frills airlines for the final three months of the millennium was mistaken. In the wake of Debonair's demise, newspapers were reporting 'A week after one of Britain's low-fare airlines went bust, a leading no-frills carrier has warned of a fares war of "bloodbath" proportions over the next two months.' Ryanair said that people were showing reluctance to travel in the dying months of the twentieth century. The no-frills survivors were forced to slash fares to attract anyone on board. In October 1999, for the first time, Ryanair offered the opportunity for flying for only the cost of taxes, fees and charges (though with a fare structure that offered this only for one-way flights and meant some real money was made on the inbound half). At Luton, easyJet announced what it claimed was the lowest air fare in Europe: £26 return on its new route to Liverpool. 'If we can make 20 or 30 pence per head at this time of year we're happy,' said a spokesman.

Shortly afterwards, AB Airlines followed Debonair into aeronautical oblivion. Once more, Tim Jeans offers an obituary – this time, so full of initials that Sweden's favourite band almost gets a mention: 'AB – poor old AB. BA were throwing capacity, and very low fares by BA standards into Gatwick, and I think AB just couldn't get to the mass that they needed to sustain profitable operations. You couldn't exist on the kind of liquidity that they had in the business. When they hit a glitch on, I think, crew training on the 737, it was really all over for them.'

EasyJet's Stelios is more philosophical: 'Neither of them were pure, low-cost carriers. I think they were sometimes referred to as local carriers for expedience's sake, for shorthand, because they couldn't be classified as anything else, but I think in reality they pursued the strategy of high cost and low fares. The swansong of Franco Mancassola's Debonair was an affordable business class with a chauffeur-driven pickup. That's not low-cost.'

'I refuse to believe that giving a cup of coffee, or not giving a cup of coffee, makes a difference on the profits of an airline,' counters Mancassola. 'Our mistake was the wrong choice of aircraft, they were very costly, not properly financed; and the rapid expansion and entrance of a lot of low-cost airlines. Ryanair and easyJet expanded very rapidly. And Go coming in – Tyson dressed in kids' clothes, with Big Daddy behind, helping him bash up the other ones. The market share that Go took away from us in Rome and Barcelona was a contribution to our shortfall. We were short by $5m when we closed. If we weren't forced to pay fuel in advance, landing fees in advance, we would have made it.'

Mancassola also believes that the European Commission let him down: 'When you start an airline, it isn't just money. The major carrier's got everything, slots, airplanes, established routes. The field has to be level, otherwise there's no way for competition to flourish, and the consumer will be taken for a ride. I am a believer in competition, and I don't believe there should be regulations, but there should be rules. Rules without freedom is tyranny, but freedom without rules is anarchy.' Sir Richard Branson believes that Debonair was not designed for success. 'They just didn't have a great brand. They didn't have a great vision. They didn't stand out from the crowd.'

Dozens of young airlines have failed to grow to maturity, leaving a trail of stranded travellers and angry creditors. (Passengers have little protection when a scheduled airline for which they hold a ticket goes bust.) The aviation sector has as low a life expectancy as dot-com companies. Perhaps that is why Debonair attracts some sympathy from Martha Lane Fox, the celebrated co-founder of the high-profile dot-com, lastminute.com. She says she is depressed by the reaction to the business closures in the late 1990s: 'I've just been very, very surprised at the glee people take when people fail.'

The causes of Debonair's demise can be argued about endlessly, but it looks to me that underfinancing and overexpansion are what put paid to the Perugia flight and the rest of the network. Any new route takes time to turn a profit. This might have happened earlier if Debonair had flown bigger, more reliable aircraft. Expansion is always a tempting option for a new airline, but the three most successful no-frills airlines – Southwest, easyJet and Ryanair – all began slowly, with a strictly limited route network. They waited until this was generating cash before launching more cash-draining services. Had Mancassola managed to acquire more finance, he could have turned the corner. At least he was in the right sector of the market, which is more than can be said for some other transport undertakings that were hit by the growth of no-frills flying.

Failure in business is typically the result of not identifying and countering a threat early enough. Traditional airlines were not alone in failing to appreciate the way that no-frills carriers would change the travel landscape. Anyone who used Piccadilly station in Manchester in the first half of 1998 will have seen a smart new Eurostar catering building being built by the entrance to the station. It was never put into use, because the trains for which it was supposed to cater never appeared. The Channel Tunnel train company promised that year that Eurostar would be running from Manchester to Paris by early summer, with direct trains from Glasgow and Edinburgh to the Continent following a short time later. The cross-Channel train operator had originally planned an extensive range of trains from Plymouth to Brussels and Scotland to Paris – indeed, part of the original justification for the Channel Tunnel was the benefits it would bring to regions outside the south-east. But by the time the trains were ready, Ryanair had established itself at Prestwick and easyJet was building up a base at Liverpool. With fares from (somewhere near) Glasgow to (somewhere near) Paris that were typically less than £100 return, and plenty of options for flyers in the north-west of England, Eurostar concluded there was simply no sustainable market for regional services.

There are other losers in the no-frills war, from the hoteliers of Rimini, who were furious when Ryanair unceremoniously pulled out of the airport and shifted all the flights down the coast to Ancona in a row about airport charges, to the rather larger community of UK travel agents.

Prior to 1995, anyone planning a weekend in Barcelona or Berlin would probably have trudged along to the travel agent and handed over at least £100 return, of which 9 per cent would have gone straight to the agent. When Debonair was still alive, it dealt happily through travel agents. (Rivals say that the extra costs helped contribute to Debonair's demise.) Nowadays, there is nothing in the cost structure of Ryanair or easyJet that allows for a travel agent's edge. 'We chucked Ryanair out four years ago when they cut commission,' says Stephen Bath, who heads the Bath Travel chain and is also president of the Association of British Travel Agents. 'Since then the service has got even worse, such as not ringing people up when the flight is cancelled.' And easyJet has done its part by slagging off travel agents in its 'Cut out the middle-man' campaign.

'The travel agency community was livid already,' recalls Tony Anderson, easyJet's first marketing director. 'They were faced with reductions in their commission from the larger airlines, so the insults from this upstart must have been difficult to bear. Indeed the Scottish Passenger Agents Association [which represents the country's travel agents] told us we'd never sell a flight in Scotland without them. Several million flights later they're looking pretty stupid now.' Early in 2002, easyJet took the battle to business travel agents, the people who arrange flights for companies. The airline 'named and shamed' big firms whose travel policies, it said, did not include low-cost airlines. The research was not flawless, though; Marconi complained that it had been unfairly singled out, and that its executives did indeed fly on no-frills airlines.

'Buzz and Go are more agent-friendly, or at least slightly less antagonistic,' says Rachel Crampton, managing director of the Norwich-based chain of Travel Centres. She believes the no-frills airlines are unaware of the proportion of bookings that go through agents. She says the travelling public should go through a travel agent so as to make sure they are getting best value for money. 'There's a big perception that they are the cheapest option, but that's very often not the case.' Crampton's company charges customers £10 extra for seats on no-frills flights.

The travel agency boss has a family connection with the independent airline business; her father, Jim Crampton, founded Air Anglia, later Air UK, later KLM UK, later Buzz. 'It started the growth in regional airports, which the no-frills airlines are now capitalising on.' Crampton senior's airline used to fly some interesting routes, such as Norwich–Heathrow in the days before the M11 was built and the journey could take five hours. The rising value of slots at Heathrow put an end to the route in the 1980s, and now Norwich airport resounds only to the occasional departure to Amsterdam or the northern part of Britain. No low-cost airline has expressed an interest in operating from there, partly because Stansted is so near and so successful. Crampton is philosophical about the rise of the sector that has cost her commission: 'They've enlarged the market, and if the travel agents get a proportion of that, that's good for everyone.'

Some charter airlines might not agree. What began as a joke, with a few silly-looking planes shuttling between England and Scotland, now comprises a big fleet of 737s, many of which are parked on the tarmac of traditional holiday airports. But the biggest players are playing down the threat. John de Vial, who looks after government affairs for the giant Thomson group, says, 'They're only just attaining a volume that is significant. They offer many headline low fares, but the reality is a bit different.' He believes that both charter airlines and no-frills operators are growing at the expense of former state-run airlines. 'Low-cost airlines are doing for the scheduled market what we've always been doing in the charter market.' Thomson's in-house airline, Britannia, tried flying a scheduled service between Luton and Belfast for a while, but could not make the success of it that easyJet has achieved on the route. For MyTravel (formerly Airtours), no-frills airlines are 'just another element of the leisure market, just something else to compete with,' according to the aviation director, Bill McGrorty. 'They may be seeing slow growth in our sector, but the main effect is that there's a whole new generation partying in Dublin or Barcelona for the weekend.' Nonetheless his company is selling its cheapest brands, 'Sundeals', as 'no-frills holidays'.

Back at Gatwick, the flight to Pisa finally starts boarding around lunchtime. Monarch, the airline whose Airbus has been hanging around waiting for its passengers and cargo since early morning, has been badly hit by the no-frills operators. In the early 90s it developed an impressive network of scheduled flights to popular Mediterranean destinations. They were put under such pressure that Monarch was obliged to take out no-frills-style advertisements with no-frills style fares, and take the inevitable hit on its revenues.

Another loser, which few people in the business talk about, is the environment. A Boeing 737 flying on Europe's longest no-frills flight, from Luton to Athens, consumes ten tons of kerosene, i.e. per passenger, roughly twenty gallons is burnt. The emission is pumped into the stratosphere. The newer the aircraft, the more efficient it is, but anyone who believes some airlines' propaganda that they're doing the world a favour by flying off on holiday should think again – it's cleaner to take out your dirty old diesel car for a run down to Cornwall. The prospect that aviation fuel, which has managed to evade tax for a century, might come under the Chancellor's microscope privately worries some in the industry.

Destinations are suffering too – some of them, like Dublin, because they are too darn busy at weekends. High-yield holidaymakers are being deterred by the prevalence of boozy young people, mostly from Britain, roaming through the city's streets every Friday and Saturday night. But there is also the chance that places falling off the no-frills map could be marginalised. Each September, Go ends its Stansted–Reykjavik flights, restoring the Icelandair monopoly for the winter. 'The extra cost of the de-icing fluid is an important element in the decision,' says Go's David Magliano. That might be an exaggeration, but the disruption to the overall schedule that weather-related delays in Iceland can have is also a significant element. Budapest and Krakow are losing out in the city-break market to Prague, which alone of the Eastern European capitals has a link to London.

The airlines' trade association, IATA, has long justified high fares by insisting that it ensured marginal places were served. This is not an entirely spurious argument. A monopoly held by a no-frills airline is only marginally less unfavourable than a traditional airline holding a stranglehold on a route.

So far, no one has started flying again from London to Perugia airport, which means that thousands are missing out on this beautiful Umbrian city. But Mancassola has ended up not far from his home town, in charge of the company that he had once bought aircraft seats from: Avio Interiors. 'The chairman invited me to dinner one night in Monte Carlo, I thought, "That's a hell of a way to go for dinner." Anyway, he met me with a proposal. I said I don't know anything about seats. He said, I want you to bring in an airline mentality. After a week, I was completely out of my depth, wondering whether I'd made a sensible decision. One night, about 7 p.m., I was in the huge factory, and there were about three 747 ship sets [consignments of seats]. I sat on one of those seats, and thought, "Jesus, have I done the right thing?" The airline world is very fast-moving and challenging. And I looked at all these seats – there must have been about a thousand – and I thought, "You know what, they're all empty, but unlike in the airline industry, they're all paid for." And that cheered me up immensely. Since then, it's been two years and it's going very well. If I leave now, it's to start another airline. If not, I'll fade away in the sunset.'

MANCASSOLA ON GO

Franco Mancassola's Debonair faced stronger competition from Go
than from anyone else. He has few words of praise for Barbara
Cassani, who founded the airline.

'If someone wants to start an airline, and is the son of the Sultan of
Brunei and has tons of money, but it's his own money, no problem.
Stelios did the right thing, and put his money where his mouth is. He
had plenty, that's great. But Barbara Cassani didn't create anything.
Everything was given to her. She didn't have to risk a dime or scratch
her head twice, because the operations manual was British Airways,
the pilots were trained by British Airways. She created nothing, and
she founded an airline. And she'd throw airplanes as far as they could
go to take market share away. We, Debonair, were the weakest because
we were running on our own money. We had to pay everything cash
in advance. But Go was British Airways, so who the heck is going to
ask Go for money in advance? So that helps the cash flow.

'If you look at pilot training, aircraft deposits, British Airways
admitted that they guaranteed the airplane. That's a huge amount of
cash. If we had had that cash we would be flying today happily. Go
was a typical example of how the European Commission, on aviation,
don't have a clue of what they're doing. Absolutely none. They allowed
state carriers to get subsidised – "One more, another one, another one
more," they allow all these big alliances, so either you sell to a major
carrier or you go out of business. What kind of competition is this? It's
not competition. Go was put into the market by British Airways, with
none of the market forces that we had to face.

'Go certainly eroded some market share that we, Debonair, with
our limited resources, could not afford to lose. But what I am really
disputing is the role of the European Commission to allow Go. In
order to play well, there must be a level playing field. If you're richer
than me and you want to start an airline, fine. But when the help of a
major carrier comes into play, which already controls a big chunk of
the market, paving the way for you to have most of your expenses
and cash flow taken care of?

'Remember their advertising? Go, the low-cost airline from British
Airways. The next moment they deny it all – "We've got nothing to
do with British Airways." It's a travesty. It wasn't a good investment
for British Airways. The fact that the shareholders forced them to sell
it means that it was a cash drain. We will never know what the
figures really were. It was a fiasco. They know it. They may say the
opposite until the cows come home, but I don't believe it.'

He is serious about returning to the industry: 'I would love to start one. I would *love* to start one. In the US, if you fail for whatever reason, a lot of time it is put down as an experience – "This guy fell from a horse, next time he'll be more careful" – so I've learned who to trust, who not to trust, and the mechanism. Would a low-cost airline flourish again? Hard to say, with these mega-alliances now – a fancy word for a cartel.'

As Franco Mancassola prepares to leave, his eyes fix mine. 'Debonair was, I believe even today, a well-planned, well-run airline. We had the cardinal sin of every airline – we were undercapitalised. Debonair never went bankrupt. We paid everybody. We just closed because we didn't have any cash to go forward. The idea was, and I still believe today strongly, to have an airline that has comfort, that has pzazz, and is affordable. We quit the race on the last quarter of a mile. And that was a great shame.'

12. 11 SEPTEMBER 2001

'Since September's horrific events, our industry has witnessed a continuous stream of cut-backs, lay-offs, aircraft grounding and airline bankruptcies'

BRITISH AIRWAYS

'My son and grandson are the most precious things in my life, and I wouldn't hesitate for a second to place either one of them on a Southwest Airlines flight'

COLLEEN BARRETT, PRESIDENT, SOUTHWEST

'If Al-Qaeda don't get you, the Deep Vein Thrombosis probably will'

MICK WEBB, RYANAIR PASSENGER

At Los Angeles International airport in 1997, a man who was wanted by the FBI for making terrorist threats was apprehended by security staff at a checkpoint. He was trying to carry a small arsenal of weapons and ammunition on to a domestic flight. Instead of being arrested, the culprit simply handed over the deadly consignment to police and continued his journey. Attempting to take a gun on to an aircraft was a felony only if the weapon happened to be loaded – carrying ammunition separately circumvented federal law. In the same year, the Federal Aviation Administration-conducted tests of airport security, in which agents tried to smuggle imitation firearms through airport checkpoints, proved dismal. Out of 173 attempts, they were caught in only 56 – worse than one in three.

In June 2000, I lived for a while at Gate 21 of Las Vegas airport. I wanted to see if I could spend 24 hours in the city that celebrates money like no other, without a cent to my name. I chose to base myself at a departure gate of McCarran International because airports in America have long functioned like community centres. Passengers and staff mingled amiably with meeters and greeters. There was no impediment to solicitors (as people asking for charitable donations are known) and do-no-gooders such as journalists on survival missions getting in the way of business. It turned out to be a remarkably comfortable experience. I spent part of the evening collecting baggage carts; each one that is returned to the machines at the passenger entrance earns 25c, which would amass enough to see me through the following day. The rest of the time I was snoozing on a bench by the departure gate. There was plenty of company: people who had been hounded out of hotels because they had gambled away the rent and had nowhere else to go before their flights home. Any of us could switch at will between landside and airside areas. The boundary was by an undemanding metal detector. My bag, full of electronic equipment, slid through the adjacent X-ray machine. The staff on duty chewed gum and looked bored, as well they might: no one had hijacked a plane to Cuba for decades, and terrorism was something that happened only in other countries.

This relaxed, comfortable world ceased to exist on 11 September 2001, along with thousands of innocent people. Nineteen hijackers took advantage of the relaxed attitude to security to smuggle blades on board four aircraft – two belonging to American Airlines, two to United. Being the biggest airlines in the world, they were prime targets; there was also speculation that their names might have attracted the terrorists to target them. The next biggest airlines, Delta, Southwest, Northwest and Continental, do not have such resonant names for people with a grudge against the United States of America. Two of the hijacked aircraft, both Boeing 767s bound from Boston to Los Angeles, were flown into the twin towers of New York's World Trade Center; they were American flight 11 and United flight 175. A third, a Boeing 757 serving as American Airlines flight 77 from Washington to Los Angeles, was deliberately crashed on the Pentagon. The fourth, United flight 73 from Newark to San Francisco, again a 757, was downed in a field in Pennsylvania after the passengers took on the hijackers. Besides the 33 crew, 214 innocent passengers and the nineteen hijackers, over 3,000 people died in the attacks – most of them in the World Trade Center.

About 2,500 flights were airborne above the US when the attacks took place, several hundred of them belonging to Southwest Airlines. 'Within half an hour of the second aircraft hitting the World Trade Center, the government mandated that all our planes be set down as quickly as possible,' says Greg Wells, vice-president for safety and security for Southwest. The US government feared that other aircraft had been captured to be used as guided missiles. Captains were told to land at the first available airport. For close on an hour, Steve Hozdulick, Southwest's director of flight dispatch, was uncertain whether any of his aircraft had been targeted. 'There was a huge sense of relief when we got them all down.' Remarkably, all but three landed at the 58 airports to which Southwest flies, which made the operational recovery easier.

It is rare that cameras catch an aircraft in the process of crashing. It is unprecedented that a fatal collision should be shown, live, to an audience of tens of millions. But 11 September was a day that shook the Western world. When the enormity of the attack on New York and Washington became apparent, President Bush talked of it as an act of war. When wars begin, people stop travelling, particularly if they have witnessed people dying as a result of doing something as harmless as boarding a scheduled flight on one of the world's biggest airlines.

Aircraft are peculiarly vulnerable to hostile acts, and passengers' alarm is heightened by the high profile that hijacks and bombings receive. The earliest act of aircraft piracy that I have been able to identify took place in Peru in 1931, when an American aviator and his aircraft were seized, on the ground, by a group with a political grievance; he and the plane were released, unharmed, several days later. Since then, aircraft have become the target of choice among terrorist groups. 'If striking terror into the hearts of people is a goal, airplane hijackings can be an effective way of getting there,' says Dr Todd Curtis, founder of the website AirSafe.com. Between 1978 and 1994, 307 fatal airline events were reported in the *New York Times*; Curtis has studied the coverage of each of them. 'One of the most widely reported involved a hijacked TWA 727 that spent several days at the media forefront. In the end, only one passenger was killed.' But the public seems singularly adept at identifying with the passengers on a jet that has come under hostile control, and fuelling their misgivings about getting on board an aircraft.

When planes crash, there is usually a temporary pause in operations at the affected airport and on the airline involved. When Concorde was lost at Paris in July 2000, Air France cancelled its departures for the rest of the day, but started them the following morning; other airlines' flights resumed almost immediately. The impact of 11 September was far more profound. For four days, not a single flight was allowed to take off from the US. Tens of thousands of passengers were stranded many miles from home, including people on dozens of transatlantic flights that did not have enough fuel to return to Europe when the order came through that US airspace was out of bounds. Every airline lost fortunes while their planes were grounded, and in the downturn in travel that followed. One individual was particularly affected, as Sir Richard Branson concisely relates. 'At nine o'clock in the morning on the eleventh of September, JetBlue was going public and the owner, David Neeleman, was going to make a billion dollars out of it. Obviously it got cancelled by what happened at 8.30 a.m.' The abandoned flotation of America's newest no-frills airline was the first of many waves that washed through the travel industry.

Within hours of the first aircraft striking the World Trade Center in New York, conventional wisdom among business and the media had reached firm conclusions about the future of aviation. Flying would be more stressful and more expensive. Insurance and security costs would rocket. Jobs and routes would be cut. While aviation would not be cast back quite to the dark ages, only the strong were likely to survive the corporate cull. 'Since September's horrific events, our industry has witnessed a continuous stream of cut-backs, lay-offs, aircraft grounding and airline bankruptcies,' said British Airways. 'The International Air Transport Association is predicting a collective industry loss of US$10 billion for 2001. It will be the biggest deficit, by far, in any single year.'

Almost every part of the travel industry was hit. Cruise lines were caught in the middle of a buying spree. Buoyed up by high earnings in the 90s, where the US market had grown steadily while overseas demand had rocketed, they had ordered billions of dollars' worth of new ships. Suddenly the market dried up, with many Americans fearing even to take the flight to Miami to board what some of them regarded as a floating target. Car-rental companies found that the decline in air travel meant there were fewer people who needed instant mobility at the end of a flight: within two months, Stelios's easyRentacar was hiring out Mercedes for as little as £1 a day. And hotels found it difficult to fill beds at almost any price; travelling in America late in 2001, I was twice asked to name my own price for hotel rooms, so desperate were proprietors for business. The verdict of most people within the travel industry was that the world had changed for ever, for the worse.

For the bereaved mourning the loss of their loved ones this was indisputable. But not everyone agreed that aviation, and in particular no-frills flying, would necessarily be grievously wounded. And there was a sense that some airlines were using the events of 11 September to justify painful measures that would have been necessary anyway.

This is a typical example of the news in the latter part of 2001: Midway Airlines announced it was to halve its workforce, cut seventeen aircraft from its fleet and abandon nine destinations, including the key cities of Washington DC and Los Angeles. 'The instant need for this restructuring has been occasioned by the calamitous drop in business traffic experienced by airlines,' said the company boss, Robert Ferguson.

How much of this was due to 11 September? None of it. Midway made the announcement four weeks to the day before the attack on America. The world's airlines, and in particular those in the US, had been feeling the effects of a downturn in business confidence already. But the hijacking of two aircraft from each of the world's two largest airlines precipitated the biggest ever slide on the stock markets, with airline stock particularly affected. Like the financial markets, successful civil aviation depends on the confidence of the participants. And plenty of people felt scared, both within and outside America, by what they had seen – amplified by further threats, and the anthrax attacks in the US.

Since cheap fares became widespread across the Atlantic, the US has been a favourite destination for British travellers, with around 2 million holidaymakers heading there each year, as well as 1 million business visits. With the exception of a few high-profile attacks on individual tourists, the US has been seen as a safe destination. That image had now been shattered. Places like the Windows on the World restaurant at the top of the World Trade Center had been a big draw for visitors, while in Washington DC you could – until 11 September – take a tour of the Pentagon. America's capital city was basically a governmental theme park which attracted millions of US citizens and foreign visitors. No one would look at either city in quite the same way again. Nor would people so readily fly to Florida for the theme-park experience. In December 2001, fares from the UK to Orlando fell from the usual rock-bottom minimum of £200 to as low as £129.

Between them, US airlines shed around 100,000 jobs because of the drop in passenger numbers. Among the major carriers there was one exception: Southwest expressed its intention to maintain services and staff at their present levels, and was continuing to hire staff. 'We were the first airline to get back out with a full schedule,' says Greg Wells, the airline's vice-president for safety and security. 'Our aircraft only make money when people are sitting on them in the air.'

On the other side of the Atlantic, the mood in the days following 11 September was grim. For four days, the skies over London were eerily quiet. Not a single aircraft adopted the usual approach to Heathrow, lining up over the centre of the capital for a direct track to touch down at Britain's busiest airport. To the east, not a single aircraft took off from, or landed at, London City airport. Among airlines that were forced to cancel dozens of flights, and pilots obliged to make awkward approaches to Heathrow, there were murmurings of an overreaction to the terrorist suicide attacks. When Washington gave the go-ahead for flights to and from America to resume, the US airlines were given a 24-hour head start. Passengers desperate to get home from both sides of the Atlantic had their stress prolonged by the delay resulting from the US Transportation Secretary, Norman Mineta, giving permission to foreign airlines to enter American airspace. Privately, some UK airline executives were seething at the implication that British security procedures were somehow inferior. BA's frosty announcement that the Federal Aviation Administration was finally 'satisfied with British Airways' security measures' was significantly terse.

It was remarkable that the FAA had doubted them. When I began my short-lived career in security at Gatwick airport, the world was a very different place. Every passenger search was carried out manually: we used hand-held metal detectors, and all cabin luggage was inspected by hand. Squads of security guards like me were bused around the airport to each gate, so that passengers were frisked at the very last moment before boarding the aircraft.

Almost all flights were treated the same way, from departures to Spain with Laker Holidays to British Caledonian flights to Libya. Only travellers to Belfast and Tel Aviv came in for special attention, having all their hold luggage checked minutely and sealed before being loaded into the hold. In my entire career, I'm relieved to say that I only ever discovered two remotely dangerous items. One was a camping gas cylinder, which I was instructed to take out on to the apron to discharge safely and return the useless canister to the passenger, who showed admirable restraint in not suggesting where I could place it. The other was a pack of ham sandwiches, whose owner enquired if he would be allowed to take them into Italy. Adopting a grave look of concern, I said I really wasn't sure, and later enjoyed them for lunch.

The flights that I took in the days immediately following 11 September, to Dublin and Charleroi, were like going back in time. Soon, though, the security procedures reverted to their previous level, though anyone who was foolish enough to try to carry on board a potentially dangerous weapon such as a knitting needle or a pair of nail scissors would have to wave them goodbye forever. Glass bottles, which have the potential for far greater harm, were still welcomed (and used) in the aircraft cabin. The attack that wounded America so badly also killed a significant number of British people, but there was not the lasting damage to confidence that many had predicted. Memories proved shorter, and a consensus built quicker among passengers that it probably wasn't going to happen to them. 'If you're an extremist seeking paradise, you're unlikely to try and get there on a no-frills flight,' says Mick Webb, a passenger on Ryanair at Stansted. 'Anyway, if Al-Qaeda don't get you, the Deep Vein Thrombosis will.'

A more sensitive soul than Michael O'Leary, chief executive of Ryanair, might have been appalled by such sentiments. But he was already telling Radio 4's *Today* programme that British Airways and other airlines were 'screwing' the government for financial support after 11 September. 'That's a bit harsh, isn't it?' interjected John Humphreys. 'It's a bit true,' said O'Leary. He and Stelios, of easyJet, took the high ground, as well as the media limelight, and were not about to relinquish their grip. 'There's no joy in running empty planes,' said Stelios. 'You can't save souls in empty churches. So very quickly I realised that unless you make a big bang in advertising, and make a big noise, you just die with lack of passengers.'

'It shows how wobbly the big carriers were – they're dinosaurs, most of them,' says Franco Mancassola, former boss of Debonair. 'It will change aviation, but not because people will be afraid. Aviation will bounce back. It's the heart of the economy. We will see airlines come and go, that's the nature of a market. Aviation left on its own, to fight on its own within the rules, will prosper. I hope new people will start airlines. We need new blood, we need new believers. And I hope the majors will not interfere too much. I'd encourage anyone to invest in aviation, because aviation has a great future.' Sir Richard Branson had been about to speak to the European Parliament when the news came through. The MEPs were offered the chance to leave, in case the parliament itself was a target, but Branson continued with his speech. As soon as it was over, he was catapulted into weeks of anxiety over Virgin Atlantic, which was more exposed than any other airline to a downturn in traffic on the North Atlantic. Even three months after the event, he used graphic language to describe the impact of 11 September: 'The plane was going straight for the ground and we weren't sure if we were going to die or come out of it. But we're just beginning, I think, to show signs of coming back now.'

Two weeks after the attack, while newspapers were full of headlines like LLOYD'S FACES ITS BIGGEST-EVER CLAIM, and AIRLINES FEAR COLLAPSE WITHOUT STATE RESCUE DEAL, easyJet and Go were already taking out ads aimed at what they saw as an expanded market. 'Get back to business – make your hard-pressed travel budget go further with Go', trumpeted Cassani's airline, while pointing out, 'Over the last couple of weeks, Go passengers have experienced very little disruption'. Overleaf, easyJet urged 'Get smart – catch the low cost shuttle!' from Luton to Edinburgh, Glasgow and Belfast.

Stelios, meanwhile, was having to deal with problems elsewhere in his business empire. Staff in his ailing easyEverything chain of Internet cafes who had bought or earned shares in the operation found the Greek entrepreneur had devalued them from £1 each to just 1p, cutting what they had believed to be a £10,000 investment to just £100. To add to his troubles, the chief executive of easyEverything, Maurice Kelly, left abruptly. Stelios himself moved in to fill the vacuum. But easyJet was performing strongly.

For the next three months, it was difficult to believe that no-frills airlines and traditional carriers were in the same line of business:

12 September: Ansett, Australia's second-largest airline, stops flying when its parent company, Air New Zealand, pulls the plug. The New Zealand prime minister is on a scheduled flight home at Melbourne airport when the news comes through; protesting Ansett workers refuse to let the aircraft leave until she is offloaded.

12 September: Southwest Airlines stops using the 'Freedom' tagline in its advertising.

14 September: Boeing announces 25,000 lay-offs.

14 September: flights resume across the US, but US airlines are given fifty new safety directives from the Federal Aviation Administration (FAA).

15 September: in my column in the *Independent*, I write, 'Last Tuesday's tragedy would be amplified still further if it were allowed to crush travellers' spirit of adventure, and the power for good that aviation represents. Airlines bring people together. That is what they are for. And, as grief resonates around the world, unity is what we need more than ever.' Colleen Barrett of Southwest later trumps this – see 1 December.

17 September: Virgin Atlantic is the first UK airline to announce job cuts; 1,200 are to go, together with the new route to Toronto that had begun only three months earlier and the prestigious service to Chicago.

18 September: Ryanair's Michael O'Leary says it is business as usual: 'Bookings have returned to normal levels, and we would expect to recover last week's slippage over the coming days with a number of seat promotions which we have planned. Advance bookings and loads remain strong, and therefore the immediate consequence of last week's events on Ryanair will not be material.'

18 September: Aer Lingus announces 1,600 job losses, a number that exceeds Ryanair's total employees.

18 September: 'Boeing came to see us,' says Stelios of easyJet. We said, "Make us an offer and we'll talk to you." We are looking to expand.'

21 September: British Airways announces at least 5,000 job cuts, and ends a number of routes including the historic link between Heathrow and Belfast.

28 September: 'The industry's got to be restructured,' easyJet's chief executive, Ray Webster, tells me. 'It's in the interests of the consumers, shareholders and staff. Because if staff are employed by companies that go belly up every time there's a recession, is that a company you want to work for?'

1 October: Continental Airlines sets out to 'improve the mix of coats and ties versus backpacks and flip-flops' – in other words, to go for business passengers at the expense of economy travellers.

1 October: just to throw a Railtrack-sized spanner in the works of both the no-frills and traditional airlines, trains on the East Coast Main Line, for the first time in a year (since the Hatfield disaster), are able to travel between Edinburgh and London in under four hours, diminishing the time advantage of the airlines.

2 October: Swissair refuses to honour its commitment to bail out its former partner, Sabena of Belgium.

5 October: Swissair announces its intention to close down in its present form at the end of October.

29 October: easyJet turns in pre-tax profits of £20.1m for the year to the end of September, almost double the previous year, and announces it would be seeking more funds with a share issue. The cash will be used to finance the takeover of intra-European slots that traditional airlines were forced to abandon. 'There's no road map to what we're doing,' said Ray Webster, the chief executive. We have to be very quick on our feet, we have to be very quick to seize opportunities.'

30 October: in Australia, Virgin Blue predicts strong profits, saying its financial position is 'incredibly strong'.

2 November: at a press conference to launch the Association of British Travel Agents' convention in Lisbon, the representative of Orlando says she is unable to reveal the downturn in visitor numbers to the city, 'because it would confuse you'. A very senior member of the travel industry observes, 'I suspect the real reason you won't tell us is because you'd lose your job if you did.' ABTA says bookings for the following summer are down 50 per cent on this point a year ago. The association's president, Stephen Bath, says, 'It's anybody's guess when confidence will return. We'll be happy if it's only 5 per cent down next summer.'

7 November: after several attempts at re-financing Sabena, the Belgian government closes down the national airline. As a result, Virgin Express loses a large proportion of its revenue.

12 November: Ryanair estimates its profits for the full financial year will top £90m.

12 November: Virgin Express apologises for the disruption caused by the bankruptcy of Sabena – 'our ground personnel are putting your bags on the aircraft themselves' – and announces new routes to Geneva, Zurich, Gothenburg and Stockholm.

12 November: at Earl's Court in London, the World Travel Market begins. At 2 p.m., the news comes through that American Airlines flight 587 has crashed on take-off from New York's Kennedy airport, killing all 260 on board the Airbus A300 and five people on the ground.

19 November: Go becomes the latest no-frills airline to announce higher profits, up by 50 per cent in the six months to the end of September.

21 November: 'More than 1,000 airplanes worldwide are being grounded because of overcapacity' – *Boeing News*.

1 December: Southwest's president, Colleen Barrett, pours out her heart to *Spirit* magazine, putting my efforts of 15 September to shame. 'As a small girl growing up in Vermont, I looked wistfully at the Christmas advertisements for the great passenger trains in magazines such as *Life*. The ads I remember most are the ones showing happy families traveling home in a brightly lit dining car against the cold, dark, snowy night. My son and grandson think of that brightness as an airplane bringing life, joy and family through a star-spangled December sky. The 32,000 Proud Americans of the Southwest Airlines Family are hard at work to ensure this brightness will prevail, not just during December but throughout the entire year.' She tells staff: 'My son and grandson are the most precious things in my life, and I wouldn't hesitate for a second to place either one of them on a Southwest Airlines flight.'

4 December: 'Congratulations, you're the forty-second passenger on today's flight. We'll make some money on the next flight, not this one.' – Southwest Airlines check-in agent, Seattle airport. One week later, Southwest announces it will be adding new routes in the coming year.

5 December: Buzz announces a 15 per cent increase in passenger numbers. Five days later, it launches nine new routes, plus four domestic services in France.

5 December: 'The freedom to go where you want to go, when you want to go, is a precious liberty,' begins a full-page ad in the *Wall Street Journal*, paid for by Boeing. 'The nation's skyways are once again ready to help you make the most of that freedom.'

8 December: at Will Rogers International Airport at Oklahoma City, I meet Tom Barry, who is going to Salt Lake City for the day to collect his grandson. He feels violated. ' I was one of the people they pulled out at random. I've been poked and prodded and examined.'

Knees jerked in all kinds of directions after 11 September. Security in the US is now so strict that many passengers are subject to multiple searches. As a ticketless traveller on Southwest, you must queue up to get what amounts to a ticket (in fact, a personal boarding card) and endure no fewer than three photo ID checks to make sure that you are who you say you are – or, at least, that the name on your boarding card and in the computer matches the (possibly false) photo ID you are carrying. Everything is slower and less flexible. Everyone behaves much more meekly (if they are passengers) or sternly (if they are staff). There are still glaring loopholes: passengers whose names are randomly selected for a further search at the gate are often warned about it in advance, giving plenty of opportunity for wrongdoers to get rid of a weapon, or to be secure in the knowledge that someone else has been picked out, not them. Overall the experience feels much more uncomfortable and less flexible, and it is also much more stringent than in the UK.

'Immediately after the 11th of September, they would have put up with anything,' says Greg Wells, vice-president for security for South-west, about the travelling public. 'There was a three-to-four week period when we were on a sort of honeymoon – whatever we did, and however we delayed the passengers, they were OK with that.' That soon changed. 'In our society today, patience isn't there. They're at the point now where they want security as stringent as it has been, only quicker and faster.' Southwest is trying to streamline its procedures, but Greg Wells does not believe that things can ever revert to the way they were before. 'We are getting back to the normal airport experience, but it's going to be a while yet. There's a lot of technology out there that we're looking at as an industry and a government. We expect we can have a more efficient, safer and hopefully not much more expensive security experience at the airports, so people can get to their aircraft and get out on time and still have a low fare.'

Across in Europe, a horrible truth dawned upon high-cost airlines after 11 September. It is neatly summed up by easyJet's chief executive, Ray Webster. 'Airlines have a very, very low marginal cost base, that's the cost of flying a flight. If you have the option of flying a flight or leaving the aircraft on the ground, the difference in flying and leaving the aircraft parked is very little. So they need very little revenue to justify flying if the aeroplane's there and the crew is there. As against if they want to get rid of the asset, and they have to get rid of the crew, the exit costs are very high.' Airlines that wanted to cut back on flying, after a decade of expansion, found it to be an expensive and painful business. Not everyone, though, was convinced that the low-cost carriers had called it right. I put it to John Wimbleton of the leading tour operator, First Choice, that the no-frills airlines had stolen the high ground in the weeks following 11 September. 'It's like selling pound notes for 99p,' he replied. 'If I could make money sending people from Scotland to Stansted for £10 I would. Nobody makes a single pound. Anyone can get a cheap headline by giving things away. They've got the high ground and they're welcome to it.'

Even before 11 September, Ryanair was already bidding for second-hand Boeing 737s; in the weeks since 11 September, the cost of these fell by one third or more. A worldwide shortage of pilots suddenly turned into a surplus. Several officers who had left Go for Virgin Atlantic returned to Barbara Cassani's airline. The traditional airlines' schedules dropped by around 20 per cent, which meant demand for aviation fuel, and the price, also fell. And airports were suddenly prepared to negotiate on previously non-negotiable charges. Aer Rianta, the leading Irish airport authority, advertised for new airlines saying it would provide free facilities for three years. But the no-frills carriers still had to face the usual autumnal problem of persuading people to get on their planes. In any normal autumn it is tricky to keep the load factors up above 70 per cent and yields reasonable. Anecdotally, there was evidence that prospective passengers started thinking more about why they travelled – a glib 'because I can' was no longer sufficient. But people don't decide to go to Barcelona because they think it will be fun flying on Iberia or British Airways or easyJet or Go – they go to see the Sagrada Familia, or the Picasso Museum, or FC Barcelona, and to visit the tapas bars and pubs. If the price was right, they would get on board.

It is not quite true to say that anyone can fill a plane if the fare is low enough, but certainly the stated aim of easyJet, Ryanair and Go to get people travelling, was achieved. The trouble is, how much were the airlines earning? A look at the fares I paid in the following three months suggested that no one was going to do well out of me: Dublin and back, and Charleroi and back on Ryanair for £20; Salzburg return for £21; one-way on easyJet to Zurich for £32.50; Vienna for £35 one-way on Buzz; and £66 return to Malaga on Go. Once the taxes had been taken off, each of these airlines would be struggling to get into double figures for their earnings from each flight. Great for the traveller, dismal for the financial directors. But besides cheapskates like me having the time of their lives, plenty of business travellers were lining up at the no-frills check-in.

Some companies had banned their executives from flying, albeit temporarily, after the attacks. When they returned to the air, with budgets trimmed back, there was a sudden interest in why some airlines charge more than others. At dawn one autumn morning at Stansted, while checking in for the flight to Charleroi, I met a rather grumpy camera crew from BBC1's *Blue Peter* programme, who had been ordered to take the cheap way to Belgium.

'People are now remarkably sensitive – in a way I've never known before – about the price of their air ticket,' says Tim Jeans of Ryanair. 'Even people who are part of large corporations are now sensitive to whether they've paid £500 or £100 for a flight to Frankfurt. There's a growing awareness that on most routes there's a choice, and if there is any element of direct budget accountability for that trip – so you, me, everyone except civil servants on junkets, basically – they will choose the low-cost option.'

Jeans himself is rarely cast as a victim, but he is living proof that it is not just the traditional airlines that have suffered. The events of 11 September 2001 had a direct impact on Tim Jeans' personal finances. Almost unbelievably, the sales and marketing manager for Ryanair had previously enjoyed free travel on British Airways – the very airline that he spends most of his professional life attacking. Once the depth of BA's problems became apparent, the airline withdrew the concession – partially. Henceforth, Jeans pays half fare.

Once 2002 began, numbers started improving. Henry Joyner, American Airlines' senior vice-president for network, said that many businesses that had taken a tolerant attitude to executives' disinclination to fly were nominating 1 January 2002 as the day when normal commercial travelling life should resume. Vladimir Raitz has seen it all before. 'People have to fly and to get around, and it took a while after the Gulf War, it may take a little longer with this war. But it will be re-established and it will continue to grow, without any doubt. Although this war against terrorism will last for a long time, after a while people will get used to the situation. And a foreign holiday has become such an intrinsic part of people's lives that it will go on. Civilisation will go to hell if such gloom persists. At the back of every traveller's mind, though, is the thought articulated by Dr Todd Curtis, head of the AirSafe.com website. 'There is no technology that can peer into a person's heart and decipher their intentions. It is difficult to stop a determined hijacker from causing mayhem on an aircraft if that person is willing to die along with the other passengers.'

13. START YOUR OWN AIRLINE, WHY DON'T YOU?

'How do you get to be a millionaire? Be a billionaire, and start an airline'

SIR RICHARD BRANSON

You've read the tangled tales of success and failure in no-frills aviation, of the fortunes to be made and lost. Now it's time to put those lessons into practice, with advice from the people who've been there, done that and have the ulcers to prove it. This chapter contains the insiders' secrets on everything from choosing your planes to selecting the uniforms, and the all-important business of convincing a wary public that you're the best thing since sliced bread – or at least Southwest.

You will need to take some tough decisions to keep costs down and passengers up. The main cost elements comprise what I shall call the five Ps, most expensive first: people, planes, petrol (all right, jet kerosene), places to put them (airports) and promotion. But the place to begin . . . is the place you begin. Until you know where your home is going to be, you can't make the other choices.

SO WHERE SHALL I START?

'There is only one London,' says Stelios of easyJet. The pool of potential passengers within an hour of the capital amounts to over 10 million, with higher-than-average incomes. London is also the place in Britain to which foreigners and Brits alike want to travel to more than any other. With luck, you will balance the routes with substantial numbers originating at either end.

'The south-east is where the biggest demand from UK travellers is concentrated,' confirms David Magliano of Go. But don't be tempted to follow his airline's example and start a second and third UK hub, at Bristol and East Midlands, until you've established yourself. 'Any company starting from scratch has to reach a critical mass and we could not do that if we had spread ourselves thinly across the country from day one,' says Magliano.

SO I HAVE A CHOICE OF THE FIVE LONDON AIRPORTS?

Six, if you count Southend – where Sir Freddie Laker began – as well as Heathrow, Gatwick, London City, Luton and Stansted. But don't kid yourself that you'll breeze into Heathrow or Gatwick and pick up the slots – the right to take off and land at particular times – that you desire. Heathrow is effectively full, with a ridiculously long waiting list of airlines wanting the right to fly from Britain's premier airport. Michael O'Leary of Ryanair has some typically robust thoughts on the place: 'Slots is just an excuse by the big guys for overcharging passengers.' He believes the constraints and delays make Heathrow a waste of time, literally. 'We get at least two more flights per day per aircraft than BA by avoiding Heathrow. We wouldn't fly from there if they paid us.' Interestingly, both Ryanair and easyJet are happy to serve Gatwick, and to pay the substantial associated extra costs, even though the Sussex facility is the busiest single-runway airport on the planet and consequently gets heavily congested. Experience shows that people will pay more to fly from a major airport like Gatwick.

SO THAT'S SETTLED, THEN: GATWICK HERE WE COME

Hang on – while Gatwick has room to increase its current 30 million passengers each year to 40 million, that will come from filling middle-of-the-day and late-evening spaces on the runway. Finding the take-off and landing slots you will need to attract business travellers, at the start of the day and in late afternoon/early evening, will be very tough. Ray Webster, chief executive of easyJet, headed south from Luton to the Sussex airport almost as soon as BA announced route cuts, and still had problems getting the slots he wanted for Britain's most successful no-frills airline. And even if you get some handy 8 a.m. and 6 p.m. rights during the winter, in summer – when the main charter season is running – you may have to change the times or cancel the flights altogether. The reason is what are known in the industry as 'Grandfather rights': airlines that have traditionally flown from Gatwick to, say, Cyprus at 8 a.m. (and back at 6 p.m.) every Friday are entitled to claim those same slots each summer. So all your loyal customers who have become accustomed through the winter to the flights to, say, Baden-Baden and back will find that the ideal departure times have disappeared – as have your earnings.

LONDON CITY?

Very handy for town, but three big negatives. You will be constrained with the aircraft you can use: the 100-seater BAe 146 is about the largest that can land there. The passenger charges are the highest in Britain because of the limited throughput of the airport and the high costs associated with running a small airport in a big city. And the airport closes down for half the weekend to give the long-suffering residents of

Docklands a break from aircraft noise. Try selling a six-day-a-week operation to the passengers, and the investors. The Israeli airline, El Al, suffers mightily from being grounded during the Sabbath.

SO THAT LEAVES LUTON, STANSTED OR SOUTHEND. HOW DO I CHOOSE BETWEEN THEM?

By asking each airport what sort of check-in facilities, slots and gates are available, and how much you will be charged for each of them. For Southend, the answers are likely to be 'plenty of space, for not very much money'; but since Laker left, the Essex airport has experienced something of a decline. The railway line from London goes past the airport perimeter, but there is no dedicated station. And the only no-frills service from Southend – to Ostend in Belgium – did not last long. So concentrate on Stansted and Luton, and try to play one off against the other as easyJet did, according to former marketing director, Tony Anderson: 'Luton was an afterthought, a bargaining chip.' When he was taken on, he was told to start looking for a house near Stansted. But Luton offered a good deal, and turned out to be a fortunate choice for easyJet, if not for Debonair. 'Luton has a fantastic catchment area,' says Anderson. But don't expect to have the upper hand in negotiations. After years in the doldrums, Luton and Stansted are now able to charge around £6 per passenger. And slots where you can get those crucial early-morning flights out are becoming scarce.

PLANES NEXT?

No, be patient. First you need to decide where to fly. That has a bearing on the aircraft you choose. 'Underserved and overpriced' is the Southwest mantra to identifying routes where low fares can prosper: where one or two traditional airlines carve up the service between them, charging whatever fares the market will bear to fly on a limited number of departures. 'The key thing to consider is can we add something by going on to a route?' says David Magliano of Go. 'Do we add choice for the consumer and create an increase in total demand? We are here to allow people to travel to more places more often through lower fares.'

Choosing a winning route is still something akin to alchemy, but there is plenty you can do to maximise your chances. The tangle of laws that govern aviation links means that you cannot simply look at a map and pick out the big cities without no-frills flights from Britain. The people of Warsaw and Budapest would no doubt welcome a low-cost alternative to the national airlines. But once you venture outside the European Union, two things happen. First, there's a good chance you won't be allowed to fly the route at all. The EU has at least theoretical open skies (though slot constraints mean that this ideal has some way to go), with any airline based in one of the member countries able to fly anywhere it chooses. As soon as you step into the rest of the world, the interests of flag-carrier airlines intervene, making it difficult for anyone else to get a look in. The only eastern European airport with no-frills service is Prague, but Go first earned the right to fly it only when BMI stopped flying there; since then, BMIbaby has joined Go on routes to the Czech capital. Second, passengers are hit by Air Passenger Duty (APD, the tax levied by the UK government) four times higher than for EU destinations. Do you really want to sweat blood to make a pound or two per passenger when the Chancellor is making £20 a head with no effort at all?

So stay inside the EU until you've got some experience. Decide whether to use primary airports like Amsterdam, Barcelona or Copenhagen, or secondary airports such as Maastricht, Gerona or Malmo. Primary destinations will cost more, but you can get away with higher fares. Secondary airports are cheaper, but require much brand-boosting to persuade people they actually want to go there. I'd suggest secondary first, for three reasons: the slot problems of major gateways; the benefits that Ryanair and easyJet enjoy, at Stansted and Luton respectively, that accrue from being the first no-frills airlines; and the chances of getting 'help' from an airport with no significant scheduled network – in other words, they'll pay you for the privilege of providing you with services.

HOW ABOUT SOME IDEAS, THEN?

From the hundreds of airports dotted around Europe, it is possible to narrow the choice down considerably. I have come up with some examples that meet the first test, at least as of April 2002: there is no competition on any of these routes. I shall explain the logic behind my selection, and also explain why others are not ideal.

I wasn't joking about Baden-Baden. With much of Europe already carved up by the existing low-cost carriers, it's a question of seeing where the remaining gaps are. The airport serving the German spa town is in a prosperous part of Europe that has good motorway links but no nearby no-frills operators. The catchment area extends far beyond the town itself, taking in the northern part of the Black Forest, the prosperous city of Karlsruhe, and Strasbourg, home to the Council of Europe and, at least some of the time, the European Parliament. Even Stuttgart is barely an hour away. These properties should help you achieve a good mix of business and leisure travel, with strong demand at both ends of the route. I also considered Dresden or Leipzig in the former East Germany, but they have two problems: a significantly longer flying time, and a relatively poor local population. One drawback for Germany as a whole is the relatively small penetration of credit-card use, but Ryanair and Go have already demonstrated that the no-frills, book-direct concept can work in the Federal Republic. You may even draw in some traffic from northern Switzerland; Basel lacks a no-frills airline, but it has a fast train service to Baden-Baden.

Spain looks another good bet, especially if you steer clear of existing operators. Santiago de Compostela, on the north-western tip, is a relatively small city, but has a wide catchment that extends east to cities like Oviedo and León, and south to Vigo and across the border to Portugal – arguably as far as Lisbon, since Go has pulled out of the capital. There is still a significant British expatriate community in and around Porto and the Duoro valley of northern Portugal, which will help sustain leisure travel all through the year. Iberia already flies from Heathrow to Santiago, but at Bilbao, further along the north coast, Go managed to carve out a whole new market when it began flights from Stansted. Thanks to Go, Buzz and easyJet, Spain has more no-frills flights from Britain than any other country, which means the population is well versed in the concept of low-cost aviation.

Finally, at least one domestic destination not currently served by no-frills airlines is a good idea, not least because it provides a potential base for expansion later on. There are plenty to choose from, including Dundee, Carlisle, Teesside and Plymouth. But the best prospects are probably at Cardiff. The Welsh capital has a vastly underused airport, and is far enough from the north of London to make driving a real pain. There is no prospect within the next twenty years of any significant acceleration in the rail service. In either direction at present, a day trip by surface transport is a nightmare – particularly to the City of London, which is well served by train from both Luton and Stansted. Wales is the only component of the UK without a no-frills airport, and the new service will act as a feeder to other low-cost carriers.

All your choices should be some distance apart, so you can then start flying between them if the market looks right; Santiago to Baden-Baden looks a promising route, and there are big savings on operations and marketing if you can establish a second base and 'join the dots'. I'm not sure how Cardiff to Baden-Baden might perform, but Ryanair seems to make money on the equally unlikely pairing of Bournemouth to Hahn.

The large Mediterranean islands of Sicily and Corsica look tempting, too, with no existing scheduled flights from the UK. Corsica is crying out for an air link from Britain. Unlike the people of much of Europe, Corsicans cannot simply jump into a car or on to a train to reach a suitable low-cost airport; the nearest, Nice and Alghero, each require a ferry trip as well. Sicily is a rich part of Italy without a no-frills option; the closest is Naples on the mainland. But there are good reasons not to choose them. Even though Calvi in Corsica was the destination for Vladimir Raitz's first-ever charter, the island as a whole has a relatively modest amount of accommodation, with much of it permanently booked up by French and Italian holidaymakers. Your customers may not take kindly to being invited to sleep in US forces tents like the first Horizon clients. Sicily looks wide open, but Ryanair regards Italy as its patch. 'If any so called "low-cost" imitator wants to throw down a challenge to Ryanair on any of our routes, anywhere, anytime, and any price then they may rest assured that we will meet every such challenge,' says Michael O'Leary. As Go found to its considerable cost when it launched the Edinburgh–Dublin route – which Ryanair previously did not operate – if the Irish airline decides to take on a rival it will shovel in capacity and loss-leader fares. That is a battle to be fought at some time in the future, when you have the cash for a long, expensive war of attrition.

GREAT: BADEN-BADEN, SANTIAGO AND CARDIFF. THEY'RE GOING TO PULL IN THE PUNTERS, THEN

Yes, at least in one direction. None have low-cost flights to London, and so the attraction to the local community will be considerable. Going the other way, sell the 'gateway' concept in the way that Ryanair has done. Baden-Baden can be marketed as the gateway to the Black Forest, and – to use the Ryanair vocabulary – Strasbourg (East). Cardiff serves West Wales and Santiago opens up northern Portugal.

CAN WE TALK ABOUT PLANES NOW?

OK. Some no-frills airlines get by with aircraft holding around one hundred people: Buzz and AirTran use BAe146s and Boeing 717s respectively. But most opt for something larger. That could mean the Airbus A320 and its derivatives (in this case, 'derivatives' being jargon for making planes longer or shorter). John Patterson, managing director of the with-frills airline, GB Airways, is such a big fan of the A320 and its longer sibling, the A321, that he has converted his entire fleet of Boeing 737s to the European plane. 'The A320 is a broader, wider aircraft which goes down very, very well with the customer.' Rumours abound that a UK no-frills carrier is about to place a big order for Airbuses. So far, though, only New York-based JetBlue uses those.

Everyone else is sticking with the jet that Southwest started off with in 1971, and which David Magliano of Go calls 'the Ford Escort of the skies': the Boeing 737. The world's most popular plane is about as exciting as a Ford Escort. But it has become the standard for every successful no-frills airline. Its sheer popularity, says Magliano, means 'planes, pilots and parts are widely available'. It is made in Renton, the Seattle suburb where Jimi Hendrix grew up; the guitarist's grave is barely a mile from the Boeing 737 factory, which overlooks Lake Washington. 'We share the shore with Bill Gates,' jokes one employee.

As you will discover when you go and see the folks at Boeing, the first journey for every one of the jets begins in Wichita, Kansas, where the fuselage is made. They are shipped from the Midwest on extraordinary-looking trains that protect the delicate skin of the aircraft embryo from trees. The journey of 2,000 miles along the Burlington Northern Santa Fe track ends when the locomotive hauls the fuselage through the factory gates, and it is transferred to a bright yellow 'dolly' for the next stage of the operation. Assembling the thing – bolting on the wings, tailplane, undercarriage and engines, and laying four miles of cable – takes eighteen working days. Only at the later stages does the interior take shape. You, the customer, supply the seats and the lavatories you want; Franco Mancassola of Avia Interiors in Italy will be pleased to negotiate on the seats, and there's a company in Camberley, Surrey, that will probably give you a good deal on the loos. Finally, the jet is tugged out of the enormous hangar on to Renton Field, where final touches are applied over the following week. The new Boeing 737's first flight is a ridiculously small distance – five miles at most – to Boeing Field, where it spends another fortnight in tests. So from departing Wichita to being ready for you to come and pick up (they never deliver), reckon on close on two months.

HOW MUCH WILL THAT COST ME?
First, a couple of things you need to know while you're talking to Boeing. Never call the aircraft the 'seven-three-seven', 'Three-seven' is sufficient (though you might have thought that 'three' is all they would need to differentiate it from the 747, 757, 767, etc.). And the three-seven comes in separate sizes, indicated by a number in the hundreds. For the industry-standard 737-700, which easyJet fits out with 149 seats, list price is about $30m. No one ever pays list price, though, and even as a first-time customer buying only three jets you can expect a bargain. That's because each aircraft manufacturer is keen that any start-up airline uses its equipment; while it is not uncommon for

carriers to switch from Airbus to Boeing or vice versa some years down the line, this will be as part of a package where the aircraft maker pays for pilots and engineers to be retrained. 'To get in now saves them an absolute fortune,' says Michael Lord-Castle, the man behind the new business-class airline, Blue Fox. So reckon on $25m each, tops (Ryanair is thought to have paid substantially less for its recent order for 100 jets). You'll need three planes to operate a sensible schedule at a reasonable frequency, and to cover for scheduled maintenance.

If you don't have $75m immediately available, there are several leasing companies that will be pleased to lend you a plane. Their pleasure derives from having bought the aircraft, often speculatively, then renting them to you at around $100,000 per month. That is a lot of cash to concentrate the mind, and is why David Magliano of Go advises, 'If you can afford to own your aircraft outright, it's a given that you will.'

Or buy second-hand; you could just follow Ryanair and place ads in the aviation press seeking cheap, 'previously operated' jets, the polite phrase for 'old'. A Boeing 737-300 could be yours for about $15m if it is in good nick (and, if it isn't, don't buy it). It's basically an earlier version of the -700, and seats the same number of passengers.

At all costs, make sure you use only one type of aircraft. All your flight crew and engineers must be able to work on all your fleet, even though your planes may come in different sizes. The Boeing 737-600, -700 and -800 are basically the Small, Medium and Large of no-frills aviation; so far, no low-cost airline has ordered the XL, the -900 seating two hundred people or more. But easyJet, Virgin Express and Go believe that one size fits all. Sir Richard Branson says that right now is a very good time to talk to airline manufacturers: 'They are hungry for people to take their planes, so try to strike a deal with them so your cash flow is good.'

WHEN SHOULD I FLY THEM?

That also depends on the exact type of aircraft you buy. Many people think that jet planes travel at the same speed. In fact, the BAe 146 is about 10 per cent slower than the Boeing 737-300, which itself plods along 10 per cent behind the 737-700. On short flights – like London to Cardiff and Baden-Baden – the difference is tiny. But when easyJet started flying its -700s to Athens instead of -300s, the time improvement was twenty minutes each way.

When you're working out your schedule, remember that there is a big difference between the airborne duration and the 'block time', which is the figures you publish in the timetable. This commences at the start of the push-back on departure, and ends when the pilot applies the handbrake at the destination airport. You have to allow for taxiing at each end of the journey, which can easily add ten minutes at Stansted or Luton, a little less at smaller, less crowded airports. You will also need to 'pad' your schedules to build in extra time for delays, though quiet airports will help. 'Flying to an airport like Hahn, our block times are 35 minutes shorter than the equivalent low-cost operation by Buzz at Stansted to Frankfurt Main,' says Tim Jeans of Ryanair. 'With a 25-minute turnaround, we're already ten minutes into the homeward journey by the time they get there. We pad, but we don't have to pad as much as the others do.'

The flying time should be an hour flat from either Luton or Stansted to Baden-Baden. Allow one hour, 20 minutes in total, and 25 minutes for the 'turn' between flights. With a 6 a.m. departure from London and the last flight coming back in at around 11 p.m., you can squeeze in five round trips every day. On paper, it looks like a neat schedule from London, with departures at 6 a.m., 9.30 a.m., 1 p.m., 4.30 p.m. and 8 p.m. A business traveller on the first flight out should arrive, local time, at 8.20 a.m., and could easily be in Karlsruhe or Strasbourg by nine. From Baden-Baden it's not so ideal, with flights leaving at 8.45 a.m., 12.15 p.m., 3.45 p.m., 7.15 p.m. and 10.45 p.m. (these are local times). But the aircraft will be actually in the air for ten hours, which on a short route is pretty good going. And, as the Southwest mantra insists, 'utilisation is the key'.

THE CREW WILL BE KNACKERED FLYING THAT KIND OF SCHEDULE SEVEN DAYS A WEEK, WON'T THEY?

They would if they were allowed to fly that many missions, but quite sensibly they're not. A hard-working captain will be airborne for only eighteen hours in a busy week.

SO HOW MANY PEOPLE WILL I NEED TO FLY THE AIRCRAFT – AND HOW MUCH WILL I HAVE TO PAY THEM?

For each plane, reckon on five crews: that means five captains, five first officers and fifteen cabin crew. One consequence of 11 September 2001 was that a looming pilot shortage failed to materialise. All summer, industry watchers had been warning that the supply of qualified pilots was not keeping pace with the increase in demand for air travel, fuelled by the success of no-frills operators. But the downturn in commercial aviation meant that hundreds of well-qualified pilots were suddenly available. Even so, the average first officer is probably not going to get out of bed (especially not for that 6 a.m. departure) for less than £60,000 per year, and an experienced captain would certainly be looking for £80,000. And that's cheap: Branson says you must 'make it clear to your pilots and crew when they join that you've got to keep fares at a decent price, say "please don't push the costs out of control". If they really want massive salaries they should go elsewhere.'

Cabin crew come a lot cheaper than pilots, not least because their training takes a month rather than several years – and because there is a seemingly never-ending supply of people who still believe that flying is glamorous and exciting. They are prepared to work for £12,000 per year (and that's after their pay has been topped up by an extra fee for every sector flown).

WHAT WILL THEY WEAR?

Anything you buy for them, though it will help you get them on your side if you involve them in the decision process. Tony Anderson, former marketing director for easyJet, relates the strange tale of choosing the cabin-crew uniforms for his infant airline, a saga that began in the chain store, Next, in a town south of Luton airport:

'We bought a stack of jackets, shirts and trousers. We pulled the stuff off the racks, piled into the car and took them back to easyLand for a modelling session by staff.' The cabin crew were relieved to have avoided the ill-fitting polyester worn by other airlines' staff. But it was clear to Anderson and Stelios that the look wasn't sufficiently distinctive.

'Then Anna, our office manager at easyLand, mentioned that she'd seen someone wandering around in a fantastic orange polo shirt with a Benetton logo. I was duly dispatched to the nearest Benetton shop in Milton Keynes where indeed there was a polo shirt and a matching sweatshirt both in garish easyJet orange, matching almost exactly the official colour. I phoned Stelios who was so enthused that he instructed me to come back to easyLand, pick him up and drive back to Milton Keynes. When he saw the shirts Stelios was suitably impressed and duly bought all the orange polo shirts and sweatshirts in the shop – about eight of each in a variety of sizes.'

Feedback from the rest of the team at easyLand was positive, so Anderson was told to talk to Benetton's HQ in Italy and place an order for 150 polo shirts and 150 sweatshirts. This proved more difficult than it sounds, as manufacturers do not keep central stocks, particularly of gaudy colours that go out of fashion as quickly as they come in. So Anderson made a road trip around London visiting Benetton stores in Islington, Brent Cross, and Oxford Street. 'God knows what the sales staff made of this strange character that came in took all the orange sweatshirts and polo shirts off the shelves and stuffed them into a large bag. By the end of the day I had accumulated around 150 shirts, which were piled high in a storage room at easyLand. I joked to Stelios that in our recruitment, which we were shortly to begin, we'd need to find twelve large, twenty medium and eighteen small staff to fit the uniforms we'd bought.'

WHO ELSE WILL I NEED TO EMPLOY?

Your chief operating officer needs to have decades of experience working for an airline. In contrast, arguably the less experience of aviation your marketing director has, the better: he or she will not be hidebound by tradition. The right information technology person is crucial; you will be selling almost all your seats on the Internet. Beyond that, you'll need people who keep any airline going: engineers, ground staff, a sales team . . . The good news is that you need not take them on as your own employees. At most airports served by low-cost airlines, the check-in staff are all bought in. For the first couple of months of easyJet's operation, the orange-clad staff were being 'wet-leased' along with the planes from GB Airways. But whether you employ direct or outsource, reckon on about ninety workers for each of your aircraft. Any more than a hundred per plane, and you are getting dangerously close to the employment levels of the larger carriers.

Pick people with care, and motivate them, says Sir Richard Branson. 'If you're starting a low-cost carrier, all your staff must feel that their mission is to enable people to fly who can't afford to fly, to help small businesses get up and running, and to help old people visit their relatives more often. It shouldn't just be a mission to worry about the shareholder's return. I think that if you can get that sort of passion into the airline, and all the staff are 100 per cent believing in what they're doing, and feeling really proud of what they're doing, and proud of the company, and proud of the brand, so they can go home and say, "I work for easyJet, I work for Virgin, I work for Laker", that's three quarters of the battle.'

One good way to generate loyalty is to have an in-flight magazine in which the staff can take pride. With luck, you can get others to pay for it with advertising. Get someone like *Rough Guides* to put together the editorial for you, to ensure a credibility that is so often lacking in the genre, or get a rival to do the work for you. Go's *One-Line Guide* is published by the same people who provide British Airways with *High Life* magazine.

OK, SO NOW CAN I START?

There's the small matter of an Aircraft Operating Certificate, which you will need to obtain from the Civil Aviation Authority. 'It's a driving licence for airlines,' says David Magliano of Go. 'It shows that not only do you meet certain standards in every part of the operation, but also that you have processes in place to maintain those standards.' When easyJet began, it flew under an AOC belonging to Air Foyle, a charter company. Being part of a bigger airline, British Airways, meant Go could have sheltered under the corporate umbrella, but Barbara Cassani chose not to do so: 'Barbara made the decision that our very first flight would be on our own AOC,' says Magliano. 'It proved to be a significant undertaking in terms of the sheer number of activities that had to be done to satisfy the CAA.'

Before you start flying, it will be handy to have some passengers well ahead of time, not least because the cash they supply in advance will make your balance sheet more fragrant. And to do that, you will need an identity.

BRIANAIR? EASYPLANE? BUZZ OFF?

No, and if you use any of those you will certainly be sued for trade-mark infringement. Either employ consultants (as Go did with Wolfe Olins) to come up with the name, or think of one yourself. Tony Ryan and Sir Freddie Laker didn't spend much time or money dreaming up Ryanair and Laker Airways, but arguably a snappy name like Go or Buzz is international and memorable. Even with expert help, picking a suitable title can be a minefield. I thought 'Climb' or 'Lift' might sound good, but they would upset air traffic control: there is plenty of scope for confusion if Climb flight one is instructed to descend.

Don't lock yourself into a particular region or ocean, as Southwest and Northwest, Virgin Atlantic and Cathay Pacific all did. You might imagine that when David Neeleman, founder of JetBlue, needed a name in 1999, he merely picked a couple of elements that combined easyJet and Virgin Blue. Not a bit of it; indeed, you could consider a few of the two hundred discarded names that David Neeleman, founder of JetBlue, rejected. There were joke ones like Dairy Air (say it out loud, in a slightly French accent); more serious options including many that uses the traditional 'Air' element: Hiway Air, Imagine Air, Fresh Air, Scout Air, Air Avenues and Air Hop. Original thinking (now that's a name in itself) began with It, Yes, The Competition, The High Road, Civilization and Idlewild (the name for Kennedy airport before the president was shot). Taxi was a favourite, until someone pointed out that, like Climb, it could lead to all kinds of confusion on the ground.

After paying $100,000 to the design consultants Landor Associates – who are behind the British Airways brand – Neeleman then settled on True Blue. Unfortunately, another company had already snapped it up. Landor halved the fee, and a company insider applied Jet in place of True. After a long brainstorming session over breakfast one day, the best I could come up with were Air OK, Beans, and Toast. But with the last two names, your rivals could have you for breakfast.

AND A LOGO?

Go paid good money for one, and won awards for it. Ryanair and easyJet did neither of the above. Anecdotal evidence suggests that good design is important for business travellers. 'People don't feel comfortable with the orange brashness of easyJet,' says Barbara Cassani of Go. Invest in your identity, and impress your customers.

SO ARE BUSINESS PEOPLE MY TARGET MARKET?

A large part of it. The natural business constituency of a no-frills carrier is the small or medium enterprise, the sort of people who keep a careful eye on costs. But set the controls for the hearts and minds of a wide range of travellers. Divide leisure passengers into two groups: those who are purely travelling on holiday, and those who are visiting friends and relations (VFR, in the jargon). The latter will be more reliable, year-round, but the former will pay higher prices at peak times. Look for balance on the route. You need to attract business travellers who will fill the plane on morning and evening flights during the week, and leisure passengers who will be attracted by cheap fares in the middle of the day. They will also be prepared to pay a premium for travel at weekends. And you will also want to achieve balance at each end of the route. On a route like Go's Bristol–Faro service, almost all the passengers originate in Britain. With a more even spread, you are less susceptible to economic cycles in one country or the other.

SHOULD I DO LOTS OF MARKET RESEARCH?

No. You could try looking round the car parks at each airport, checking out the geographical codes on the licence plates to gauge the catchment area. But most low-cost routes establish a market that no one was certain existed. The most reckless route that Ryanair ever opened was Bournemouth to Hahn, on Valentine's Day 2002. 'I can't be confident that route is going to be a great success,' said Tim Jeans, the airline's sales and marketing director, before the launch. 'Did we research [the Bournemouth–Hahn] route and try and prove to ourselves that that would be the case beforehand? No, we didn't. I'm a great optimist.' A few months later, he was proved right, with excellent loads and yields on the Dorset to the Hunsrück route. Market research is not a discipline that is much used among airline entrepreneurs like Sir Richard Branson, whose principle market research for getting into the airline business was to find that the reservations number for PEOPLExpress (the low-cost carrier then flying between Gatwick and Newark) was permanently engaged.

But know your enemy. The competition is anyone who can carry a customer on the route they wish to travel, be they low-cost, traditional or charter airlines. On domestic routes, trains and motorways are the alternatives. With the possible exception of motorways, everyone will be doing their utmost to spoil your party. Be prepared for vicious competition.

WHERE DO I ADVERTISE?
Anywhere you can: press, the sides of taxis, billboards on your rivals' turf. Be prepared to spend a fortune: on an average flight, the earnings from half-a-dozen seats will be eaten up by promotional costs.

SHOULD I USE TRAVEL AGENTS?
Incentivise them a little, with a few pounds for each booking they make on the Internet. But don't get caught up with paying the 9 per cent commission that is still the norm in much of the aviation industry. In 1999, Stelios was watching his distribution costs tumble as the number of people booking online increased. Meanwhile, British Airways was paying more to sell its seats – mostly through agents – than it was on putting fuel in the planes. In reality, though, the vast majority of your seats will be sold direct to the public, over the Internet. The other no-frills airlines have done the work for you: travellers know how the low-cost concept works, and they also know how to book flights on the Internet.

HOW MUCH AM I GOING TO CHARGE?
On your first few flights, a flat fare of perhaps £20 each way, including all taxes, fees and charges. You'll be losing a small fortune, but you'll get your name known. You must then quickly master the black art of yield management – getting the maximum fare from each seat, while leaving as few as possible unoccupied. To understand the principle, visit the

No.1 Oriental Buffet in Whitworth Street, Manchester. Between noon and 4 p.m., you can eat all you like for £5.50. From 4–6 p.m., it rises by £1; and after 6 p.m., by £2. On Saturday evenings, you can add another £1, almost double the base price. There are various specials offered during the week to attract students. Exactly the same product costs different prices at different times. That principle works for airlines just as it does for Chinese food, with the extra sophistication of rewarding the early booker. The No.1 Oriental Buffet could probably increase its occupancy still further by lopping a pound or two off for people who are prepared to commit a week in advance. That would boost the restaurant's 'load factor', but it would deplete the average amount that each diner pays – the yield. These are the two key measures in aviation. You want both of these to be as high as possible, though the natural tendency is for them to work in different directions: fares come down, load factors increase; fares go up, load factors decrease.

Yield management explains the first principle of air travel, that the person next to you has always paid less than you have. Start off by assigning a certain number of seats to each price band. On the Monday morning departure to Baden-Baden, you will want to make very few cheap seats available, because you can look forward to filling the flight with high-revenue business travellers. But that 10.45 p.m. departure from Germany is always going to be a 'dog flight' – nothing to do with passports for pets, but the industry's acknowledgement that a flight is 'non-optimally scheduled', i.e. you're really going to have to bribe people to get on board. So put plenty of seats on sale at low prices, and keep checking – micro-managing – each departure to make sure that you're filling the plane at the best prices you can. Expect that last flight of the day to generate an average fare of a fiver.

It's a long-held myth that the later a passenger books a flight, the cheaper it becomes – that is partly the way that traditional airlines used standby flights to try to tackle the Laker Skytrain. In practice, people who book the day before are those who will pay the most to guarantee a place on board. So on the 6 a.m. to Baden-Baden, and even the 10.45 p.m. from there, keep a few seats free for the people who are prepared to pay £150 for a one-way flight. That's still a heck of a lot less than Air France to Strasbourg.

DISCOUNTS FOR YOUNGSTERS?

No. Be tough on children, and tough on the causes of children – international aviation rules dictate that anyone aged two or over must occupy a seat. On with-frills airlines, there is a case for offering some sort of discount to children between two and eleven (the usual limit) because they are less likely to be knocking back one Jack Daniel's after another. On no-frills flights, since costs are effectively the same regardless of age, it makes no economic sense to offer a discount for anyone who has lived for more than 730 days. Ryanair takes this one stage further by imposing a £5 'administrative charge' on infants.

Sex is no doubt the motivation of some of the passengers, especially if you fly to romantic places like Paris or Venice. But deter in-flight intercourse; about the only place it can happen is in a lavatory, which will inconvenience the other passengers no end. And, if your staff comprise one or both of the participants, you will soon get a salacious reputation in the tabloids, with attendant headlines alluding to the easyVirtue of flight crew.

DO I REALLY HAVE TO FILL UP ALL THE SEATS?

No. If you are Ryanair, then selling just more than half is enough to break even. Sometimes, though, you may want to fill up more than all the seats.

SURELY YOU DON'T MEAN OVERBOOKING?

I surely do. It's good for you, and for your passengers. Travellers, and airlines, should be in favour of overbooking. The practice of selling 'confirmed' seats to more people than can fit on a plane is an overwhelmingly positive phenomenon. It helps keep fares down and increases the opportunities for travel. Only when an airline fails to cope adequately with the consequences of everyone turning up does it turn into a negative. If the European Commission were to carry out its threat to put an end to overbooking, all scheduled airline passengers would suffer.

Airlines overbook because passengers aren't perfect. On the average no-frills flight, around 5 per cent of people holding reservations for a particular flight will fail to show up. So it is fair for the airlines to assume that one in twenty passengers will be a 'no-show', and to accept bookings for seven seats more than are fitted to the typical 737. This enables you to fly with a higher load factor (i.e. with more of their seats filled), the per-passenger cost decreases and fares can be lower than they would otherwise be. A second benefit is that more people are able to travel: if airlines stopped accepting bookings once a plane reached 100 per cent capacity, some prospective travellers would be denied the chance of boarding the flight of their choice, even though – most of the time – there is room for them on board.

SO IF THERE'S NOTHING WRONG WITH OVERBOOKING, WHY DO PEOPLE GET SO UPSET ABOUT IT?

Because sometimes an airline's desire for full planes backfires, and more people turn up than there are seats available. That itself is not a problem, unless you handle the consequences ungenerously or ineptly. As travellers, we almost all have our price. Sure, there are a few passengers on most flights who simply have to get to their destination, for personal or professional reasons. But most of us will, if the price is right, agree to defer our journey.

An overbooked flight is a problem that can easily be solved without anyone getting upset. You just need to throw money at it. Since the profit motive brings the situation about, some of your earnings from the many occasions when it guesses right must be given out when the bet goes wrong. Americans, who are by far the leading consumers of air travel, are well used to the idea. If a flight is looking dangerously oversold, announcements will be made at the gate asking for people who are prepared to postpone their travel plans. The initial bribe is often low – maybe £100. As the minutes tick away until departure, add other sweeteners, like a free round trip to anywhere the airline flies. Mostly, though, money talks. If boarding has been completed and there are still confirmed passengers waiting at the gate, increase the bribe until space is found. The result of this aeronautical auction is that the people who really need to travel are able to do so. Meanwhile, the passengers who take the bribes feel chuffed. Over time, passengers become rational participants in this system. Many travellers, me included, build in as much flexibility as possible to flight plans. If an option to offload voluntarily comes up, then there are plenty of willing takers. As a Continental Airlines flight prepared to depart from Seattle to Cleveland, I witnessed (all right, took part in) a race to the front of the plane to claim the $300 (£210) being offered so that two unaccompanied minors could travel to see their father in Ohio. Running an airline is a high-stakes business. Be prepared, when the overbooking trump lets you down, to improve the odds in favour of passengers and switch the people who are currently involuntarily denied boarding into willing volunteers.

ANYWHERE I CAN MAKE MORE MONEY?

Inflight sales, an opportunity that existing no-frills airlines rarely seize. For example, do a deal with the local rail or bus company to sell tickets in flight. They weigh next to nothing and take up minimal space, yet you can sell them at a profit to passengers who really don't want to be bothered faffing around to find the right change and persuade the ticket machine to work. The same hassle factor means you should make a handsome profit selling pre-stamped holiday postcards for the destination – ideal for people who are going over for a quick weekend – with a reminder of the local rendition of Great Britain, Deutschland or España to help the passenger address the thing. Charge £10 for the right to check in fifteen minutes (instead of half-an-hour) before departure. And offer to transfer bags (e.g. Cardiff–Stansted–Santiago) in return for the same fee.

WHEN I'VE SOLD ALL THE SEATS I CAN, IT'S EASY: THEY DELIVER THEMSELVES TO THE AIRPORT?

Treat the business of getting people on planes as a military exercise, advises Richard Garrett. He is the former army officer who looks after Ryanair's airports in continental Europe. 'It's all about people and equipment coming together to perform a set drill.' But don't neglect the human side. Remember that check-in isn't like a supermarket check-out. Airports are curious places where the staff are familiar and comfortable with the environment and its geography. So, too, are some of the regular travellers. But no-frills airlines also attract a large number of people who have never travelled before. Many passengers are under stress, heading for events like weddings or funerals. The scope for problems is immense. To make sure people get on the planes on time, 'push from the check in, pull from the gate,' urges Garrett. 'There should never be a void. Attract people to the gate. Make them hungry to get on the plane.' And that means not having a seat assignment for each passenger. 'People are far more comfortable if there's a seat reserved.'

ONCE WE'RE GOING, IT'S ALL DOWNHILL, ISN'T IT?

No, and letting the eye stray from the ball operationally or strategically is what has brought the downfall of many airlines. Minimise your risk. Short term, keep marketing aggressively. 'It's like a shark,' explains Tim Jeans, sales and marketing director of Ryanair. 'When you stop swimming, you sink.' In off-peak travel periods, set up a promotion with a newspaper. You will get lots of publicity, they will attract readers, and if you stipulate the right conditions you should make sure you don't 'cannibalise' the people who would have paid high fares to travel with you.

WHAT IF THINGS GO WRONG?

Not 'if' – 'when'. Deal intelligently with problems. Suppose a plane 'goes technical' – how do you cope? Try to hire one in on the ad-hoc market, but be warned that you could face a five-figure bill. Instead, you may want to be cruel to holidaymakers to be kind to business travellers.

A two-hour delay on a weekday morning domestic flight, or a service to an important foreign business destination, is likely to cause more upset than the same delay on a 'sunshine' destination such as southern Italy, Spain or Portugal. For business travellers, a two-hour wait could wreck the whole trip, while for people going on a fortnight's holiday it will barely merit a mention. So if you are forced to choose (and you most certainly will be), go for the option that minimises the damage to your credibility. Delay the Santiago flight so that people can get to Baden-Baden on time.

Long term, limit the downside by hedging. You will be earning cash in pounds and euros, but spending in dollars. So use the financial instrument of hedging to limit your exposure to sharp currency fluctuations. Buying fuel ahead is also essential, to minimise the chances that OPEC can put you out of business.

You will also need a crisis-management plan for use if your aircraft is in an accident. Rent space from British Airways at its Compass Centre at Heathrow, which is where you handle all the calls from distraught relatives, and make sure your PR people can handle a crisis as adroitly as a seat sale.

IF A FLIGHT IS LATE AND PEOPLE DECIDE NOT TO TRAVEL, SHOULD I OFFER REFUNDS?

No. Full-fare passengers who opt not to travel can be allowed to re-book on another flight, or use the money paid towards a different departure. But for everyone else, make the cancellation charge exactly equal to the fare paid. You will make a lot more money out of people who don't fly than those who do.

WON'T I END UP ON WATCHDOG?

Quite possibly, but some no-frills operators see the BBC1 consumer programme as an opportunity to preach the low-fares mantra.

SMOKING?

Don't allow it. A couple of months after Go got going, the airline had a highly publicised incident at Milan where the captain kept passengers grounded until the one who had been smoking owned up – and he himself was arrested by Italian police for imprisoning the passengers. But it brought home the point that Go was flying to Milan.

THE GIANTS HIT BACK

The one certainty about starting a no-frills airline is that the competition will be queuing up to put you out of business. Flying from London to Cardiff, for example, is certain to generate a reaction from the train operator, First Great Western. To Santiago, Iberia will hit back with lower fares on the route. And Air France is likely to respond similarly to new flights from London to Baden-Baden that threaten its lucrative traffic to Strasbourg.

The biggest threat, though, could come from Europe's biggest airline. In February 2002, British Airways' chief executive, Rod Eddington, outlined the airline's plan: 'We must transform British Airways into a simpler, leaner, more focused airline.' The plan includes high-frequency, lower-cost flights designed to appeal to leisure and business travellers alike. This sounds remarkably similar to the no-frills proposition – and BA is even turning its Gatwick short-haul operation into a Boeing 737-only fleet. New airlines will ignore it at their peril.

British Airways' great strength remains its home airport. Heathrow is the most accessible airport for the majority of people within Europe's biggest catchment area, and offers the widest range of flights. Whoever possesses the largest number of slots has a unique asset – and that is the happy position for BA.

GIMMICKS SEEM TO WORK WELL IN GENERATING FREE PUBLICITY – ESPECIALLY WITH HIGH-PROFILE PERSONALITIES

They certainly do. Sir Richard Branson has performed countless stunts for Virgin Atlantic, while camera-friendly Stelios – who, these days, devotes only a small amount of his time to easyJet – is always wheeled out ahead of the brainy backroom boss, Ray Webster. Television is a crucial medium these days, but the cost of reaching a substantial audience is so high that any publicity you can generate for free is valuable. An airline needs a leader who projects and promotes the company. Branson says he is 'trying to make sure that if someone's picking up the phone to book a flight, then the first one that comes to their mind is Virgin, rather than American or BA. It also helps to do it all with a little bit of panache, and style and fun, and make people smile, and try and do it in such a way that gets on the front page.'

AND WHAT IF I CAN'T MAKE MONEY?

'Accept that one day you may have the embarrassment of failing, and of having a bankrupt company in your hands, but you'll have great fun in the process,' advises Branson. You'll learn a lot, give a lot back and you should never be embarrassed about failure if you've given it your all.'

14. A LIFE IN THE DAY

'There's a challenge every day in the airline industry not to do something stupid'
MICHAEL O'LEARY, CHIEF EXECUTIVE, RYANAIR

'We may annoy you at times, but by God we give you good value'
BARBARA CASSANI, CHIEF EXECUTIVE, GO

Author's note: Not even Stelios has invented easyTimetravel. While all these events happened during 2001 and 2002, by necessity they did not take place on the same day. Instead, to compile this chapter I spent a day at Athens, a day at Hahn, a day shadowing Barbara Cassani (with her knowledge) and a lot of time in Brussels and elsewhere in Europe. I have also spent more of my life than I care to remember at Stansted and Luton. All times are in GMT.

2.45 A.M., ATHENS: EASYJET FLIGHT 453 FROM LUTON TOUCHES DOWN

The longest year-round no-frills route is no problem to fill in summer and at Christmas, but for much of the year the easyJet link between Britain and the Greek capital is barely profitable. One reason: easyJet's twice-daily departure is up against a competing airline that hasn't quite got round to making a profit for thirty years. The Athens service, though, is an important statement by the airline's owner to his contemporaries in Greece. Stelios Haji-Ioannou has taken on the established airlines; he has already outlasted Branson's Virgin Atlantic on the route; and he makes money, unlike strike- and loss-prone Olympic Airways.

The Greek national carrier was started half a century ago by another shipping magnate, the billionaire Aristotle Onassis. Soon, though, it was taken over by the Greek government. Olympic Airways last made a profit in 1971. Every time an attempt is made to straighten out the organisation, to rationalise the fleet and network, and to reduce the wastage and overstaffing, one or more groups of the airline's employees threaten to strike, safe in the knowledge that the Greek state will underwrite the pay deals.

Airlines have a peculiar vulnerability to the threat of industrial action – it is the next worst thing to rumours of bankruptcy. As soon as prospective passengers get a whiff of the notion that an airline's flights might be grounded, they book on other carriers. At once, the airline's cash flow is hit. The Greek unions are no fools: from past experience, they know that ultimately the government is going to pick up the tab.

So they are hardly underambitious about demands for more money, fewer hours and extra perks. Seeing the potential for turning around Europe's worst-managed airline, British Airways became involved in 1999. BA talked about an alliance, and even put in an executive, Rod Lynch, to run the operation in the hope that Olympic could be made profitable. After a year, Lynch walked out, unable to find a way through the morass. The last time I flew from Heathrow to Athens on Olympic, the airline operated a Boeing 747 in each direction. It was the exact opposite of no frills. The forty or so passengers on board enjoyed an especially comfortable flight, since each of us had ten seats to choose from, and 0.3 of a stewardess to wait upon us. That is the competition that easyJet is up against on its longest route.

4 A.M.: AIRBUS A6: VICTORIA COACH STATION–STANSTED AIRPORT

You think you have problems with your journey to work? At least you don't have to brave the maddest bus in Britain, the A6 between London and Stansted.

As anyone trying to run a company at the Essex airport knows, the big problem with Stansted is that it is in the middle of nowhere. While London's other airports are surrounded by residential areas, and benefit from the labour pool and good transport links that go with them, the only nearby town of any size to Stansted is Bishop's Stortford with a puny population base for meeting the staffing needs of Europe's fastest-growing major airport.

Plenty of staff have to come in from London. The first Stansted Express train from Liverpool Street starts meandering northwards at 5 a.m., and makes half a dozen stops; the trip takes nearly an hour. So unless you have a car, the only way you will make it in time for a 5.30 a.m. start at work, or to check-in as a passenger for a flight any earlier than 6.30 a.m., is on the Airbus.

At 4 a.m., the A6 is the only show in town at Victoria Coach Station. A couple of bleary American visitors have had problems with the terminal name; in US transport vocabulary, 'Coach' means 'Economy Class'. At around ten past four, the bus sets off through the silent streets of London.

On the longest day of the year, when dawn begins around now, the trip must be a delight – a tour of some of London's most popular tourist attractions. It takes in Hyde Park, Marble Arch, Oxford Street and even Lord's Cricket Ground. But for most of the year, all you see is the occasional destination sign that, for anyone familiar with London's geography, is not encouraging. A bus with this trajectory, aiming north-west from central London, is heading not for Stansted airport, but for Birmingham. This uneasy feeling continues to Golders Green Tube station. To me, this seems like something of a gratuitous stop, because the Tube does not start running for another hour or so. Unsurprisingly, no one gets on. But the schedule appears to allow for the driver to take a cigarette break – and then, when he is good and ready, a sharp change of heading, around the North Circular in the direction of Southend.

One hour after leaving Victoria, the bus is still orbiting the capital. Finally, it obeys a signpost pointing to Stansted airport.

5.30 A.M.: BUZZ FLIGHT 2580, STANSTED–VIENNA

At around the time the passengers aboard the Airbus A6 get their first sight of the gleaming terminal through the gloom, a stewardess – who deserves to remain anonymous – is already on duty, preparing for the Buzz flight to the Austrian capital. She was one of the KLM UK cabin crew who, at the end of 1999, found themselves suddenly having to change their mindsets. Overnight, from 2 to 3 January 2000, they had to stop giving out first-rate meals, drinks, hot towels and chocolates, and start selling food. The old put-down about stewardesses being tea-ladies of the air seemed about to resurface.

You might imagine that cabin crew on no-frills airlines have the most unfulfilling jobs imaginable. In the classless low-cost society, there is no chance of working your way upwards – first, ministering to the premium passengers who are screened from the riff-raff; then working up the career ladder, and the airline class structure, to becoming cabin services director on a jumbo and seeing the world from a series of luxury hotels. But my new acquaintance is enjoying herself. 'Some of the girls stayed with KLM UK, but they only do Stansted–Amsterdam now.' She is glad she switched to Buzz, and not just because of the extra variety. 'You get much nicer people. On KLM UK they don't even say good morning.' And, she is glad to say, 'We get lots of people who've never flown before, pensioners who might not even have been out of the country before.' What Buzz does not get, so far, is A-list celebrities to match Princess Diana, who flew once on KLM UK. The best she can suggest is the racing favourite, Frankie Dettori. He is a regular; after the private aircraft accident that claimed the lives of the flight crew and almost his own, he now flies only on scheduled airlines. And the Dutch soccer star, Ruud Gullit, was on one of the flights; she was concerned that he was being pestered so much for autographs that she asked the captain to switch on the seat-belt sign early.

6 A.M. (7 A.M. IN GERMANY): HAHN AIRPORT

The information desk at Hahn airport, perched on a plateau above the Moselle, is open for business. The staff occupy a desk at one end of the big, bright box that comprises the passenger terminal. By common consent it is a vast improvement on the former terminal, which was the Officers' Mess of the old US Air Force base. During the cold war, Hahn was an essential base for the defence of the Western world against the Warsaw Pact countries. The Berlin Wall came down in 1989, but the Americans hung on until 1993. When they finally went home in 1993, hundreds of local people lost their livelihoods. Many of them had worked at the base, while others rented property or supplied goods to the military. To try to revive the community after the US pull-out, the regional authority pumped millions of Deutschmarks into the airport. And today is payback day. Hitherto, Hahn's only scheduled routes have been Ryanair's flights from London Stansted, Glasgow Prestwick, and Shannon in the west of Ireland. Later this morning, a special flight from Dublin is due to arrive with three dozen worthies on board. Within the next few hours, one of Europe's sleepier aviation backwaters is to reveal a new identity as a leading hub with six new links to airports in Italy, France, Norway – and Dorset.

7.15 A.M.: EASYJET FLIGHT 12

The flight has arrived at Luton airport from Edinburgh, and has 25 minutes to be transformed into flight 11 back to the Scottish capital. The choreography involved in making sure the plane is able to depart on cue is impressive. The baggage handlers and refuellers are already waiting when the 737 emerges from the gloom to draw up at the stand. Sets of stairs are eased into position at the front and rear doors on the port side, and a member of cabin crew flings open each door. At almost the same time, the forward hold is opened and unloading begins. With no class structure (and consequently no need to prioritise bags belonging to premium passengers), and a company ban on transferring bags from one flight to another, the baggage handling is a breeze – until a passenger fails to board in time, and his or her luggage has to be found and unloaded before the plane can leave. As the empty baggage carts fill up, the bags for the departing flight trundle up to wait their turn. 'Turn' is the key word; in the lexicon of no-frills airlines, it translates as 'how quickly can we get the plane airborne again?' The pit-stop mentality prevails.

One stage that could, in theory, be omitted is filling up with fuel. The tanks on an easyJet 737 hold sufficient fuel to fly from Edinburgh to

London and back three or four times. But no captain would seriously countenance that. Fuel adds weight, which means you consume extra fuel to lift it. It also makes landing more problematic; every pilot wishes their aircraft to be as light as possible at the point where they have to reacquaint it with the ground, and no captain wants his plane to be carrying an excess of inflammable liquid. So the optimum fuel load is: enough for the planned journey; enough in reserve for a prolonged holding pattern or a diversion, or both; and a little bit for luck, because running out of fuel is almost the worst thing that can happen to a plane. The pilots are calculating the load, studying the flight plan, and running through a daunting number of checklists. They may also be talking to air traffic control, given that all manner of planes – from Far Eastern arrivals coming in over Clacton, to military jets limbering up in Lincolnshire – are clamouring for a space in the crowded skies between Bedfordshire and West Lothian.

The cabin crew, meanwhile, are relaxing over a cup of coffee with their feet up. Only joking. On easyJet, professional flight attendants risk the accusation that they are not merely flying tea-ladies, they are flying cleaners. Every airport has a cleaning company that can remove rubbish from the seat-pocket, wipe the tray-table and, on a bad day, mop up sick. But they cost money. No frills means no cleaners, or rather requires the cabin crew to clean up after the passengers during the brief stop on the ground. They also conduct a security check, inspecting the overhead lockers. And they check the takings for the catering trolley, and restock it for the journey north. Unlike Southwest Airlines where, along with the peanuts, you get juice or coffee, easyJet gives nothing away beyond a plastic cup of water. Having departed from the Scottish capital at 6 a.m., the flight crew will have completed two sectors and nearly 700 miles of travelling before 9 a.m. The arriving passengers took five minutes to clear the plane; the new consignment took eight minutes to board.

I watched the people checking in for flight 11, and looked at those arriving on flight 12. Almost all are male, and most are wearing jackets and ties. Either the recession is biting, or increasingly many businesses realise that, for a simple day trip between the Scottish and English capitals, a fare of around £100 is a better business proposition than a £300 fare on British Airways or BMI from Heathrow. Or it could be a matter of time management: easyJet has the first flight south from Edinburgh, and the last one home.

The passengers have one other thing in common: to a man and woman, they look exhausted. The northbound contingent have one more chore when they get through to the departure lounge; a market researcher working for the Civil Aviation Authority who is politely demanding 'Where have you come from this morning? How did you travel to Luton today? Are you travelling for business or pleasure? How much did you pay? How many times have you flown in the last twelve months? Have you travelled on any of the low-cost airlines in the past year? Where to? How many people live in your household?'

9 A.M.: ENTERPRISE HOUSE, STANSTED AIRPORT

'Passion . . . commitment . . . teamwork' is one of the messages that pops up on the computer screensaver at Go's headquarters. The reception area is decorated with all kinds of notices, including a poster offering the services of a head masseuse. By the end of today, I may need one.

I am here to spend a day shadowing Barbara Cassani, the only woman to run an airline. Her first task of the day – not counting the two-hour commute from her home in Barnes, west London, to the Essex airport – is to cross the footbridge that cuts through the atrium of Enterprise House and walk into a bare, glaringly lit room to chair the weekly Communications meeting.

At the meeting is a mixed bunch of experienced airline staff and outsiders, such as Clive, Go's new tax accountant. He has recently arrived from a firm of funeral directors. A colleague explains: 'He's used to repatriating dead bodies. We told him, "Same kind of thing, only live passengers".'

The average age of the circle of twenty people looks to be around thirty, meaning that many of them had not even been born when Southwest Airlines started up. Of the twenty, I am the only one wearing a tie. (Most people appear to be segregated by clothing: there is a woolly jumper corner over by the window, and a blue-shirted contingent near the door.) I am also the only one who is not directly concerned with running Go, the newly independent no-frills airline. This is the regular Wednesday occasion when every senior manager finds out what is happening across the airline. Less than a month after 11 September, with other airlines shedding workers in their tens of thousands, the mood is upbeat.

First, the detail of the past week's performance is picked over: the number of flights on time (which means anything up to fifteen minutes late), the percentage of bookings online – and the proportion of abandoned calls to the reservations centre. 'Yesterday we had only seventeen abandoned calls in one hour. We're overstaffed'. If this comment sounds odd, it is because one of the measures of productivity of a call centre is the proportion of the public who give up. Were it zero, that would suggest that there are underemployed staff sitting around waiting for the phone to ring.

The news from Newcastle is good. The previous week, Go had said it would start flying to Tyneside from Stansted. The team that had been at the airport to sort out the logistics for the operation reported their reception had been 'very warm – it was almost Bristol-ish' [a reference to Go's arrival at Bristol airport the previous year]. Newcastle United want to charter the aircraft.'

The discussion then takes a turn that many other business people would find strange: 'We're going to reward passengers on our routes that are doing well,' says David Magliano, the airline's sales and marketing director. In other words, Go is to cut fares on its successful Mediterranean routes to Malaga, Alicante and Naples. The airline has also celebrated its top place in a *Business Traveller* survey of no-frills airlines by buying the most high-profile poster site on the approach to Luton airport to advertise the fact. 'It'll be there for a year,' says Magliano. Ray Webster, chief executive of easyJet, will pass it every day on his way to and from work.

Northern Ireland's first minister may be surprised that he made it to the agenda of the Communications meeting at Go. 'Trimble's pulling in his people,' observed the finance director. He predicted the effects on bookings 'if the peace process implodes'. Magliano warns that, if the Americans extend the bombing of Afghanistan into Iraq, 'we'll see a spike in oil prices'.

9.15 A.M.: VIRGIN EXPRESS HQ, BRUSSELS AIRPORT

The yield managers for continental Europe's leading no-frills airline are getting into their stride, fixing fares by the hour. Every departure on every route that the Belgian airline flies is 'micro-managed' to make sure the maximum earnings are squeezed out of each flight. Half a dozen earnest young men are peering at screens showing how many people have booked, and the fares they have paid, on flights that won't take off for another month. If there are too many passengers paying too little, they will tweak fares upwards; too few people, and the price comes down. These days, finding the best price for a flight is as tricky a matter as choosing the optimum moment to back a horse at Doncaster.

9.30 A.M.: RYANAIR FLIGHT 23, BEAUVAIS–DUBLIN

The plane is directly overhead Heathrow airport. It is a shimmeringly clear day, and west London is laid out like a map beneath us. Captain

X dips the starboard wing to give me a better view of the metropolis. 'See, that's City airport down there.' I know his real name, but this encounter took place just prior to the events of 11 September 2001 when attitudes to flight-deck visits were very different. I had approached Captain X on the ground at Beauvais airport in northern France, and told him I was a journalist who would like to interview him. He agreed.

Once the flight to Dublin is in its cruise phase, he asks the lead stewardess to summon me to the cockpit, where he tells me about his day.

'We started in Dublin this morning, flew to Paris Beauvais, we're on our way back as I speak to you, and then we're going to turn around and go to Brussels Charleroi, and then back to Dublin and home for lunch.'

Nice work if you can get £75,000 a year for it, which is the going rate for Ryanair captains. Their German counterparts are earning up to three times as much working for Lufthansa, which is perhaps why Michael O'Leary and his team see the opportunity to expand low-cost aviation in Germany. I am sitting in the jumpseat of a Boeing 737-200, which is the elderly workhorse of the Ryanair fleet. We are flying directly over the busiest international airport in the world. From our vantage point six miles up, we can see other airports; Gatwick just swept past to port, and the captain's momentary manoeuvre allowed me to see London City. Everything is going according to plan.

The flight plan is a computerised print-out that gives the crew all the information they need for the flight. It is basically a list of the navigation beacons over which flight 23 will pass. The plan also predicts the fuel required, and allows the crew to compare what's in the tanks with what should be expected during the course of the eighty-minute flight. It also predicts the ground speed, allowing for the wind, and the frequencies for those navigation beacons. Even in the cruise, when you or I might be tempted to do some sightseeing and take in the view, Captain X and his colleague are working. 'We write everything down that we get from air traffic control, our radar heading, or frequency change, we copy it. We compare the times we estimate overhead the beacons, and the minimum fuel that we must have, with what we actually have. We keep an eye on it to make sure our fuel situation is normal, and our times are normal.' Another document, the voyage report, records where the aircraft has been, and when: 'the flights, the schedule times, the off-blocks times, which is when we started to push back to when we set the parking brake at the end of the flight, the flight times, our fuel – what we uplifted, what we arrived with – the crew, their duty times, which have to be kept very strictly monitored. The number of passengers, cargo, the delays, the reason for delays, and this is all put into the computer and analysed.' Maybe that £75,000 salary is not enough, after all.

I ask Captain X if he has favourite airports. 'I tend to like the smaller airports like Beauvais. I like that family atmosphere. You met me walking around the aircraft having a stroll, and I like that type of operation. It's a lot less congested so when you land, you literally taxi off the runway and you park. Let the passengers get out, go to the terminal building, get on their bus, then new passengers come on board, we turn the aircraft around, and between landing and taking off we can do it in 25 minutes when we're landing in secondary airports. And I like that.'

And least favourite airports?

'It would be airports that are difficult to make an approach in that they're very short, or high grounds so they tend to be very windy. Dublin winds tend to be very strong. Leeds-Bradford springs to mind, it's not that I dislike it, but it's harder work flying into an airport like that.'

10 A.M.: ENTERPRISE HOUSE, STANSTED

'Ken – you're in charge of quality. Do you want to find a solution?'

Barbara Cassani's inner cabinet is congregated for the Decisions meeting, to sort out some of the thornier problems of running an airline, and Ken New, quality manager, is under some pressure. One afternoon the previous week, every flight between Scotland and Belfast had run four hours late because of an error about maintenance. Every aircraft requires a daily check by engineers. A Boeing was erroneously scheduled without a hop back to Stansted for maintenance, so the jet had missed its routine examination. Getting another aircraft to replace it, either from within Go or as an ad-hoc charter, proved difficult. 'That was a huge number of passengers inconvenienced as a result of one mistake,' says Captain Ed Winter, chief operating officer for the airline. He looks like a taller, friendlier version of Denis Healey, but I sense that you would not want to be on the wrong side of him. 'We haven't seen disruption like that since 11 September. There must be a process to make sure that cannot happen again.'

At least the delays did not create any disruptive passengers. The 'self-loading cargo' that we passengers comprise (a widely used industry expression, but not one that I ever heard at Go) present a constant challenge, especially when we drink too much. This was the root cause of a big air-rage incident the previous week in which a passenger broke another's nose ('We had to get the seat covers changed' . . . 'the police let him off with a caution'), and another when a group on a Stansted–Naples flight decided to stage a mass mooning.

10.05 A.M.: GATWICK
Britain's leading police officer specialising in air rage is preparing to board easyJet flight 838 to Amsterdam. Chief inspector Mike Alderson's final destination is The Hague, where a seminar on disruptive passengers is taking place. He is to urge the airlines to root out possible problems on the ground.

10.30 A.M.: APPROACHING CORK AIRPORT
'Jesus Christ, that's not Shannon!' exclaims the passenger in the window seat as the plane from Stansted breaks through the clouds on its final approach and the distinctive sight of Kinsale harbour appears. Almost at once, the captain makes an announcement that Shannon airport is closed because of fog, and that the aircraft will instead land at Cork. The passenger in the middle seat is Jamie Bowden, who has recently left British Airways after twenty years' experience across the airline, and is now engaged in PR consultancy. BA hired him back to mastermind the relaunch of Concorde. Now he is off to see the management of Shannon airport about some work. He checked with Aer Lingus, who wanted £350 for a day trip, and settled for £75 return on Ryanair.

Once on the ground, passengers are told, 'we're getting coaches to take you to Shannon'. Bowden asks a member of staff how long that might take. 'Three hours, and it's a grand journey.' He decides the beautiful scenery will not make up for a missed meeting, and opts to fly straight back to Stansted on the same plane.

'You didn't stay long,' says a stewardess who recognises him from the outbound trip. As the plane levels off, Bowden tells the sorry story to this sympathetic ear.

'You probably need a cup of tea, then.' Bowden gratefully accepts. She returns with the brew, and asks for £1. 'But all my money's in my jacket, which you asked me earlier to put in the overhead locker.'

The passenger in the next seat pays the stewardess for Bowden's tea. 'I don't believe it,' he says. 'Eight weeks ago I was flying on Concorde, today I'm having to scrounge money off a stranger to get a cup of tea.'

11 A.M.: ENTERPRISE HOUSE, STANSTED
'I want us to be as proud of our toilets as we are of the rest of the airline. And at the moment, I'm not.'

Barbara Cassani has moved on to operational issues, and the 'lavs', as cabin crew around the world call aircraft lavatories, are causing her concern. 'I've been doing a lot of research into toilets,' pipes up Go's cabin-crew manager, Andrew Goodrum. The problem, as Cath Lynn, head of customer service, succinctly puts it, is that 'toilets stink'.

Flight crew have been complaining that there is an unpleasant odour from the forward lavatory. The discussion opens what I hesitate to call a can of worms. 'In all my time at Go, I've never seen a toilet truck at the front of an aircraft,' says Dominic Paul, who has the unwieldy title of director of people services and business development. Ed Winter ripostes that 'they must get attached sometimes'. The rule is that a toilet truck, which empties the tank where waste is collected, should service each inbound international flight. In contrast, domestic flights have the tanks emptied only on request from the crew (do not read this as an interesting commentary on foreign habits – overseas flights are longer than the typical one-hour domestic hop in Britain). The cost to the airline is £7 per visit.

Some fingers are pointing at the insanitary habits of men. Passengers choose between the forward or rear lavatory depending on gender rather than where they are sitting on the plane. Men, exhibitionists that they are, tend to stride blithely to the front of the aircraft. Once in the forward lavatory, they treat it with less respect than do the women. Female passengers, meanwhile, are shy about bodily functions and tend to retreat to the rear. They leave the lav as they would wish to find it. But the habits of cabin crew are coming in for scrutiny at the Decisions meeting, too. 'I'm getting all kinds of debris, cafetières, ice tongs, coffee grounds,' says Mike Williams, the chief engineer. 'We get through a hell of a lot of toilet motors.' Cath Lynn promises to get tough on toilet blockages, and tough on the causes of toilet blockages.

'I'm polishing my Exocet,' says Andrew Goodrum, cabin crew manager. 'I'm just not ready to fire it.'

11.20 A.M.: RYANAIR FLIGHT 7751, DUBLIN–HAHN

Don't bother checking on the website for this flight. It has only ever flown once. And while no one on flight 7751 has paid a European cent for the flight, the fact that it is in the air at all is causing inconvenience to fare-paying passengers. This morning, one Ryanair 737 has already 'gone technical' before it had even left Charleroi (not, I should say, with a toilet-related problem). The airline could use all the Boeings and crews it has to operate the normal schedule. But one has been commandeered by the chief executive, Michael O'Leary, and his senior managers for a day out in Germany that they intend to milk for all the PR value they can muster.

A brass band and a coachload of local schoolchildren waving German and Irish flags wait in a torrential downpour on the apron at Hahn airport to welcome O'Leary. Flanked by the region's finance and labour ministers, O'Leary claims his airline will carry 1.5m passengers in the first year on its nine routes from Hahn, and would force the German national carrier, Lufthansa, to cut its fares by €200m (£120m). He says Ryanair's fares will be one sixth of those presently prevailing: 'Lufthansa won't know what hit 'em.' The airline announced fares of €61 (£38) to Bournemouth and Bergamo (in northern Italy), and uses BA's Frankfurt–Southampton and Lufthansa's Frankfurt–Milan fares for comparison.

11.30 A.M.: ENTERPRISE HOUSE, STANSTED

'The administrators have contacted us and asked if we'd like to buy Ansett,' says Ed Winter, chief operating officer for Go. The Decisions meeting is on to post-11 September matters – and what a management consultant might call threats and opportunities. The perceived increase in risks from terrorism leads to a discussion on whether passengers should be asked for photographic ID on domestic and Irish flights. The consensus is that they should, but before action is implemented a reporter for the *Daily Telegraph* travels on a Go flight from Edinburgh to London under an assumed name. The story is splashed on the front page of the travel section.

More optimistically, the downturn in the aviation business has provided the opportunity to obtain aircraft and crew more easily and cheaply than before. 'The market is changing dramatically,' says Ed Winter. 'You can get two old dogs for the price of one new one. Boeing field is stacked up with white tails' (the term for new aircraft that are built speculatively, without a definite buyer, to keep the production line going).

The meeting also learns that 'three of the captains who left us to fly for Virgin Atlantic are coming back'. But the government does not appear to be listening to Go's demands about fair treatment for airlines. 'You could make a career out of talking to the government,' says Stephen Horner, the network director. 'I've wasted time waiting to hear from the Treasury. The reply was, "we might get a letter back to you by 11 October, and here's your customer service number". We've made our views known, they haven't given us the courtesy of a reply.'

Andrew Cowen, director of finance and strategic planning, has had no more luck in his dealings with the Secretary of State for Transport: 'I got the most bullshit letter back I've ever seen from Stephen Byers.'

Back at their unoccupied desks, the screen saver is repeating the Go mantra: 'passion, commitment, teamwork'.

11.45 A.M.: HAHN AIRPORT

After a press conference in which the most testing question was what might tempt the Germans to fly to Bournemouth ('climate, culture and warm beer,' responded O'Leary), the crowd of 200 is treated to a video about Hahn airport, featuring the information desk staff with a high-kicking routine to the heavily amplified sounds of Van Halen's 'Jump'. The location is a departure lounge, cordoned off from the travelling public who are checking in for the flight to Stansted. The children have long been dried off and loaded back on to their coaches, while the adults tuck assertively into some of the Moselle's finer wines. Almost all the promotional lighters have been swiped, but most of the Ryanair T-shirts remain unclaimed. It is a fascinating milieu of bewildered local bigwigs unused to their national airline being slagged off by an Irish rival, Frankfurt-based business journalists complaining about the long journey to Hahn from continental Europe's financial centre, and the entire senior management team for Ryanair, becoming increasingly boisterous as the party continues.

12 NOON

Enterprise House is abuzz. As Barbara Cassani chairs a meeting on a personnel matter to which, understandably, I am not invited, I perch at the reception desk for Go HQ. It beats even easyJet and Ryanair as the most no-frills reception. The desk stands at a crossroads, where the corridor linking each end of the office meets the path between the door to the outside world and the canteen. 'Crew bag – do not offload', reads the tag on one stewardess's case (passenger bags are fair game, then, I conclude). A group of Spanish cabin crew arrives; with a year-round presence in Spain, Go chooses to recruit the country's nationals, and offers cash to British cabin crew prepared to learn foreign languages.

12.30 A.M.: CUSTOMER SERVICE DEPARTMENT, RYANAIR, DUBLIN AIRPORT

Siobhan O'Neill is checking to see how fast her team is working through today's pile of correspondence. 'We have less than one person in every thousand complaining,' she says with a fair amount of pride. For some weary passengers, the very notion of a customer service department at Ryanair may sound like a contradiction in terms, and the task of running it the worst job in the world. But O'Neill – who joined Ryanair in 1989 as a secretary, and now has a staff of four – enjoys her work. 'We get complaints in, we get queries, we get compliments, some people can be very irate but there are some lovely people here, and we all work very well here. We just get on and do the job. The main thing is that we answer the letters as quickly as we can and get an answer to the passenger, because the worst thing that can happen is a passenger can have a problem and get no answer to it.'

Ryanair insists that all correspondence is in writing (and only English is acceptable). 'We can't take calls because people will stay longer on the phone than they're meant to,' says O'Neill. 'We investigate the problem and respond back to them as quickly as we can, on the same day if possible.'

As with any airline, bags get lost, and it takes time (and a lot of money) to reunite them with the owner. That is the leading cause for complaint. Next are delays, usually caused by poor weather or technical problems. And a number of people ask for their money back. 'Everyone has very genuine circumstances and unforeseen reasons as to why they need a refund,' say O'Neill. 'Obviously we can't provide refunds and we'd explain to them why we can't. For delays, we'd advise the reason for the delay and include a letter for insurance purposes, because they can claim from their insurance.'

That is not strictly true, because most travel insurance policies kick in only if you miss a connection on your outbound journey, or if your delay is twelve hours or longer – a most unusual event on short-haul airlines.

O'Neill's boss, Michael O'Leary, is rather more robust when I talk to him about customer service. 'We don't go in for all the old bullshit that British Airways and the other airlines have gone on with for years. They'll rape you for the airfare of £500 or £700, and then pretend they're giving something they're not. We have a very well-defined product. It doesn't mean we can eliminate all delays, it doesn't mean that we won't cancel less than one tenth of 1 per cent of flights, and in those cases we will not give you anything and we make no apologies for it. People who arrive at airports with no money in their pockets and expect us to put them up in hotels or feed them simply because there's a delay will not get fed on Ryanair. But they will not be charged the extra £500 every time they fly with us either. What we're trying to do is to wean people off this notion that air travel is some first class, intercontinental, *Titanic*-like experience – it isn't, this is a bus service.'

'Every passenger expects when they travel, quite rightly, a high level of service. And I think certainly at Ryanair we aim for a high level of service by offering very friendly, professional service from our frontline staff to our airline crew to our complaints department turnaround times,' says O'Neill. She travels on Ryanair herself, but increasingly on publicly available fares rather than the airline's concessions, which are available only for standby travel. 'When you're only paying £9.99, it makes sense to go confirmed.' She flies as much as she can: 'When I get on a flight, I like to see how people react.' On a recent flight to Italy, the passengers applauded after the landing. It's nice to see that side because I only tend to see the very negative side when they complain.' Complaints outnumber compliments by a ratio of fifty to one, but O'Neill sifts them out and posts letters of praise on the Ryanair website. Some people also enlist her to help with their love lives: 'People telling us they met someone on a flight, and they fell in love with them, and they can't get in touch with them, and can they get their contact details? Of course we can't give out the details. If we can find out who the passenger was – they might have their name – we would look them up on the system, and then we'd ring the other person and say, "Do you want me to send on this letter?" '

Before we part, I need to ask: does Siobhan O'Neill send out many cheques?

'No, I don't send out many cheques.'

1 P.M.

Lunch with Barbara Cassani is a disconcertingly informal experience. The trim, blonde 41-year-old leads me through the building works that constitute Britain's fastest-growing airport and into the terminal at Stansted. Go's chief executive flutters past the check-in desks, pausing to talk to staff, to introduce herself to unfamiliar faces – and to explain that the bloke with the tie and the tape recorder is a writer following her in action for the day.

We go to the sandwich counter at Boots, but I guess the most powerful woman in British aviation would prefer it to be Prêt à Manger, which she often cites as a model of good customer service. At least today she is taking a few minutes for lunch, rather than working straight through: 'I pepper my day with popping into the different parts of the operation, like sitting on the phones [in the call centre] at lunchtime.'

1.30 P.M.: LUTON AIRPORT, EASYJET FLIGHT 451 TO ATHENS

Check on the easyJet website and you will see that fares for flight 451 to the Greek capital on any given day are generally much higher than for flight 453. That's because the daytime departure, 451, is very civilised, departing Luton at lunchtime and arriving in Athens in good time for dinner. In contrast, the night flight sets off at around pub closing time and arrives at an hour when any civilised person is sound asleep. It neatly sums up the appeal of no-frills airlines: the passenger can decide whether convenience or cost is the more compelling. During the day, one expensive Boeing is tied up for around nine hours for just one return hop, but passengers who value their sleep are prepared to pay for the privilege. At night, when the aircraft would otherwise be parked, passengers willing to travel are rewarded with fares that reflect the low marginal costs involved in flying to Greece in the middle of the night.

The aircraft pushes back exactly on schedule, much to the relief of the crew. On board is Stelios, the airline's chairman, off to Athens to see family and friends – and to inspect the new airport. As soon as the seat-belt light goes off, he starts work, moving through the cabin, speaking to each and every passenger.

2 P.M.: JOB CENTRE, STANSTED

Following 11 September, dozens of airlines laid off thousands of UK employees. Stansted was especially hard hit, with Continental Airlines dropping its bold new route to Newark, and the Star Alliance (represented by Lufthansa and SAS) closing down all operations at the airport. The sacked workers are keenly aware that the no-frills airlines are still expanding, and they are queuing up for interviews.

Those who decide to apply for Ryanair need not spend too long perfecting the CV. 'The only restriction to becoming a member of Ryanair's cabin crew is age,' says Sharon Fitzsimons, cabin services manager for Ryanair. 'You must be at least eighteen years of age. Other than that, you need to have an outgoing personality, be willing to work hard, and be good at dealing with people.'

4.30 P.M.: ENTERPRISE HOUSE

The first blocks of red appearing on the computer screens are causing a certain amount of alarm at the hub of Go's activity: the Operations room. A corner of the building overlooking the apron is filled with screens, telephones and worried-looking people – all of them, in my experience, men, though Go has one female operations manager. The game of three-dimensional chess that the duty managers of the no-frills networks play all day (and, in the case of easyJet and Go, all night) requires them to deal with hiccups ranging from breakdowns on the Stansted Express or the M11 to oversleeping staff.

The operational hub of each no-frills airline is a sophisticated computer monitoring system that represents each flight as a bar on a screen. At Stansted, planned flights appear in blue, completed ones in grey. Delays are picked up in red. When circumstances conspire to delay many flights, the image can look fairly bloody. Patches of red are beginning to show up this afternoon – most immediately flight 514 from Edinburgh, which is running half an hour late.

'It was a flight holding inbound because of weather here, then we picked up an air traffic delay northbound,' says one of the people with furrowed brows – Nick Chapple, operations control manager. 'We schedule so tightly that it's very difficult to pick up once you start getting delays – it tends to roll on.'

'We are flying our aircraft between eleven and twelve hours a day,' says Go's chief operating officer, Ed Winter. 'A traditional airline will probably only get seven or eight hours a day out of their aircraft, because they concentrate on the key business travel periods of the day. High utilisation is one of the key ways we can offer such low fares. We do have 100 per cent days, and we do celebrate them. We give all the staff on duty a little present that day.' That may give you some idea of how rare they are.

Plenty of unforeseen events can interfere with what should be a routine operation. Luggage has gone missing, or the baggage belt breaks down. Passengers dawdle in duty-free. The refueller, caterer or dispatcher may be held up working on another delayed flight. 'Firebreaks' are built in to the system in the middle of the day: 'Gaps built in deliberately, so you can catch up and move things around,' says Winter. And, unlike other airlines hidebound by arcane working rules, crews' planned destinations can be switched at short notice. Flight crew who might be expecting a day in the sun in Spain could find themselves in Scotland. 'That's the difference between us and the more traditional airlines,' says Winter. 'Traditional airlines have got complex industrial agreements. So if a crew comes in expecting to go to Alicante and you want them to go to Glasgow, that's not always possible. There are often quite difficult arrangements to get round.'

There certainly are. A British Airways pilot who reports for work expecting to fly to Stockholm, may find that the rostered destination has been changed to Rome. To compensate for what is hardly a huge inconvenience, the airline is required to 'draft' them – an industrial agreement which can involve a payment of £750 for a pilot, just for doing his or her job of flying a Boeing for two hours to a European destination, and two hours back to Heathrow.

The single cause that the traveller is likely to hear delays attributed to is air traffic control. There is some agreement about the worst regions; the area between the south of Germany and Milan, overflying Switzerland, is a notorious bottleneck with too little capacity and too much traffic. Clacton is another one, because many aircraft coming into the London terminal area from northern Europe, Scandinavia and almost anywhere in Asia will at some point end up over the Essex resort, and pressure has been increased because of the rapid rise of no-frills flying. The north-west of England, and in particular the Wirral peninsula, is another pinch-point. Faced with an air-traffic delay, airlines can consider alternative routes, and weigh up the cost of a twenty-minute delay against ten minutes' extra flying time, and the fuel consumed. 'Sometimes we find ourselves flying between Dublin and London at 16,000 feet simply to avoid some of the congestion at the higher levels,' says Tim Jeans of Ryanair.

The airlines pay air traffic control authorities handsomely for the privilege of being told where, and when, to go. Jeans says what are known as en route charges are 'a big thorn in our flesh'. He complains: 'It's frankly a lot of money for a service which has very little accountability to its users. I recall the famous meltdown in June 2000. Fleets were grounded for thirty-six hours while they put a fault right. Was there any ability to claim against Nats [National Air Traffic Services] for that? Not at all, they're unaccountable.'

4.35 P.M.: EUROCONTROL HQ, BRUSSELS

Ian Jones is at his office opposite the NATO building in the Belgian capital, feeling aggrieved at the way that his organisation is so often blamed for delays. He is head of operations for Eurocontrol's flow management division. 'We get blamed for everything. As an air traffic controller I can tell you the truth, supported by all the statistics we have, that 80 per cent or more of all flights, every day in Europe, take off with no air traffic delay at all. It's the other 20 per cent that causes the grief. But it's easy for the girl at the check-in desk to say, "Oh it's due to air traffic." First of all it's very difficult for the passenger to challenge that, and secondly we're remote, faceless, hidden behind large steel doors in protected centres and therefore we're easy victims. What we're trying to do is get all the aircraft that want to get away by eight o'clock, away at eight o'clock to wherever they're going.'

4.50 P.M.: BBC RADIO FIVE LIVE, *DRIVE* PROGRAMME

From a live outside broadcast at the information desk of Hahn airport, the nation hears about Michael O'Leary's plans to 'stuff it to Lufty' with

Ryanair's new hub. The German national carrier does not immediately rise to the bait. 'Lufthansa watches its competitors closely,' says Peter Middleton of the German carrier. 'The airline welcomes competition and is in a strong position to meet any challenges.'

5 P.M.: CITY HALL, THE HAGUE

Chief inspector Mike Alderson is talking at the Air Rage seminar. 'Nobody has to be a disruptive passenger, it's not compulsory, it's not written on the ticket. You have a bad journey round a motorway, a bad check-in, your partner's giving you earache – all those sorts of things. Airlines can recognise that those stresses exist during the journey, they can look at check-in, they can look at the way that people go through central search, they can look at the departure gate.' But Alderson is reluctant to subscribe to the theory that air rage is getting worse. 'I'm perhaps a jaundiced policeman, I've been in the police service for over twenty-four years now. My experience is that people have always been angry.'

Air rage is not a huge problem in the low-cost sector, partly because the flights are so short – and because no-frills airlines don't hand out unlimited free drinks. 'We fly about two thousand football supporters every week from Dublin to Old Trafford or Liverpool,' says Tim Jeans of Ryanair. 'I could count on the fingers of one hand the number of times things have got out of hand.' The trick, he says, is to fly 'a brand new 737 that goes on time'. And when it doesn't, it helps if a passing Ryanair executive can demonstrate what's happening. 'I was at Bristol when we had to cancel our flight to Dublin. Passengers were crowding around complaining, so I went into the back office and printed out the weather report that showed fog and drizzle had made visibility below the limits for the 737 that was flying.'

Everyone agrees that alcohol is the single biggest contributor to air rage. Since no-frills airlines do not give away free drink, some passengers decide to take their own on board. 'People can be animals, real monsters,' says Luke Deals, a former steward on Go. 'The number of arguments you would have from people bringing their own alcohol on board was amazing. And when you tell them it's not legal, they say, "we've done it before".' Tim Jeans of Ryanair is concerned about the earnings his airline loses from such self-catering: 'They can bring their own food, but they can't bring their own alcoholic drink. You wouldn't bring your own drink into a pub and say, well, thanks very much for the environment. If we choose to tell people they can't bring their own drink on to our plane then that's our right, and it's not infringing on anyone's civil liberties, it's just our bloody right. It's our plane and we'll tell people what they can eat and drink on it.'

5.10 P.M.: EASYJET FLIGHT 451 PULLS UP AT THE GATE IN ATHENS, TWENTY MINUTES EARLY

To many trained eyes, as well as untrained ones, all easyJet's jets look identical. The airline got rid of its old Boeing 737-200s – the stubby ones with a couple of puny-looking engines – soon after it began operating. They were replaced by -300 series planes, with big, meaty engines, and extended cabins holding 149 passengers. Then Boeing stopped making the -300s, substituting the -700; same looks, same length, same capacity, but better performance. In particular, the new version goes faster. The higher speed is barely noticeable on most short hops, but on the 1,500-mile flight to Athens, it shaves twenty minutes off the flying time.

Stelios is a little tired and hungry. Tired because he has been talking to every one of the hundred-plus passengers, and then I interviewed him for half an hour; hungry because, unlike his rivals on the route, easyJet does not serve an elaborate meal on the flight. Some people, me included, have bought on-board snacks or tucked into pre-prepared picnics, not least because eating alleviates the potential for tedium inherent on a three-hour, forty-minute flight. But Stelios is adamant that his policy is the best one, particularly since most of his flights last two hours or less.

'On a short flight it's irrelevant. A four o'clock departure out of Luton lands in Nice at seven – why the hell would you want to eat? Would you eat at five today, and at nine again? No.'

He is bade farewell by the passengers, who share a mix of admiration – for what a young man has achieved, and gratitude – for getting them to Greece for a fair price, and early to boot. Every appearance he makes on the airline boosts his stock, and gives the passengers something to gossip about. Despite the unfortunate Blair Holiday Project that went scarily wrong in August 2001, easyJet attracts plenty of celebrities. But Stelios says he doesn't believe in product endorsement: 'The seven million passengers we carried last year are the biggest endorsement – not the fact that a celebrity has flown with us.'

Inside the terminal, Stelios is greeted like the celebrity he is in Greece, by a team of easyJet employees, who proceed to whisk him around the new airport. The airport at which the 737 touches down looks strangely unfamiliar to anyone who had the misfortune of using the old Athens airport. Last time I was there, switching terminals necessitated a £5 taxi ride. Fortunately, one of the world's least attractive airports was replaced in 2001 by a trillion-drachma, state-of-the-architecture construction on a rural site twenty miles east of Athens.

Eleftherios Venizelos airport is both harder to pronounce and reach than the old one, Hellenikon, which was within spitting distance of the Parthenon. The new airport has already been rechristened Spata, after the nearest town. It is spacious and well designed. For non-smokers, the best news of all is that secondary smoking is no longer a compulsory part of the airport experience.

Judging from the number of television satellite trucks outside, and the clutter of cameras, lights and journalists inside, though, there is a big story happening today. Not a crash, nor a hijack, but agonising teething problems.

Olympic Airways' computer system keeps spitting out boarding passes that quote a gate number for the old airport. Not surprisingly, this leads to chaos. The highly sophisticated baggage handling system has jammed; at least one foreign airline blames misuse by Olympic staff. The Greek Minister of Transport has stepped in to take personal charge of sorting out the problems.

Because Greece is scattered across dozens of islands, and there are huge Greek communities in places like Toronto, New York and Melbourne, air travel is crucial to the country, and with Athens at the hub of the network, the implications are very serious when things go wrong. While British Airways, easyJet, and Virgin Atlantic flights all depart to London on time, Olympic passengers to Heathrow are delayed for five hours and finally arrive at around two o'clock next morning. A subject of considerable discussion in aviation circles: will Olympic Airways still be flying, with its familiar tail-fins bearing the Olympic rings, when the Games take place in Athens in 2004? The money is on the Greek airline staggering on, for reasons of national prestige, as it has for decades.

5.30 P.M.: STANSTED EXPRESS, STANSTED AIRPORT–TOTTENHAM HALE

'I've got one speech. I got a really expensive speechwriter to write it for me. I just change it. If it's a small group and it's safe I'll speak off the cuff.'

It is speaking season for Barbara Cassani. Being bright, articulate and influential, Go's chief executive is in demand at events across Britain and abroad. Tonight, the Association of MBAs has booked her for a meeting to be held at the British Medical Association (confusingly, BMA) at Tavistock House near Euston. Cassani judges this one will be worthwhile as an opportunity to speak directly to around 200 powerful business people, to get them on her side and, indirectly, to sell them some air travel on Go. BT, with one of the biggest travel budgets in the UK, is sponsoring the event. The audience will also include representatives from her airline's suppliers such as BAA and National Air Traffic Services.

6 P.M.: SOMEWHERE IN SCHLESWIG-HOLSTEIN

The writer Darius Sanai is not having a good day looking for Lübeck airport. 'Try getting there, in a rental car, from Hamburg. The airport isn't even marked on Michelin or Kummerley & Frey maps. At the Lübeck autobahn exit, a taxi driver just shook his head and said we'd never find it. You have to negotiate the whole of the city, some horrendous traffic jams, a couple of back lanes and a country road to get there.' It took him an hour and forty minutes to cover the 40 km from Hamburg. 'But running into the terminal we saw all our fellow passengers sitting around at the gate. There had been a delay. Great – could we get on? "No" said the man at check-in. We showed our locator number and e-mail confirmation, and pointed out the passengers reading magazines and drinking beer just a few metres away through the metal detector. "No," he said. The flight wasn't full, but we had missed the official check-in time and we weren't getting on. OK?'

The reason for enforcing a strict 'minus 30 closure', according to Richard Garrett, who manages the 'out-stations' for Ryanair, is to encourage the others. 'If a passenger gets away with it in Nimes, they'll try to get away with it in Stansted.' The former army officer says, 'When you come to an airport, you have to play by the airport's rules. I want everyone to travel on time.'

7 P.M.: VIRGIN EXPRESS HQ, BRUSSELS

At eight in the evening, central European time, Neil Burrows is locking up his office and going home to a handsome and stylish town house in one of the finer quarters of the Belgian capital. 'I generally work about eleven hours a day during the week. But then of course I pick up quite a lot of phone calls when I go home. I set aside a portion of the weekend to work in my study. But I think if you have the opportunity to have an influence on a growing, thriving organisation, the line between work, creation, and satisfaction is very, very blurred. It's not work if you can see the results, and changes and improvements of it. When an artist paints, how much of it is work and how much of it is the joy of creation?'

7.30 P.M.: OUTSIDE THE BRITISH MEDICAL ASSOCIATION, TAVISTOCK HOUSE, LONDON

Not everything is going according to plan for the great and good business leaders. The 200 guests at the MBA meeting at the BMA, plus the star guest, Barbara Cassani, plus assorted fire appliances and their crews, are standing around in Burton Street, London WC1 while a fire alarm is investigated. Eventually we are allowed back in. 'I bring congratulations from the firemen,' says the host. 'They say you are one of the most orderly groups of people they have ever had to evacuate.' I lean against one of the mahogany columns in the assembly room to watch the address, and to listen to the comments of the audience. 'She looks amazingly human,' whispers one woman, who also looks human.

Cassani talks passionately about her airline, and why it is 'uniquely positioned to grow even faster' since the events of 11 September. She discusses the details of running the organisation: it costs £200 to kit out a member of Go's staff, compared with £2,000 at British Airways. Then she questions the very qualification that unites the audience. 'I think your MBA's a waste of time. Common sense rules the day.'

8 P.M.: HAHN AIRPORT

Nadine, the youngest of the information desk officials at what is now Germany's fastest-growing airport, asks me what sort of pizza I would like. Being a Ryanair passenger, and therefore unaccustomed to hot food, I am taken aback, but recover quickly enough to ask for a *funghi*. The pizzas are delivered from the nearest takeaway, eight miles away. Over dinner, Nadine's colleague Christine tells me she lives in the nearest village. Its population is fifty.

8 P.M.: CHARLEROI

An obscure but handy rule known as IATA Resolution 735d decrees: 'The receiving carrier agrees to transport the listed passengers (irrespective of class, service or routing) at no additional charge to the forwarding carrier.' It gets a mention on the standard Flight Interruption Manifest (FIM), the document you get if you are Involuntarily Re-Routed (IRR) when your flight goes awry. Many airlines, including Ryanair, have 'mutual aid' agreements to carry each other's passengers when things go wrong. The problem, for the hundred-odd passengers at Charleroi hoping to reach Pisa, is that no other airline uses 'Brussels South' airport.

Massimo Bonechi from Florence is due to be at work in about twelve hours' time. 'It's a low-fare condition,' he says philosophically. 'No hotel, no taxi, but they said they would keep the airport open if we want to sleep on the floor.' One group of passengers had their inbound flight cancelled on the way up, too. But Bonechi has made contact with a group of attractive young women and says he is planning 'a certain amount of mingling' during the night.

9 P.M.: BRITISH MEDICAL ASSOCIATION, LONDON

Barbara Cassani is surrounded. After a flawless speech, she takes fifteen minutes of questions. Speaking off the cuff, she showed fresh reserves of energy and defiance: 'I did value-added for a decade; I'm now into really low prices'; 'We may annoy you at times, but by God we give you good value.'

Her show ends to resounding applause. Cassani steps from the stage and is promptly enveloped by people. Just as doctors are weary from people seeking opinions or – worse – giving their views, so an airline executive needs the patience of several apostles to put up with a mix of tirades against aviation. Even worse are those who are keen to give advice on just how to run an airline. Plenty of people want to tell Cassani just what they think about no-frills flying ('I flew on easyJet and they were four hours late – I won't ever use them again') and quiz her on everything from her future plans to the airline's policy on disabled travellers. From the fringe of the throng surrounding her, it is difficult to make out more than the odd line of her responses. 'I'm sorry we let you down.'

A brief opinion survey shows that Barbara Cassani has converted a good proportion of her blue-chip audience. At the end of another thirteen-hour day, she takes a taxi home to Barnes.

9.55 P.M.: EASYJET FLIGHT 23, LUTON–EDINBURGH

The last two flights to Scotland are timed to leave Luton at the same instant, and arrive in Edinburgh and Glasgow seventy minutes later. Today, the departure to the capital wins the race to the runway. With seven flights a day each way between Luton and Edinburgh, a dedicated Scots executive can spend fourteen hours, forty minutes in London – or at least in Luton – and still be home in Edinburgh the same day.

10.10 P.M.: RYANAIR FLIGHT 883: CARDIFF–DUBLIN

At the only significant Welsh airport, final preparations are being made for the flight to Dublin. Why should the only link between the capitals of Wales and Ireland take off so late in the evening? Not even Tim Jeans, the man responsible for selling the flight, knows. 'Scheduling is a black art, manipulated by schedulers to make it seem even blacker than it

If you're not enjoying your flight, remember it could be worse. This is the standard US government advice, issued by the State Department to travellers on African aviation:

> You may have difficulty securing and retaining reservations and experience long waits at airports for customs and immigration processing. If stranded, you may need proof of a confirmed reservation in order to obtain food and lodging vouchers from some airlines.
>
> Flights are often overbooked, delayed, or cancelled and, when competing for space on a plane, you may be dealing with a surging crowd rather than a line. Traveling [sic] with a packaged tour may insulate you from some of these difficulties.
>
> All problems cannot be avoided, but you can:
>
> Learn the reputation of the airline and the airports you will use to forestall problems and avoid any unpleasant surprises.
>
> Reconfirm your onward or return journey immediately upon arrival.
>
> Ask for confirmation in writing, complete with file number or locator code, when you make or confirm a reservation.
>
> Arrive at the airport earlier than required in order to put yourself at the front of the line – or the crowd, as the case may be.
>
> Travel with funds sufficient for an extra week's subsistence in case you are stranded.

need be. Why particular planes turn up at particular times at certain airports is a mystery even within the airline.'

11 P.M.: HAHN AIRPORT

'BORN-muth.'

The staff at the information desk at Hahn have been meticulously friendly and hospitable to the alien writer. I have heard how local people come along to the new terminal for a Sunday afternoon treat, to look at a shiny new international airport that has replaced the heavy military presence of a nation that defeated Germany in the Second World War. But as the incoming Ryanair flight is announced as late, and weariness takes over, they are in the mood for some payback.

'How do you say this? Bern-a-MOOT?'

Christine used to work at the air force base, and now works on the information counter. She is having problems with Ryanair's latest destination, Bournemouth. She has mastered Stansted, Prestwick and Shannon, but is looking to me for advice on how to pronounce the name of the next British destination.

'BORN-muth,' I repeat, and then write the phonetic pronunciation on a square of paper that, I am pleased to say, is still Sellotaped to the computer screen from which they make the announcements about delayed flights.

Once the final flight departs, the information desk staff have to secure the airport. Any stray passengers are booked into a local hotel for the night. But the information team have to wait until the courtesy car arrives and takes away the passenger before they can go home. 'We never run out of hotel rooms,' says Christine. From the tales I have heard during the evening, that is just as well. I have been regaled with stories of romances broken because one partner was waiting at Frankfurt Main while the other one arrived at Hahn. Tonight, everyone is going home alone.

15. WHERE NEXT?

GO FLIGHT 115: STANSTED–MALAGA

Frank Butcher eases himself into seat 20A aboard Go flight 115. Mike Reid, the much-loved actor from *EastEnders* is a convert to no-frills flying. 'I don't fly from anywhere except Stansted,' he says. Most of the remaining passengers to Malaga recognise him, but do not intrude. A few years ago, many of them would have had the notion that highly paid soap stars must fly in business class, and that to find an *EastEnders* actor on a cheapie implied something scandalous. No more. That was then, as was this:

'Want a cheap flight to Madrid? Try Aerolineas Argentinas from Heathrow. Rome? You'll need Kenya Airways. Copenhagen? The Brazilian airline, Varig. But don't go direct, book through a bucket shop.'

In 1996, that was precisely the advice I gave readers wanting budget flights within Europe. The traditional airlines kept fares high, because the only significant competition was aboard short-haul legs of intercontinental flights on obscure airlines, sold through discount agents. British Airways' profits were flying high, and all was well within the cosy world of aviation. Yet in six years, our perceptions of travel in Europe have been comprehensively overturned. The murky twentieth-century history of commercial aviation – which, all too often, wasn't commercial but was a rip-off – has been left behind. For almost a century, powered aviation was viewed as a black art that somehow evaded the normal rules of economics, just as many believed flight transcended the laws of physics. As that notion disappears, and venture capitalists start eyeing up the prospects from new no-frills opportunities, our outlook on travel is changing too.

In 1998, when Go first announced £100 flat fares on its first three routes – to Rome, Milan and Copenhagen – the London *Evening Standard* splashed the news across the front page. By 2001, cheap flights had become so much an accepted part of life that the newspaper barely mentioned the offer of 300,000 free flights from Ryanair. Passengers, at least in Britain, have become blasé about cheap travel, and much more knowing about the airline industry. 'The travelling public has recognised that they have being paying an awful lot for frills,' says Neil Burrows, managing director of Virgin Express. Travellers, he believes, are starting to assess what exactly they are paying for: 'They look at the difference between the traditional airline's fare and that of a low-cost carrier, and think, "Well, they have to pay for the same fuel, the same technical and engineering quality because of the CAA, similar landing fees." You then start to think, "Gosh that was a jolly expensive newspaper. And that orange juice when I got on – that cost a few quid as well." '

Travellers also possess a new mental map of Europe. No-frills airlines will take you to all sorts of places that, five years ago, you never knew existed. 'Charleroi is the de facto airport for all the expatriates in Europe,' says Joe Lister, an Englishman working in Luxembourg. 'You can tell when Ryanair is doing a special, because everyone disappears.' Hahn is less favoured by the British community living in Benelux, because public transport is poor and the road links are difficult in winter. But both are prominent on the twenty-first-century map of Europe that has been redrawn so dramatically. What happens next? That the changes in flying in Europe in the last six years have brought many questions with them is clear; but what are some of the answers? And what does the future hold for the no-frills passenger?

HOW MANY NO-FRILLS AIRLINES WILL THERE BE IN TEN YEARS TIME?

In Europe, it depends who you ask:

'One or possibly two' – Michael O'Leary, chief executive, Ryanair. 'We have a long track record, and we're the most profitable and best financed. For easyJet, Go and Buzz, the jury is still out.'

'Two or three' – Stelios, easyJet.

'I don't think any of us should be complacent about newcomers coming in and showing us a thing or two' – Barbara Cassani, chief executive, Go.

'You don't get consolidation until the market is mature. We're nowhere near market maturity yet.' – Tony Comacho, commercial director, Buzz.

'The new airline is an independent and valuable addition to the BMI family and we believe it will have a long and successful future' – Nigel Turner, mastermind of BMIbaby – the sixth low-cost carrier in Britain.

What everyone agrees is that, in the words of Henry C. Joyner, senior vice-president planning, American Airlines, 'Europe has the potential for explosive growth.'

WHO WILL BE ON BOARD?

Anyone and everyone, according to the no-frills airlines that have set the controls for the hearts and minds of Europe's travellers. Tim Jeans of Ryanair: 'I saw Sir Peter Davis, the boss of Sainsbury's, the other day. He'd travelled with us to Alghero because that was his only means of getting direct to Sardinia. With these leisure routes we are introducing people to the airline, to the fact that no frills is just as good as flying economy in a full-service airline except that you don't get a doggy bag thrust into your lap. There are converts coming back at the end of the summer and looking on the website and finding that Ryanair is an alternative for their destination, and often for their staff. Remember the captain of industry goes to Alghero and he says, 'Jeez, that's all right, I'll bloody make sure they all go with Ryanair to Glasgow on their next sales meeting.'

WHERE WILL THE NO-FRILLS AIRLINES FLY TO NEXT?

Don't expect a rapid increase in the number of destinations. The next few years will be largely taken up with joining the dots on existing networks, and adding frequency on existing routes. There are good commercial reasons for doing this. The marketing costs at a particular airport are pretty much the same whether an airline has one flight a day to one place, or many flights to several destinations. Operational costs per passenger fall as the number of flights from a location rises, and the opportunities for minimising disruption increase. So expect easyJet to boost its services from Gatwick and Palma; Ryanair to convert one of its Italian destinations, probably Bergamo, Treviso or Trieste, into a hub; Go to establish a base at Newcastle – serving the Mediterranean – and Bologna; and Buzz to build up its French domestic network.

WHERE WILL THE NEW DESTINATIONS BE?

Executives of the no-frills airlines won't say, but they are looking hungrily at the anticipated expansion of the European Union in 2004, when former communist countries sign up for the free trade agreements. The best opportunities are in Hungary, Poland and Slovenia, with some relatively wealthy people but minimal opportunities for cheap flying from those countries. Go, with its existing routes to Prague, is well placed to exploit the new markets, but Ryanair has the advantage of a presence in both Salzburg and Trieste, which already attract passengers from the Czech Republic and Slovenia respectively.

WHAT ABOUT FURTHER AFIELD?

'I don't think their customers would be prepared to put up with the service they provide for that length of journey,' says John Patterson, managing director of GB Airways, the airline that faces the strongest competition from no-frills carriers on Mediterranean routes. 'I'm talking about Morocco, the Canaries, and Madeira, where our competition is from national carriers or charters.'

Not everyone agrees: the longest sectors flown at present are to Athens on easyJet, and in summer to Reykjavik on Go. The fact that holidaymakers put up with minimal legroom on narrow-bodied charter flights as far as the Gambia suggests there could be a demand to places like Istanbul or Cyprus; neither is much further than Athens.

WHY NO TRANSATLANTIC NO-FRILLS FLIGHTS?

With two caveats, because there's no point. The no-frills airlines get the prime cut of their cost advantages from the high utilisation of aircraft and staff. On a typical transatlantic route from London to most places in the US, the aircraft can operate only one rotation (there-and-back trip) in 24 hours anyway, so there is little more that can be squeezed out by an assiduously low-cost operator, the advantage is eroded to the point where any savings are minimal. 'The controllable costs where you can make a difference are swamped by uncontrollable costs like fuel and air traffic control charges,' says Stelios of easyJet.

Next, passengers on long flights are prepared to pay a premium for frills, which is why British Airways' superior service to Australia can command higher fares than, say, Malaysia Airlines. And fares are at historic lows anyway: in low season, you can fly between London and New York for a pre-tax fare of around £118 return, which is exactly what Sir Freddie Laker charged for his Skytrain service when it began a quarter of a century ago.

Those caveats. One: in high season, when the benchmark UK–US fare can rise to £400–£500 return, there is some scope for a low-cost operation using a cheap, old aircraft like a DC10 or a 'classic' Boeing 747 with high-density seating; the problem is, what do you do with the plane for the rest of the year, outside the June–September and Christmas/New Year peak? Two: the new long-range Boeing 737s can be '180 ETOPS-certified' to fly long distances over water, with the nearest diversion airport three hours away. While passengers would not necessarily want to be scrunched up in a 737 from London to New York, it is not beyond the bounds of possibility that some UK–Canada services could start up. Glasgow–Halifax, Nova Scotia, is just over 2,500 miles, while Liverpool–St John's, Newfoundland, is a shade over 2,100. This translates to a comfortable six hours' flying time outbound and five inbound (because of the effect of the jet stream), which could extend the daily utilisation of the aircraft very effectively if combined with a couple of round trips to the Mediterranean. There is no existing competition on what would be the epitome of 'long, thin' routes, and there would be a fair amount of 'ethnic' traffic in both directions, given the strong ties between the north of Britain and the Maritime Provinces of Canada. But don't put your pension on it.

WHAT ABOUT DOMESTIC FLIGHTS IN THE BIG EU COUNTRIES LIKE FRANCE, GERMANY AND ITALY?

If you believe the Eurocrats' line, any European airline can fly anywhere it wishes. Debonair put a toe in the water in Germany in 1996, with domestic flights from Moenchengladbach to Munich, a move 'that went straight up the nose of Lufthansa', according to Debonair's founder, Franco Mancassola. 'They tried every trick in the book to ground us.' Buzz tried the French market for the first time in summer 2002 but found itself up against Europe's best network of high-speed trains. An attempt to inject some competition into Italy, called National Jet Italia, was closed down in 2001 by its owner, British Airways.

So the omens do not look especially promising. Despite the EU's protestations, obstructions remain. For some European countries, state airlines have always been symbols of national virility rather than profit-making service providers. 'Nation states believed that to be a nation you needed a flag, a national anthem and an airline. The first two come cheap but the third is extremely expensive,' says Bob Ayling, British Airways' former chief executive and the man who gave Go the go-ahead. Indeed, on the day in April 1997 when the new aviation liberalisation rules came into effect, staff at Air France went on strike in protest at what they regarded as a threat to their livelihoods.

Some within no-frills airlines believe that all kinds of forces are at work to make sure the free-market runway is anything but level. I was aboard a Ryanair flight from Biarritz to Stansted that was ready to leave ten minutes early. Yet we ended up departing late, for reasons which, hinted the captain, could be chauvinism on the part of air traffic controllers. 'All the Air France aircraft are moving around,' he said, 'but we're not being allowed to go anywhere.'

One domestic market that should be particularly promising is Greece, where the flag-carrier airline is apparently still blissfully unaware that the world has changed for ever. Olympic Airways of Greece is cruising serenely towards the cherished role of official Olympic airline for Athens in 2004, even though it last made a profit, probably, around the time England last staged the Games. Stelios of easyJet has explored the possibility of a Greek operation. But with two regional carriers – Air Aegean and Axon Airlines – already competing on the primary routes to Thessalonika, Heraklion and Rhodes, and a modest population base, a broader-based Eastern Mediterranean operation taking in Cyprus and Lebanon might be a better plan.

WHAT SORT OF COMPETITION WILL THE NO-FRILLS AIRLINES FACE?

That depends, as so much in no-frills aviation does, on who you talk to. Michael O'Leary of Ryanair says, 'There's going to be three or four very large connecting hubbing carriers – based around the British Airways, Lufthansa and Air France families. They'll have all the frills and control all the connecting traffic and the hubs. Connecting carriers don't compete with the low-fares carrier: even though BA flies from Dublin to London, 80 per cent of the people are going to be on connecting flights. The big guys will cede all point-to-point flying to the low-fares airlines.'

Already there has been evidence of the erosion. When the winter 2001/2002 schedules came into effect, SAS abandoned the Stansted–Copenhagen route because of the competition from Go. Virgin Atlantic withdrew from its one short-haul route, Athens, which was the only route on which it faced no-frills competition. Alitalia threw in the towel (or should that be the silk scarf?) in its battle against Go, and ended all its flights from Gatwick to Bologna and Venice. Some of these airlines could be merely regrouping in order to launch their own low-cost operations, as BMI did in 2002 when Go moved on to its patch at East Midlands airport. But on routes where passengers have a choice between frills or not, many of them are choosing the latter. In case any traditional airline thought of calling in a no-frills boss to step in to sort it out, forget it, says Stelios: 'I don't think I know how to turn around the supertanker called British Airways that is heading for the rocks.'

In contrast, John Patterson of GB Airways, which flies to Mediterranean destinations on behalf of BA, is confident his airline has a future: 'When people get on board our aircraft in Malaga it really does feel to them like a scheduled operation. They go, "Oh, it's BA, look at those leather seats." So you really do get a premium. We don't equate ourselves with Go or easyJet in terms of the way we do it, we certainly compete with them, and what we're trying to provide is a different standard, but at the cost that does attract the customer.'

NO-FRILLS AIRLINES EMPLOY FEWER PEOPLE – SO IF TRADITIONAL AIRLINES DECLINE, SURELY SOME PEOPLE WILL LOSE THEIR JOBS?

'A job in aviation – glamorous, secure, well-paid employment.' The speaker raised an ironic cheer from a despondent audience of airport executives at a conference I attended one month after the terrorist attack on America. He went on to introduce a session on employment with the words, 'For those of you about to be sacked, this is the one to listen to.'

The same week, I spent some time observing life at Heathrow airport. At Terminal 1, eight ticketing agents staffed the BMI British Midland desk, selling tickets on routes that competed with no-frills airlines. For most of the time, they were unoccupied, occasionally fiddling with a stapler or tapping a few keys disconsolately on the antiquated keyboards they used. Sometimes a traveller would approach the desk, and the answer seemed always to be the same. 'If you want to travel on the earlier flight to Dublin, that'll be £48.' 'If you've lost your ticket, I can reissue another one, but it'll cost £35.' This kind of micro-enterprise is probably self-sufficient, in that enough cash can no doubt be taken to pay the salaries, but I doubt it contributes either to the airline's bottom line or future customer relations.

'How do I get to Stansted? I'm going to fly on Ryanair' and 'That's the last time I fly BMI' were two typical reactions from passengers. When adjustments to tickets for a one-hour flight cost more than the entire flight on another airline, things are likely to change. BMI's chairman, Sir Michael Bishop, fought the cause of the traveller for years in trying to drive fares down. Now, his airline looks part of the establishment – except in the eyes of readers of the magazine, *Wanderlust*. In 2001, they were asked to name their favourite budget airline. I don't know which will have annoyed Sir Michael Bishop more: appearing in the top three of the 'Top Budget Airline' awards – when it should, by rights, have featured in the 'Top Major Airline' category – or coming only third, behind Buzz and Ryanair.

MORE FLYING WON'T DO MUCH FOR THE ENVIRONMENT, WILL IT, IN TERMS OF NOISE, POLLUTION AND CONGESTION?

No. The skies of Europe were reaching their limits at certain times of day, until two events. The first was the attack on America on 11 September, which cut the amount of air traffic; the second, the introduction in January 2002 of Reduced Vertical Separation Minima from 29,000 to 41,000 feet – in other words, slicing the sky more thinly between 5.3 and 7.5 miles high to create an extra six flight levels. The effects of both events are likely to be cancelled out in a few years by increased air traffic.

More radical solutions are possible. Europe taxes most things, but not aviation fuel, which is one reason the airlines can afford to slug it out in the skies between Edinburgh and Dublin. The residents of those cities, plus the people who live around Stansted and Luton, are unlikely to welcome yet more flights. The introduction of a tax on fuel has always been fought on relatively flimsy grounds – that it is an international commodity that needs to be sold at roughly the same price everywhere to avoid distortions such as aircraft carrying unnecessarily large loads of fuel from countries where it is cheap. A tax on fuel could raise a fortune for national and European coffers, and stifle growth.

Another possibility is that the EU could step in to cap the number of flights between cities with fast rail links. With Brussels barely two and a half hours from London, served by trains that typically run half empty, does it make sense to have 34 flights each way, each day, consuming fuel, slots and airspace? A limit would impact directly on Ryanair and Virgin Express. One more prospect that is under active consideration in the US is a 'gold card' arrangement that would give airlines that were prepared to pay extra the right automatically to go to the front of the air traffic control queue. The ability to get you to your destination on time is one of the frills that airlines will be able to market.

ARE THERE OTHER IMPEDIMENTS TO EXPANSION?

Not all airlines relish competition, and many nations design rules to protect their existing carriers. In the quest for low-cost aviation, governments have generally proved, in the memorable phrase of the late satirist John Wells, 'about as useful as a one-legged man at an arse-kicking party'. Franco Mancassola, the founder of Debonair, says, 'I never understood why politicians meddle in the airline business. They don't meddle in the shoe business.'

It is over thirty years since Freddie Laker wanted to meet the demand for low-cost flying between London and New York, and spent years in legal battles for that right. The same kind of official obstructions remain in force in many parts of the world. A service from Luton or Stansted to Tangier in Morocco would be operationally little different to a flight to Malaga – it is only eighty miles further. But the chances of such a route taking off are remote. Once out of Europe, the attitude to cheap flying changes dramatically.

For British travellers, the big issue could be slots. The most desirable one- and two-runway airports in the world are Gatwick and Heathrow. The business vision of both easyJet and Virgin Express encompasses airports like these; indeed, they already serve Gatwick and Heathrow respectively. But most of the slots are the prized possessions of incumbent airlines, particularly British Airways. Franco Mancassola, founder of Debonair, says this is an outrage: 'You've seen British Airways dropping routes from Heathrow, but protecting the slots. I was on the radio with [former BA boss] Bob Ayling. He said "Why should we give up the slots? We developed them." Excuse me, haven't you got things the other way round, didn't the slot develop you? If you give me five slots at 8 a.m. to Frankfurt, and I give you five to Frankfurt at 11 a.m., I'll do better than you, guaranteed, even if you're British Airways. It's the slot that allows the airline to prosper, not the other way round, like Mr Ayling was wanting the world to believe.' Mancassola says the slots should be shared out so that low-cost airlines 'can have a share of the good pie, as well as the bone that is thrown at them'.

There are also some arcane ownership and control laws, some of them almost a century old. They were designed to make airplanes available to the government in case of an armed conflict. But many aircraft are leased from companies that prohibit their use in war zones. 'It limits the ability of our industry to prosper and expand because it cannot take advantage of capital that may be available in countries of which the airline is not a citizen, says Mancassola.

One more threat: the no-frills airlines themselves. 'The bigger you are, the more sclerotic you become,' says Sir Bob Geldof, latterly of the Boomtown Rats and currently on the board of the travel website, deckchair.com.

WHAT ABOUT THE NEXT ECONOMIC DOWNTURN?
While no airline relishes a recession, the no-frills carriers believe that a downturn could actually strengthen their hand. Businesses will focus more rigorously on keeping travel expenditure under control, runs their argument, to the benefit of airlines that themselves keep costs, and fares, low. Dr Keith Mason of Cranfield University, author of *Europe's Low Cost Airlines*, says 'In the short-haul market, the additional benefits aimed at the business traveller are becoming less highly valued.' Stelios agrees: 'A recession would be a very good test, and I think we're going to do very well out of it.'

ANY OTHER THREATS?
Safety is the main concern of every no-frills airline. If any one of them were to suffer a crash, the effects would reverberate across the industry in the way that the ValuJet disaster in the Everglades awoke anxieties about low-cost carriers. The level of aviation security worldwide is also a factor in people's propensity to travel by air. More incidents such as the would-be suicide bomber aboard an American Airlines flight from Paris to Miami just before Christmas 2001, that caused security to become even tighter, would blunt still further the edge that air travel has.

One other threat – or possibly an opportunity, depending on which side you're on – is internal to the airlines. If you work for a no-frills airline, you are no doubt keen to benefit personally from the growth of the industry. In other words, you would like higher wages. The question being asked prior to 11 September 2001 was: who would throw the first industrial-relations spanner into the well-oiled machine that delivers no-frills flights? Those crews, Boeings and support teams have been calibrated to work at full throttle. But strikes, or even the threat of a strike, can wound an airline deeply: people simply stop booking and switch to other carriers or means of transport, rather than take the risk of having their travel disrupted.

Every no-frills flight requires a minor miracle of co-ordination to be fulfilled. There must be space at the departure airport – in the terminal for the passenger, and somewhere to park an aircraft that is ambitiously scheduled to shuttle to and from Luton or Stansted half a dozen times a day. The airline has to organise the ground staff and crew the jet, and air traffic control must find a path through the complex and crowded skies over Europe. And, upon arrival, baggage handlers must be on hand to unload the luggage, with airport ground staff on hand to check in passengers for the return flight. When any element of this three-dimensional jigsaw goes awry, even something as trivial as a passenger dawdling in duty-free and causing the plane to miss its slot, the whole system can quickly seize up. Before 11 September, everyone was watching anxiously to see the consequences of a worldwide shortage of pilots. Their industrial muscle had already pushed annual earnings for captains on some airlines to $300,000. In addition, every other small cog in the big machine, from check-in staff to aircraft refuellers, is conscious of their critical role and their potential for disrupting a complex, fragmented business. One small example: a holiday flight to Athens has to traverse the airspace of a dozen different countries. The repercussions of just one nation's air traffic controllers walking out will be visible on the radar screens across Europe. As with increased security, anything that makes air travel less comfortable leads people to consider other modes of transport, or simply not to travel.

HOW WILL NO-FRILLS AIRLINES SELL THE SEATS?

The Internet, almost exclusively. If ever two concepts were made for each other, they were the World Wide Web and no-frills flying. The airlines are seeking to offload sizeable quantities of a generic yet perishable product to a large number of individual purchasers. The offer, and order-taking, are straightforward and extremely cheap operations. Unlike the books and records sold by, for example, Amazon.com, the great trick is that there is nothing to deliver. People take delivery when they turn up at (they hope) the right airport on the right day at the right time. If they go missing, usually that is the end of the story; there is nothing to replace. The consumer is rewarded for using the Internet with a discount compared with reservations by phone or through an agent. Better still, the traveller can arrange all the other elements of their journey, from hotels to car rental, online.

Not everyone agrees. Sir Bob Geldof, rock star turned high-powered businessman, believes the social experience of shopping will never be lost: 'It's too much fun. I buy records down at the record shop, because the guy wants to talk about what's new, because he knows what I like. "Check this out" – and he'll play it and there'll be someone else that'll say, "Yeah that's OK, but their first one's better." Shopping online is consumer wanking. You're just there by yourself and you think, yeah I like that, then you come when you finally make your purchase.'

Many satisfied customers would not agree with the masturbation analogy, though the sites should start to give more solitary pleasure when they become smarter, as they begin to understand users' travel patterns. If you always fly from Glasgow Prestwick, for example, the site should offer that as the first option you see, rather than a tedious scroll through from Aarhus to Friedrichshafen first.

HOW MUCH WILL FLIGHTS COST?

'We passionately believe that even today, Ryanair's air fares are too high,' says the airline's boss, Michael O'Leary. 'They'll have to go much, much lower in the next ten or twenty years.' On average, much the same as they do at the moment: around £60 for the typical flight, perhaps a few pounds less on Ryanair. Within that average, though, there will be wide variations, from the lowest possible fare of around £10 (assuming taxes and other marginal charges are levied) to a maximum of £200 or more for desirable flights.

WHAT SORT OF PLANES WILL THEY USE?

The folks at Boeing assume the Boeing 737 will be the choice for the next couple of decades, which is perhaps bad news for planespotters. The one point of interest could be the 'winglets' that can be applied to these planes, which improve performance – for example, making transatlantic flights more feasible (but not much). The older, noisier 737-200s should disappear soon, priced out by noise levies at airports and low efficiency. Airbus, the only other maker of medium and large jet aircraft, is desperate for a stake in the fastest-growing sector of aviation, and has come up with a configuration for its A319 that has 150 seats – one more than easyJet's 737 – which attracted the attention of

---

FREE FLIGHTS AT LAST
You can fly completely free of charge, but there are two catches:
the flights are strictly one-way – from Stansted airport to Knock,
in the west of Ireland – and you have to be dead. Coffins, and
their occupants, making the final homecoming to County Mayo
are the only freight that Ryanair carries. The short turn-rounds on
which the airline relies to make maximum use of planes and
crews do not allow for the regular carriage of cargo. But the chief
executive Michael O'Leary, makes a single exception out of
respect for Mayo families.

---

the Luton airline's chief executive, Ray Webster: 'We feel it is important
to consider all the options,' he said, no doubt safe in the knowledge that
Boeing was listening and knows it does not have a divine right to build
planes for Britain's biggest no-frills airline.

ANY CHANCE OF A FEW, WELL, FRILLS ON NO-FRILLS AIRLINES?

Ryanair is promising to carry a million passengers a year for nothing
within five years, and hoping to earn cash from new interactive screens
on each seat back. The idea is that people will pay to watch programmes
such as sports events, and that the earnings from those will more than
offset the marginal cost of carrying discretionary passengers. People with
flexibility – retired or unemployed people, and the growing number of
freelance workers – will increasingly be tempted on board to soak up
the excess supply, and their inflight spending will help to build those
profits. In America, the no-frills airlines have always had some frills,
with JetBlue offering 24-channel television (free) and all-leather seats.
The problem with in-flight entertainment is that it is expensive and of
limited use on a typical ninety-minute flight. And since 11 September,
traditional airlines have cut back on frills. Flying is becoming about as
thrilling as a bus ride.

WHY STOP AT PLANES – WHY NOT NO-FRILLS TRAINS, BUSES, RENTAL CARS, CRUISE SHIPS, HOTELS . . .?

They already exist, as anyone who has travelled on a Connex train or
Portuguese bus, or stayed at a Campanile hotel will know. The most
promising targets for the no-frills concept are package holidays – and
Airtours is already selling its Sundeals brand as 'no-frills holidays'.

0800WHAT DRIVES THE PEOPLE AT THE TOP?

'We have a mission. We believe we can transform air travel around Europe, but it's going to take us another ten or fifteen years to do it' – Michael O'Leary, chief executive, Ryanair.

'We actually care about what happens to you on your journey with us, and we're going to try and make it as pleasant as possible. Do not expect to have a five-star lunch or dinner when you come on board, because you haven't paid for that. Consumers in airlines are like consumers in anything else. What they're looking for is great value' – Neil Burrows, managing director, Virgin Express.

'We change the way people live their lives. I joke that I'm waiting for my Nobel Peace Prize for services to humanity' – Barbara Cassani, Go.

HOW WILL OUR TRAVEL HABITS CHANGE?

There will be more of it. Business travellers can make typically twice as many trips on no-frills airlines than on traditional carriers. Well-to-do Londoners will swap the country cottage in Wales for an apartment in the south of France or a finca in Majorca: the commuting time and travel costs are much the same, and the climate tends to be more agreeable. Families will become more adventurous, substituting the Mediterranean package with island-hopping around Greece or sightseeing in Italy, once they realise the costs are about the same. Priorities will change, too: we will focus less on the journey, as it becomes more routine rather than a once- or twice-a-year event, and more on the 90 per cent plus of a trip that is not spent in an aircraft. Luxury hotels in Amsterdam and Barcelona already report a boom in business from easyJet passengers, who conclude it is far more important to spend cash on a hotel – where you are likely to spend a fair amount of time – than on a flight lasting around an hour.

Today, you can expect to travel from London to Rome for around £100, the same as it was thirty years ago, when £100 was worth nearly £900 at today's prices. You won't get rubber chicken (though go ahead and bring some on board if you wish), because you won't pay for it. Thanks to the pioneers who realised that aviation was for the masses, the traveller in the first decade of the twenty-first century enjoys a degree of freedom no previous generation has ever known. On the new map of Europe, Madrid and Munich are as easy and cheap to reach from south-east England as Manchester. The travelling public has voted with its credit cards (or debit cards, to avoid those £3 supplements), and will not go back to the bad old days.

The closest analogy I can come up with for the no-frills revolution is the way that punk took the music world by storm – and surprise – in the mid-seventies. When the prevailing artists grew old and their music

THE WITH-FRILLS EMPIRE STRIKES BACK?

What's to stop the traditional airlines hitting back? A good person to answer that question is John Patterson, former director of strategy for British Airways and managing director of GB Airways which flies in the colours of, and on behalf of, BA. He believes his current airline already has low costs, and has just added another daily flight from Gatwick to Malaga, making it easily the leading Mediterranean destination served from Britain. The market justifies the expansion, he says. 'The reason everybody is attracted to Malaga is because the whole place from Algeciras all the way through to Motril is growing like Topsy.' When he travels to southern Spain, he tries to count the number of cranes and 'gets fed up after about ten minutes when you pass about fifty. The place is a building site and that means that demand's there, if you're flying from the right place at the right time – which we are.'

In many other airlines, the old joke about asking for directions in rural Ireland applies: the response – 'I wouldn't start from here.' Would any traditional airline start from its present position? Certainly British Airways relishes its slots at Heathrow, but it could certainly do without the baggage of the past, going back to pre-privatisation days when, as effectively a branch of government, the airline had bottomless pockets and everyone knew it.

A job in a state-owned airline has traditionally been regarded as among the cushiest of postings, with low expectations of productivity and high expectations of earnings and pension rights. 'The traditional carriers will completely reconstruct themselves,' says Ray Webster of easyJet. 'A lot of them will disappear. The days of countries having airlines will disappear. Airlines will exist in the same way banks exist, they'll exist because a market of opportunity exists and they're well-run businesses.' Webster gets support from a former Labour MP for Islwyn: 'I've never discovered a justification for taxpayers' money being used to sustain airlines. Commuter rail – yes, it's a fundamental social necessity. But I've got no difficulty at all in being an avid pursuer of the denial of state aid and the promotion of commercially viable, competitive airlines that offer a fair deal to the air user.' What he thinks is important because he is Neil Kinnock, deputy chief commissioner, and former transport commissioner, of the European Union.

Perhaps the sharpest edge that the no-frills airlines have on their traditional competition is the absence of a history, and in particular no tradition that airlines are run for the benefit of the staff rather than the passenger. Three leading no-frills figures tell different stories. 'My aunt worked for British European Airways thirty years ago,' says one, 'and she's still entitled to free tickets.' Another recalls that in the pioneering days of commercial aviation, crews who were obliged to stay overnight abroad were put up in luxury hotels, and given generous allowances. They still are. A third asserts that the complex system of extra payments for flight crews means that, on occasion, they have been known deliberately to slow down or take an unnecessarily meandering route in order to qualify for a lunch allowance. An on-time arrival at the stand at 11.55 a.m. might not earn them anything, but turning up six minutes later would trigger bonuses. Such practices could persist while there were regular government-sanctioned fare increases.

'We've got a very sick, unsustainable industry,' says Ray Webster of easyJet. 'The only way to fix the body is to undergo treatment, moving the whole industry into a pro-competitive environment where there's an incentive for efficiency, and to ensure that it's the fittest that survive. That will mean that some of the airlines that are less well placed, and less well run, don't survive. But I think everyone is going to be a lot better off as a result of that. In five or ten years' time, you'll either travel round Europe on high-speed trains or low-cost airlines.'

bloated, when Led Zeppelin had released one too many albums and Phil Collins and Yes refused to keep quiet, rock had to be reinvented – it was unsustainable. In the same way, air travel could not carry on as it was, charging crippling fares to sustain viciously high costs.

Southwest, who (some say) started it all, just managed to complete the transformation of aviation within a century of its invention. In October 2001, the airline opened its latest base in Norfolk, Virginia. This is the closest airport to the windswept shore where the Wright brothers spent three hungry years pioneering powered flight. Within a century of the first take-off on 17 December 1903, the ordinary working man or woman of Kitty Hawk, Kill Devil Hills or Dismal Swamp has easy access to low-cost air travel, in the same way that most of Britain's population can benefit from cheap seats.

When people learn foreign languages, the first verb to be taught is *to be*. Once the concept of existence has been mastered, the next verb is *to go*. The no-frills airlines allow more people, more often, to travel. Business people can do more deals, clubbers can do more dancing, travellers can enjoy more sex and shopping in exotic places, and everyone who travels can find more common ground with the people they meet. In a world that needs to be brought closer, that must be a force for good.

NO-FRILLS FLYING: A USER'S GUIDE

WHERE CAN I GO?

From Britain, almost anywhere within a two-hour flight of Britain, at least if you live in the south-east of England. This is a comprehensive list as of summer 2002; some routes may be dropped, and many more are sure to be added over the next few years. Nations are listed alphabetically (with England, Northern Ireland and Scotland listed separately for ease of reference). Within each country, destinations are listed clockwise from the capital (or, at any rate, the closest airport to it).

AUSTRIA

GRAZ

Fly from: Stansted (Ryanair)

Airport: six miles south of city centre; bus 630 and 631 hourly, fare around £1.50.

Main attraction: the World Heritage Site at the centre of Austria's second city.

Also handy for: Slovenia and Croatia, whose frontiers are 30 and 60 miles.south respectively.

KLAGENFURT

Fly from: Stansted (Ryanair)

Airport: four miles north-east of city centre; frequent buses.

Main attraction: the Italianate city centre, and the surrounding castles.

Also handy for: Ljubljana; the Slovenian capital is 50 miles south.

SALZBURG

Fly from: Stansted (Ryanair)

Airport: three miles east of city centre; frequent trolleybuses (the only such mode of transport at any airport in western Europe).

Main attraction: the beautifully preserved home town of the von Trapp family.

Also handy for: Hitler's tea house at Berchtesgaden, across the border in Germany; and the city of Linz, where the dictator grew up.

BELGIUM

BRUSSELS

Fly from: Heathrow (Virgin Express)

Airport: National, seven miles north-east of the centre, frequent trains.

Main attraction: the Grand' Place, one of the finest city squares in the world. And the food.

Also handy for: Antwerp (direct buses from the airport, taking 45 minutes), Bruges and Ghent (direct trains).

CHARLEROI
Also known as: Brussels (South)
Fly from: Liverpool, Prestwick, Stansted (all Ryanair)
Airport: four miles north of Charleroi (frequent buses); thirty miles south of Brussels (buses connect with flights, in theory).
Main attraction: the much-overlooked city of Namur, 25 miles east.
Also handy for: the Ardennes and the Waterloo battleground.

CZECH REPUBLIC

PRAGUE
Fly from: Stansted and Bristol (both Go), East Midlands (Go and BMIbaby)
Airport: seven miles north-east of city centre; frequent buses.
Main attraction: central Europe's most beautiful city.
Also handy for: the castles of Bohemia, Plzen (the lager capital of the world) and Dresden, across the border in Germany.

DENMARK

COPENHAGEN
Fly from: Heathrow (Virgin Express, via Brussels), Stansted (Go)
Airport: eight miles south; frequent trains, taking twelve minutes.
Main attraction: an intensely human city, with free rental bikes to help you explore.
Also handy for: Hamlet's home town of Elsinore, the extraordinary Louisiana modern art museum, and Malmo in Sweden – direct trains across the Oresund Link from the airport.

ESBJERG
Fly from: Stansted (Ryanair)
Airport: six miles north-east, regular buses.
Main attraction: the unspoilt island of Fanø, just offshore from Esbjerg.
Also handy for: Legoland; and Odense, home town of Hans Christian Andersen.

AARHUS
Fly from: Stansted (Ryanair)
Airport: six miles north-west, occasional buses.
Main attraction: Denmark's lively second city, with a big student population.
Also handy for: Legoland; and lightly travelled north Jutland.

ENGLAND

NEWCASTLE
Fly from: Stansted (Go)

Main attraction: post-industrial city with some dynamic new tourist draws.

Also handy for: Sunderland, Hadrian's Wall, Durham.

NEWQUAY
Fly from: Stansted (Ryanair)

Airport: six miles east of the resort; take a taxi.

Main attraction: surfing on Cornwall's wild north coast.

Also handy for: anywhere west of Plymouth.

FRANCE

PARIS
Fly from: Stansted (Buzz)

Airport: Charles de Gaulle, fifteen miles north-east of city centre; frequent fast trains.

Main attraction: the world's most popular tourist destination.

Also handy for: Disneyland Paris (direct trains, fifteen minutes); Parc Asterix (direct buses, thirty minutes).

BEAUVAIS
Also known as: Paris

Fly from: Prestwick, Dublin, Shannon (all Ryanair)

Airport: three miles east of town centre (take a taxi), fifty miles north of Paris (buses connect with flights).

Main attraction: extraordinary medieval cathedral of which only half remains.

Also handy for: Compiègne, Rouen, Chantilly.

DIJON
Fly from: Stansted (Buzz)

Airport: three miles south-east, frequent buses.

Main attraction: a handsome city that serves as capital of Burgundy, and has a strong line in mustard.

Also handy for: the vineyards of Burgundy.

GRENOBLE
Fly from: Stansted (Buzz)

Airport: 25 miles west – almost halfway to Lyon – at the confusingly named village of St Étienne de St Geoirs. Take a taxi to the nearest sensible station, Rives, ten miles east.

Main attraction: a spectacular location, with successful music and theatre festivals.
Also handy for: the French Alps and the Rhone Valley.

LYON
Fly from: Stansted (Go)
Airport: Satolas, fifteen miles east; frequent buses.
Main attraction: gastronomic capital of France, and a superbly three-dimensional city.
Also handy for: French Alps.

ST ÉTIENNE
Also known as: Lyon
Fly from: Stansted (Ryanair)
Airport: ten miles north-west; regular buses.
Main attraction: the Modern Art Museum
Also handy for: the Massif Central.

NICE
Fly from: Gatwick (easyJet), Heathrow (Virgin Express, via Brussels), Liverpool, Luton (both easyJet)
Airport: six miles west; frequent buses.
Main attraction: walking the Promenade des Anglais, and stuffing your face with seafood.
Also handy for: Monaco, Italian Riviera, ferries to Corsica.

TOULON
Fly from: Stansted (Buzz)
Airport: fifteen miles east, just south of Hyères; take a taxi.
Main attraction: the boat across to the amazing marine National Park of Port Cros.
Also handy for: St Tropez.

MARSEILLES
Fly from: Stansted (Buzz)
Airport: twenty miles north-east; frequent buses.
Main attraction: ancient seaport, one of Europe's most cosmopolitan cities.
Also handy for: the weird and wonderful landscapes of the Bouches-du-Rhône.

MONTPELLIER
Fly from: Stansted (Ryanair)
Airport: eight miles south-east of city centre; buses hourly or less.

Main attraction: a handsome, atmospheric city with a large student population.
Also handy for: the Camargue.

NÎMES
Fly from: Stansted (Ryanair)
Airport: seven miles south-west; regular buses.
Main attraction: marvellous Roman remnants.
Also handy for: Arles and Avignon.

PERPIGNAN
Also known as: Barcelona
Fly from: Stansted (Ryanair)
Airport: four miles north-east; buses, but not on Sundays.
Main attraction: the sleepy city with a railway station that Salvador Dali nominated as the centre of the universe.
Also handy for: the eastern Pyrenees, Spain's Costa Brava.

CARCASSONNE
Also known as: Toulouse
Fly from: Stansted (Ryanair)
Airport: three miles east; regular buses.
Main attraction: sublime walled city, with an extraordinary Cathar history.
Also handy for: the eastern Pyrenees, Andorra.

TOULOUSE
Fly from: Stansted (Buzz)
Airport: four miles north-east; frequent buses.
Main attraction: civilised, well-proportioned city with intriguing odd corners.
Also handy for: the Airbus factory, where you can see planes being built (but not the sort that you arrived on); Lourdes; and Tony Blair's holiday home.

BERGERAC
Fly from: Stansted (Buzz)
Airport: four miles south-east; take a taxi.
Main attraction: Wine.
Also handy for: Périgueux, the heart of the Dordogne.

LIMOGES
Fly from: Stansted (Buzz)
Airport: six miles north-west; take a taxi.

Main attraction: porcelain and enamel.
Also handy for: the unspoilt terrain of Limousin.

BIARRITZ
Also known as: Bordeaux
Fly from: Stansted (Ryanair)
Airport: three miles south-east of Biarritz, six miles south-west of Bayonne (regular buses), but within walking distance of Biarritz station.
Main attraction: chic seafront, and Bayonne – capital of the French Basque lands.
Also handy for: western Pyrenees, San Sebastian (Spain).

BORDEAUX
Fly from: Stansted (Buzz)
Airport: six miles west; regular buses.
Main attraction: home to France's finest wines and merchants.
Also handy for: the Atlantic coast.

LA ROCHELLE
Fly from: Stansted (Buzz)
Airport: two miles north; walk or take a bus.
Main attraction: blissful Atlantic port city, with easy access to the Ile de Ré.
Also handy for: the oyster beds of the Charente-Maritime.

POITIERS
Fly from: Stansted (Buzz)
Airport: two miles west; regular buses.
Main attraction: fine Romanesque churches.
Also handy for: Futuroscope, the European Park of the Moving Image, on the northern outskirts.

TOURS
Fly from: Stansted (Buzz)
Airport: five miles north-east; take a taxi.
Main attraction: a classic French city with a spectacular cathedral.
Also handy for: the great wine towns of the Loire, such as Chinon, Saumur and Vouvray.

BREST
Fly from: Stansted (Buzz)
Airport: seven miles north-east; occasional buses.

Main attraction: because the city was comprehensively trashed in the Second World War, the reason to come here is for access to western Brittany.
Also handy for: anywhere in Brittany, Nantes.

DINARD
Fly from: Stansted (Ryanair)
Airport: four miles south; occasional buses.
Main attraction: the gently fading grandeur of a leading resort.
Also handy for: St Malo, Rennes.

CAEN
Fly from: Stansted (Buzz)
Airport: four miles west; take a taxi, or walk to bus line 1 in the village of Carpiquet.
Main attraction: a fortress, two abbeys and some fine Normandy cuisine.
Also handy for: the World War II landing sites on the Channel coast.

ROUEN
Fly from: Stansted (Buzz)
Airport: six miles south-east; take a taxi.
Main attraction: the cult of Joan of Arc, who was burned at the stake here; a Gothic cathedral; and half-timbered houses.
Also handy for: Claude Monet's home in Giverny.

GERMANY

BERLIN
Fly from: Stansted (Buzz)
Airport: Schonefeld, twenty miles south-east (frequent trains).
Main attraction: the dazzling new capital of united Germany.
Also handy for: Potsdam, Dresden, Leipzig.

MUNICH
Fly from: Stansted (Ryanair)
Airport: twenty miles north; frequent trains.
Main attraction: the beautiful capital of Bavaria.
Also handy for: the German and Austrian ski resorts.

FRIEDRICHSHAFEN
Fly from: Stansted (Ryanair)
Airport: three miles north-east of city centre; frequent trains.
Main attraction: the birthplace of the Zeppelin, with a Museum on the airship.
Also handy for: Liechtenstein.

FRANKFURT
Fly from: Stansted (Buzz)

Airport: Main, eight miles south; frequent trains.

Main attraction: fine riverside views, a marvellous Modern Art Museum, and the airport itself – an architectural attraction in its own right.

Also handy for: the fine city of Heidelberg.

HAHN
Also known as: Frankfurt

Fly from: Stansted and Bournemouth (both Ryanair)

Airport: eight miles east of Traben-Trarbach.

Main attraction: the beautifully intestinal Moselle Valley, with picturesque towns beneath expansive vineyards.

Also handy for: the stunning Roman city of Trier.

DÜSSELDORF
Fly from: Stansted (Buzz)

Airport: six miles north; frequent trains.

Main attraction: walking the banks of the Rhine.

Also handy for: Cologne, Aachen, Maastricht.

LÜBECK
Also known as: Hamburg

Fly from: Stansted (Ryanair)

Airport: five miles south of Lübeck (frequent buses), forty miles east of Hamburg (buses connecting with flights).

Main attraction: well-preserved Hanseatic city, hub of the world's marzipan trade.

Also handy for: Kiel, Schleswig, Rostock.

GREECE

ATHENS
Fly from: Luton (easyJet)

Airport: twenty miles east; frequent buses.

Main attraction: the miraculous Parthenon, and beneath it the old Turkish quarter of Plaka.

Also handy for: the islands, thanks to the direct bus connection to the port of Rafina.

HOLLAND

AMSTERDAM
Fly from: Belfast, Edinburgh, Gatwick, Glasgow, Liverpool, Luton (all easyJet)

Airport: eight miles south-west; frequent trains.

Main attraction: depending on your inclination, either superb seventeenth-century architecture, or legally available sex and drugs.

Also handy for: Leiden, Haarlem, The Hague.

EINDHOVEN

Fly from: Stansted (Ryanair)

Airport: four miles north west of city centre; frequent services on bus 11 from the Central Station.

Main attraction: a tranquil Dutch city.

Also handy for: Maastricht, Dusseldorf.

REPUBLIC OF IRELAND

DUBLIN

Fly from: Birmingham, Bournemouth, Bristol, Cardiff, Edinburgh, Gatwick, Leeds/Bradford, Liverpool, Luton, Manchester, Prestwick, Stansted, Teesside (all Ryanair)

Airport: seven miles north of the city centre; frequent buses.

Main attraction: the only capital in the world where the Irish pubs are genuine.

Also handy for: the Wicklow coast and mountains; and, at a pinch, the Mourne mountains of Northern Ireland.

CORK

Fly from: Stansted (Ryanair)

Airport: seven miles south of the city centre; frequent buses.

Main attraction: unreconstructed cityscapes and great music.

Also handy for: Kinsale, and all of Ireland's largest county.

KERRY

Fly from: Stansted (Ryanair)

Airport: three miles south-east of Killarney; take a taxi.

Main attraction: the mountains, lakes and seashore of Kerry.

Also handy for: the far south-west of Cork.

SHANNON

Fly from: Stansted (Ryanair)

Airport: twelve miles south of Ennis and fifteen miles west of Limerick; rare buses.

Main attraction: a bizarrely huge 1960s airport, which is still a hub for the Russian airline, Aeroflot.

Also handy for: the Clare coastline, including the Cliffs of Moher, plus the Aran Islands and the city of Galway.

KNOCK
Fly from: Stansted (Ryanair)
Airport: seven miles south of Charlestown; take a taxi.
Main attraction: the 'Knock special', a toasted sandwich about two inches thick, served at the airport cafe.
Also handy for: the Connemara coast, including Westport.

ITALY

ROME
Fly from: Stansted (Go and Ryanair), Heathrow (Virgin Express, via Brussels)
Airport: Go and Ryanair fly to Ciampino, twelve miles south; awkward bus/rail connection. Virgin Express flies to Fiumicino, twenty miles west, with a faster but more expensive connection.
Main attraction: more history than any other city in Europe.
Also handy for: the lakes north of Rome, the Mediterranean coast south of it.

PESCARA
Fly from: Stansted (Ryanair)
Airport: three miles south-west; regular buses.
Main attraction: lovely ten-mile long sandy beach.
Also handy for: the beautiful Gran Sasso d'Italia range.

NAPLES
Fly from: Stansted (Go)
Airport: six miles north; frequent buses.
Main attraction: graciously decaying Mediterranean port where the pizzas are close to perfection.
Also handy for: Pompeii, Sorrento, Capri and the Amalfi coast.

ALGHERO
Fly from: Stansted (Ryanair)
Airport: eight miles north-west; take a taxi.
Main attraction: the north-western corner of the least-discovered (by the British) large Mediterranean island.
Also handy for: the rest of Sardinia.

PISA
Fly from: Stansted (Ryanair)
Airport: two miles south; frequent buses, regular trains, or walk.

Main attraction: the Leaning Tower, now open for business again.
Also handy for: Lucca, a much more attractive and less touristy city twelve miles north; and Florence, with direct trains from the airport.

GENOA
Fly from: Stansted (Ryanair)
Airport: four miles east; regular buses.
Main attraction: the home of Columbus and pesto.
Also handy for: the Italian Riviera, and in particular the Cinque Terre – five towns squeezed between the mountains and the sea.

TURIN
Also known as: Milan
Fly from: Stansted (Ryanair)
Airport: eight miles north; frequent buses.
Main attraction: northern Italian architecture on the grandest of scales.
Also handy for: the Italian Alps.

MILAN
Fly from: Heathrow (Virgin Express, via Brussels), Stansted (Go)
Airport: Linate, four miles east; frequent buses.
Main attraction: a city dripping with style and sprinkled with fine art.
Also handy for: lakes Como and Maggiore (though Malpensa airport, served by Alitalia, is a lot handier).

BERGAMO
Also known as: Milan Orio al Serio
Fly from: Stansted (Ryanair)
Airport: three miles south-east.
Main attraction: the Citta Alta, the medieval and Renaissance quarter that dominates the city.
Also handy for: lakes Como and Iseo.

BRESCIA
Also known as: Verona
Fly from: Stansted (Ryanair)
Airport: twelve miles east; occasional buses.
Main attraction: the delicate Piazza della Loggia, and the cathedral with the third-highest dome in Italy.
Also handy for: Lake Garda.

TREVISO
Fly from: Stansted (Ryanair)
Airport: three miles south; occasional buses.

Main attraction: lots of canals, but more like Amsterdam than Venice.

Also handy for: Venice (buses connect with flights), the eastern Italian Alps.

VENICE

Fly from: Stansted (Ryanair)

Airport: six miles north; frequent (and expensive) boats; frequent (and cheap) buses.

Main attraction: the fabulous city, for which you must suspend disbelief.

Also handy for: Treviso.

TRIESTE

Fly from: Stansted (Ryanair)

Airport: 25 miles west; buses connect with flights.

Main attraction: a chunk of Austria-Hungary wedged into a corner of Italy.

Also handy for: Slovenia, the northern Croatian coast.

BOLOGNA

Fly from: Stansted (Go)

Airport: four miles north; frequent buses.

Main attraction: intensely atmospheric and artistic city.

Also handy for: Florence (frequent fast trains).

FORLI

Also known as: Bologna

Fly from: Stansted (Ryanair)

Airport: three miles south-east; take a taxi.

Main attraction: a palio (crazy municipal horse race) that is less touristy than that in Siena.

Also handy for: Ravenna (European home of the mosaic), and the resort of Rimini.

ANCONA

Fly from: Stansted (Ryanair)

Airport: seven miles west, in the town of Falconara.

Main attraction: a lovely crescent-shaped harbour, though desecrated by twentieth-century war.

Also handy for: eastern Umbria; and boats across the Adriatic to Croatia.

NORTHERN IRELAND

BELFAST INTERNATIONAL

Fly from: Bristol (Go), Edinburgh, Glasgow, Liverpool, Luton (all easyJet), Stansted (Go)

Airport: twelve miles west of Belfast; buses every half-hour.
Main attraction: a handsome Victorian city that is slowly reclaiming its
former civility.
Also handy for: counties Antrim, Armagh and Down.

DERRY
Fly from: Stansted (Ryanair)
Airport: five miles north-west of the City of Derry; hourly buses.
Main attraction: the views from the city walls.
Also handy for: counties Donegal, Londonderry, Tyrone and Fer-
managh.

NORWAY
TORP
Also known as: Oslo
Fly from: Stansted (Ryanair)
Airport: close to Sandefjord.
Main attraction: the port of Larvik, ten miles south-west.
Also handy for: Oslo, fifty miles north; connecting buses.

PORTUGAL
FARO
Fly from: Bristol (Go), Heathrow (Virgin Express, via Brussels), Stansted
(both Go), East Midlands (Go and BMIbaby)
Airport: three miles west; regular buses.
Main attraction: a compact, lively town with strong African influences.
Also handy for: the Algarve coast, Spain's Costa de la Luz.

SCOTLAND
EDINBURGH
Fly from: Belfast (easyJet), Bristol, East Midlands (both Go), Gatwick,
Luton (both easyJet), Stansted (Go)
Airport: six miles west of Edinburgh; frequent buses from Waverley
station.
Main attraction: the Royal Mile leading to the Castle; the elegant New
Town; and the port of Leith.
Also handy for: Stirling, Perth, Dundee.

PRESTWICK
Also known as: Glasgow
Fly from: Stansted (Ryanair)
Airport: two miles north of Ayr; half-hourly trains.

Main attraction: the Robert Burns connection.
Also handy for: Dumfries and Galloway, Glasgow (33 miles).

GLASGOW
Fly from: Belfast (easyJet), Bristol (Go), East Midlands (Go), Luton (easyJet), Stansted (Go).
Airport: six miles west of Glasgow; frequent buses from city centre.
Main attraction: the Charles Rennie Mackintosh architecture and design.
Also handy for: Stirling, and the beautiful, fragmented region of Strathclyde.

INVERNESS
Fly from: Luton (easyJet)
Airport: seven miles north-east; occasional buses.
Main attraction: the five-mile walk along the river to Loch Ness.
Also handy for: the wild north and north-west of Scotland.

ABERDEEN
Fly from: Luton (easyJet)
Airport: four miles north-west; frequent buses.
Main attraction: the leafy Old Town, and the strange old fishing community of Footdee.
Also handy for: the Dee Valley, including Balmoral.

SPAIN

MADRID
Fly from: Heathrow (Virgin Express, via Brussels), Liverpool, Luton (both easyJet)
Airport: eight miles north-east; frequent buses and Metro trains.
Main attraction: some of Europe's finest art galleries scattered around a city that celebrates life.
Also handy for: the gorgeous cities of Toledo, Avila and Salamanca.

BILBAO
Fly from: Stansted (Go)
Airport: six miles north.
Main attraction: the Guggenheim museum, which looks like a collage of the offcuts from the Boeing factory.
Also handy for: San Sebastian, Santander and the Basque region of Spain.

GERONA
Fly from: Stansted (Buzz)
Airport: six miles south-west; take a taxi.

Main attraction: a dramatically beautiful small city with a fascinating Jewish quarter.

Also handy for: Figueres (for the Dali Museum) and the Costa Brava.

BARCELONA

Fly from: Bristol (Go), East Midlands (BMIbaby), Gatwick (easyJet), Heathrow (Virgin Express, via Brussels), Liverpool (easyJet), Luton (easyJet), Stansted (Go)

Airport: eight miles south-east; frequent buses, regular trains.

Main attraction: superb location, architecture and nightlife.

Also handy for: the Roman city of Tarragona, plus the Port Aventura theme park.

PALMA

Fly from: Bristol (Go), East Midlands (BMIbaby and Go), Gatwick, Liverpool, Luton (all easyJet)

Airport: six miles east of Palma de Mallorca; regular buses.

Main attraction: Palma, one of the most underrated Spanish cities – a more manageable version of Barcelona.

Also handy for: the beaches of Arenal (two miles from the airport), and the remainder of the world's favourite holiday island.

IBIZA

Fly from: Stansted (Go)

Airport: four miles south; take a taxi.

Main attraction: the island's small capital is a shimmering white town.

Also handy for: the clubs and beaches dotted around the island; and the ferry to Formentera, unspoilt and beautiful.

ALICANTE

Fly from: Bristol (Go), East Midlands (BMIbaby and Go), Stansted (Go)

Airport: eight miles south-west; regular buses.

Main attraction: Alicante is worth an afternoon, but the city of Valencia – a hundred miles north through mountains – is much more enticing.

Also handy for: the Costa Blanca, including Benidorm.

MURCIA

Fly from: Stansted (Buzz), East Midlands (BMIbaby)

Airport: twenty miles south; take a taxi.

Main attraction: a Renaissance city built on top of an Islamic city, which itself rested on the foundations of a Roman colony.

Also handy for: the relatively unspoilt Costa Calida.

MALAGA

Fly from: Bristol (Go), East Midlands (Go), East Midlands (BMIbaby and Go), Gatwick (easyJet), Heathrow (Virgin Express, via Brussels), Liverpool, Luton (both easyJet), Stansted (Go)

Airport: six miles west; frequent trains and buses.

Main attraction: a splendidly preserved Old Town, with the impending interest of a Picasso Museum to honour the city's most celebrated son.

Also handy for: the Costa del Sol and the inland mountains.

JEREZ

Fly from: Stansted (Buzz)

Airport: five miles north-east; regular buses.

Main attraction: the sweet, heavy atmosphere that drapes itself over the home of sherry.

Also handy for: the port of Cadiz, the Costa de la Luz, and the city of Seville.

SWEDEN

STOCKHOLM

Fly from: Heathrow (Virgin Express, via Brussels)

Airport: Arlanda.

Main attraction: Gamla Stan – the Old Town – and the other islands across which Stockholm is scattered.

Also handy for: Uppsala, the beautiful university town close to Arlanda airport.

SKAVSTA

Also known as: Stockholm

Fly from: Stansted (Ryanair)

Airport: seven miles west of Nyköping; buses connect with flights to reach Stockholm.

Main attraction: the nearby city of Norrköping, a kind of Scandinavian Manchester with well-renovated industrial revolution architecture.

Also handy for: Stockholm (sixty miles north-east).

VÄSTERÅS

Also known as: Stockholm

Fly from: Stansted (Ryanair)

Airport: four miles south-east of Västerås; buses connect with flights to reach Stockholm.

Main attraction: the Vallby Friluftsmuseum, an open-air collection of historical wooden houses.
Also handy for: Stockholm (sixty miles east), and central Sweden.

GOTHENBURG
Fly from: Heathrow (Virgin Express, via Brussels) and Stansted (Ryanair)
Airport: Ryanair flies to Save, eight miles east; Virgin Express flies to Landvetter, fifteen miles east; regular buses from each.
Main attraction: Gothenburg's maritime museum, the world's largest.
Also handy for: northern Denmark, a couple of hours across the Baltic.

MALMÖ
Also known as: Copenhagen
Fly from: Stansted (Ryanair)
Airport: twenty miles south-east; regular buses.
Main attraction: the view of the Oresund Link to Denmark; and the historic university city of Lund, twenty miles north.
Also handy for: Copenhagen (bus connects with Ryanair flights).

SWITZERLAND
GENEVA
Fly from: Gatwick (easyJet), Heathrow (Virgin Express, via Brussels), Liverpool, Luton (both easyJet)
Airport: three miles north; frequent trains and buses.
Main attraction: the shimmering lake and a fine Old Town.
Also handy for: the French Alps.

ZURICH
Fly from: Gatwick (easyJet), Heathrow (Virgin Express, via Brussels), Luton (easyJet)
Airport: eight miles north; frequent trains.
Main attraction: the prettiest financial hub in Europe.
Also handy for: 'Europe's Niagara', the modest falls on the Rhine an hour north.

You can also fly within continental Europe, on the no-frills networks of Buzz, easyJet and Ryanair. Europe is unusual in that there is international low-cost flying. Almost everywhere else in the world you will be confined within the same country, so to get cheaply from, say New York to Vancouver, you would need to fly on JetBlue to Buffalo, cross the US–Canada border to Hamilton and board a WestJet flight for the rest of the journey.

WHO CAN I FLY WITH, AND HOW DO I BOOK?
BMIbaby (0870 60 70 555, www.bmibaby.com)
Buzz (0870 240 7070, www.buzzaway.com)
easyJet (0870 6000 000, www.easyJet.com)
Go (0870 60 76543, www.go-fly.com)
Ryanair (08701 569 569, www.Ryanair.com)
Virgin Express (0800 891199, www.virgin-exp.com)

All of these airlines impose a penalty on people who do not book via the Internet (though they present it as special online discount). Abroad, the best way to book is also via the Internet, not least because it saves on international phone calls.

The following options can be expected to expand widely over the next few years:

AUSTRALIA
Virgin Blue: www.virgin-blue.com.au

BRAZIL
GOL: www.voegol.com.br

CANADA
Tango: www.flytango.com
WestJet: www.westjet.com

SOUTH AFRICA
Kulala: www.kulala.com

US
AirTran (Atlanta hub, with flights north-west to Minneapolis, north-east to Boston, south-east to Miami and south-west to Dallas): www.airtran.com

JetBlue (New York State, and flights from JFK to the West Coast and Florida): www.JetBlue.com

Southwest (nationwide network): www.southwest.com

Spirit (Florida to Chicago, Detroit, New York and Atlantic City): www.spiritair.com

Vanguard (coast-to-coast flights via Kansas City hub): www.flyvanguard.com

HOW DO I KNOW THAT I'VE GOT THE BEST DEAL?
It's impossible to be sure that the person in the next seat will not have paid less than you, but you can improve the odds in your favour by

shopping around assiduously. Until 1995, whatever your intended journey, there was a pretty good chance that a decent travel agent would find the best-value flight for your destination. These days, you have to do the leg-work – or rather the mouse-work – yourself. Never assume that the traditional airlines will be more expensive, particularly at busy times when no-frills fares are at their highest.

WHAT ABOUT THOSE GIVEWAY DEALS: £9.99, £5 AND EVEN FREE?

Look out for newspaper special offers promoting very low fares, but to get some even better bargains sign up online with Buzz, easyJet, Go and Ryanair. They will often send out deals that are available only to e-mail subscribers.

The very cheap seats will be restricted to off-peak flights – forget Friday and Sunday evenings. Maximum availability is likely to be on Tuesdays and Wednesdays. On a route with more than one daily flight, there is likely to be a very early or very late departure that is not 'optimally scheduled', and therefore has to be sold at distressed rates.

KNOWING THE NO-FRILLS AIRLINES, THERE'LL BE LOTS OF CONDITIONS ATTACHED?

First, you'll almost always have to book on the Internet, because the only way they can offer prices like that is to cut out reservations staff. If you see a headline figure like £5 return, bear in mind that all the taxes and charges will add around £20 to that. Some airlines will insist that you stay away for one or two nights, but you can sometimes get around that by buying two one-way tickets. And if for any reason you can't travel on the days in question, you can kiss your cash goodbye. But they're so cheap that people are learning to book a whole series of these days out and just decide to go or not depending on the weather or how they're feeling on the day.

CAN BUSINESS TRAVELLERS BENEFIT FROM THESE CHEAP FARES?

Yes, though people travelling on business often prefer Heathrow, Glasgow or Manchester airports to Stansted, Prestwick or Liverpool. And if you need to change your plans then you'll lose your money. But crafty business travellers use these flights because, on a midweek trip to Sweden, you can save many hundreds of pounds.

WHAT ABOUT CHILDREN?

Adulthood begins on the second birthday, say the no-frills airlines. The traveller has to occupy a seat whether aged two, forty or eighty (no senior citizen discounts, either). If you want to do anything difficult like send a child unaccompanied, choose a 'frilly' carrier.

HOW MUCH LUGGAGE CAN I BRING?

The usual 20 kg (44 lb) on most of them, but only 15 kg on Ryanair; you could end up paying more for the extra weight than you did for the fare.

WHAT RIGHTS DO YOU HAVE WHEN YOU BUY A NO-FRILLS FLIGHT?

Not many, unless you bought it as part of a package holiday. 'A passenger is in a weak negotiating position compared to the airline when buying a ticket or subsequently making the flight' says the European Commission about aviation in general. He or she is subject to conditions of carriage and to business practices decided by the airline, but will frequently be unaware of the exact terms and have little alternative to accepting them even if dissatisfied. The customer's position is further weakened by the obligation to pay for the service before actually taking the flight.' When things go wrong, many traditional airlines will offer far more than the terms and conditions demand, such as a taxi home if your flight arrives after public transport has shut down for the night.

'Whilst we do empathise with some of our customers in difficulty, you will understand that the economics of short-haul low-cost flying cannot sustain too many taxi fares of £60,' says Stelios of easyJet. We are not responsible for ground transport and passengers should build that cost (with some contingency for delays) into their travel budgets.' His airline refunds passengers whose flights are delayed by four hours or more. 'My approach to customer service has always been to under-promise and over-deliver. The idea that airlines are a bottomless pit and if you complain loud enough you get paid off is one of the legacies of the flag carriers.' Stelios says he wants to change the public's perception. 'Whimsical demands for "compensation" not only increase the cost of flying for everybody, but also they never leave anybody completely satisfied. That's over-promising and under-delivering.'

ATOL, ABTA, AITO, IATA – ARE THEY ANY HELP?

Probably not. The Air Travel Organiser's Licence (ATOL) scheme was set up by the Civil Aviation Authority after one tour operator collapse too many. It covers package holidays that include air travel, but the vast majority of these are on charter airlines.

The Association of British Travel Agents (ABTA) has a scheme for what's called 'non-licensable' activities, such as self-drive or coach holidays, and guarantees your money back if you buy through an ABTA member. The Association of Independent Tour Operators (AITO) has its own bonding scheme, but few member companies use no-frills airlines. The International Air Transport Association is the trade body that dreams up these rules and regulations, and naturally wish to endow the airlines with maximum options.

AS AN INDEPENDENT TRAVELLER, I FIX UP EVERYTHING MYSELF. WHAT RIGHTS DO I HAVE?

Far fewer. If you pay with cash or a debit card direct to a scheduled airline, and it goes bust, you have no rights at all. Paying with a credit card gives you some protection if the booking is for over £100. Most travellers on no-frills flights arrange their own accommodation, which does not count as a package for the purposes of the rules.

MY TRAIN TO THE AIRPORT BROKE DOWN AND I MISSED THE FLIGHT – AM I ENTITLED TO A SEAT ON A LATER PLANE?

No. The train company will point to its terms and conditions and, if you're lucky, offer you the value of your rail ticket back. No-frills airlines say you should (a) allow plenty of time to reach the airport, and (b) be insured against failure of public transport. In practice they will usually try to get you on the next flight out, with a payment of £25–£50 per person.

WHAT HAPPENS IF I TURN UP AT THE AIRPORT AND FIND THE FLIGHT IS DELAYED?

You sit and fume. Under the 1929 Warsaw Convention, the airline is merely expected to get you from A to B, possibly via C, in a manner of its choosing, with reasonable despatch. You are not entitled to food, drink, or accommodation. Most airlines – with the exception of Ryanair – will provide these in the event of a long delay.

THINGS GOT WORSE – I MISSED A CONNECTION

If you have made two separate bookings, on different airlines, as is likely to be the case if one or both is on a no-frills airline, then you are in trouble if the first flight goes awry. Suppose you fly on Ryanair from Prestwick to Stansted, and plan to arrive two hours before a Go departure to Bologna. If the first flight is so late that you miss the connection, there is no liability on the part of Ryanair to help you out. Nor is Go obliged to rebook you on its next flight. Your only recourse is claiming on travel insurance, and even then the insurer will want evidence that you were not cutting things too fine by allowing insufficient time between flights.

BUT I'M TRANSFERRING AT LUTON FROM ONE EASYJET FLIGHT TO ANOTHER

Tough. Like all the airlines, easyJet emphasises it is a point-to-point carrier. This means each flight is self-contained; unlike with-frills airlines, you will not see your luggage seamlessly transferred, nor will you get both boarding passes. One of the things you are not paying for is the cost of being looked after.

AVIATION GLOSSARY: HELPING YOU DECIPHER THE JARGON OF AIRLINES

ABTA Association of British Travel Agents, a trade body that gives some protection to customers of member companies.

Ad-hoc charter hiring an aircraft to cover a gap in a fleet, usually caused by mechanical problems. European Aviation and Titan are among the companies that regularly fly for no-frills airlines.

Apex Advance Purchase Excursion, which used to be the standard cheap ticket on scheduled flights. You had to book a couple of weeks in advance, stay away at least one Saturday night and pay heavily to change reservations. These are still often cited as a good deal, but have rather been left behind. Similar restrictions, though, are often applied to some cheap seats on no-frills flights.

choose as in 'You'll be able to choose your own seat on board very shortly', announced by airlines that don't pre-assign seats. Loosely translates as 'join the massive scrum at the gate if you want any chance of a window seat'.

damp lease you rent the plane and the pilots, and supply your own cabin crew.

dry lease you rent only the plane, and supply your own pilots and cabin crew.

ETOPS Extended Twin-engine Operations over water, which means flying a plane with two engines, such as the Boeing 737, a long way from suitable diversion airports. It means these planes can fly quicker and cheaper courses, and make journeys that would not otherwise be allowed.

fifth-freedom the right, under the 1944 Chicago Convention on international air travel, for an airline to fly between two points, neither of which is in its home country. All airlines from EU member states have fifth-freedom rights within the Union.

HAG – Have A Go a term used by check-in staff for a passenger who arrives after the check-in deadline but is permitted to try to get to the gate in time to catch the plane. Very rare on no-frills airlines because they do not want to jeopardise their schedules, and across aviation in general since 11 September 2001 because of increased security concerns.

hotac hotel accommodation for cabin crew. Smart airlines such as Ryanair sometimes persuade the local authority, such as the one at Charleroi, to pay the bill.

IATA International Air Transport Association, the airlines' cartel. Its main purpose is to set standards and fix fares. Even though some no-frills airlines are members, the fare-fixing aspect is irrelevant.

no-show failing to turn up at the check-in desk before the flight closes. On most no-frills fares you lose the money paid for the flight. Theoretically you can apply for a refund for taxes and charges, but the process is sometimes made so difficult that people rarely bother.

oversold overbooked, ie selling more seats for a flight than the number the plane actually holds. Common practice in aviation, because of the large number of no-shows, with set penalties for the airline to pay an affected passenger.

published fare a fare that appears in airlines' manuals. Tends to be used to distinguish 'official' fares from those sold more cheaply through discount agents.

reprotect transfer to another airline, usually in the event of a mechanical failure or a scheduling change.

self-loading cargo passengers.

standby a standby ticket used to be the only cheap way to fly around Britain and across the Atlantic. Passengers would hang around at the airport to see if there was room on board for them. Even once on board, it was possible to be tapped on the shoulder just before take off and asked to surrender your seat to a busy full-farepaying executive. Nowadays, standby tickets no longer exist, and the term refers only to people – who will have paid a variety of fares – hoping to travel on a fully-booked flight.

wet lease you rent the plane, the pilots and the cabin crew.

white tails aircraft that have been built without a specific customer. In 2002, there were increasing numbers of these at Airbus and Boeing.

INDEX